The GE Way Fieldbook

Jack Welch's Battle Plan for Corporate Revolution

The GE Way Fieldbook

Jack Welch's Battle Plan for Corporate Revolution

Robert Slater

McGraw-Hill

New York   San Francisco   Washington, D.C.   Auckland   Bogotá
Caracas   Lisbon   London   Madrid   Mexico City   Milan
Montreal   New Delhi   San Juan   Singapore
Sydney   Tokyo   Toronto

Library of Congress Cataloging-in-Publication Data

Slater, Robert
  The GE way fieldbook : Jack Welch's battle plan for corporate revolution /
  by Robert Slater.
      p.   cm.
  Includes bibliographical references and index.
  ISBN 0-07-135481-6
  1. Welch, Jack (John Francis), 1935–   2. General Electric Company—Management.
  3. Chief executive officers—United States—Biography.   4. Industrial management—
  United States.   5. Leadership—United States.   I. Title.

HD9697.A3 U5677 1999
658—dc21
                                                                    99-049177

McGraw-Hill

A Division of The McGraw·Hill Companies

1 2 3 4 5 6 7 8 9 0 DOC/DOC 9 0 9 8 7 6 5 4 3 2 1 0 9

ISBN 0-07-135481-6

Printed and bound by R. R. Donnelley & Sons Company.

McGraw-Hill books are available at special quantity discounts to use as premiums
and sales promotions, or for use in corporate training programs. For more information, please write to the Director of Special Sales, McGraw-Hill, 11 West 19th Street,
New York, NY 10011. Or contact your local bookstore.

This publication is designed to provide accurate and authoritative information in
regard to the subject matter covered. It is sold with the understanding that neither
the author nor the publisher is engaged in rendering legal, accounting, or other professional service. If legal advice or other expert assistance is required, the services of
a competent professional person should be sought.
—*From a Declaration of Principles jointly adopted by a Committee of the American Bar
Association and a Committee of Publishers.*

 This book is printed on recycled, acid-free paper containing a
minimum of 50% recycled, de-inked fiber.

To Jeffrey Krames,
for the major role he has played
through the years in my book-writing career

Contents

BOOK 2
The GE Way: The CEO in the Field

List of Exhibits

How to Get Started

Why a GE Way Fieldbook?

Jack Welch is arguably the most lauded CEO in the world. In the winter of 1998–1999, the accolades poured in for Welch, frequently proclaiming him one of the great business leaders of all time.

Such leading magazines as *Time, Fortune,* and *Business Week* all lavished praise upon him. They described him at times as the best CEO in America; at times, these magazines credited GE with being the best-run company in the nation.

Few business leaders have been followed as closely by the media as Jack Welch—and with good reason. In 1999, only one company was more valuable than GE (the one out in Redmond, Washington, headed by that Harvard dropout).

Welch built GE into the most successful American corporation of the late twentieth century by forging and then implementing a series of business strategies that have become his trademark: *Business is simple. Don't make business overly complicated. Face reality. Don't be afraid of change. Fight bureaucracy. Get boundaryless. Use the brains of your workers. Find the best ideas, inside or outside your company, and then put those ideas into practice.* These strategies and others have formed the building blocks of Jack Welch's battle for corporate revolution.

The Welch strategies have been described in a number of popular business books of the past decade. I myself have written three, the most recent of which is *Jack Welch and the GE Way* (McGraw-Hill, 1998). Most of these books describe the aforementioned business strategies, and others as well, and give an excellent overview of what Welch and GE have accomplished. What *The GE Way Fieldbook* sets out to accomplish is not simply to explain the strategies but to offer a blueprint of how other companies can implement those strategies expeditiously and seamlessly in their own businesses.

The fieldbook genre is a relatively new one, and there are only a handful on the bookstore shelves. The popular ones have focused on implementing a certain set of business techniques: for example, *The Fifth Discipline Fieldbook: Strategies and Tools for Building a Learning Organization* by Peter Senge, Art Kleiner, Charlotte Roberts, Richard B. Ross, and Bryan J. Smith (Doubleday Currency, 1994). That fieldbook shows how to create a learning organization. In contrast with the other fieldbooks, *The GE Way Fieldbook* is the first of its kind to focus on the inner workings and business strategies of a specific company.

How Does a Fieldbook Differ from Other Business Books?

Even a quick glance through these pages will show you that a fieldbook contains far more visual material than a traditional business book. Since the goal of the fieldbook is to show you how to implement an entire set of business techniques, such a book requires a far more didactic or instructional format than found in other business books. While we include much of the GE story throughout the book, the primary objective is to provide a road map for those wishing to implement GE's practices in their own organizations. As a result, most chapters include not only textual material but also self-assessment exercises, action steps, and internal GE documents. It is worth noting that these documents, most of which have been provided by General Electric, have never appeared in book form.

What's in the Fieldbook?

This fieldbook has been designed to be as user-friendly as possible. With that in mind, the book is organized into two sections:

Book 1 is called "The GE Way: A Fieldbook for Corporate Revolution." It contains four learning modules which focus on the initiatives and programs that have helped GE to create a learning organization that is boundaryless with the highest levels of quality:

- The leadership module

- The empowerment module

- The organization module

- The customer module

Within each of the modules, we have included several chapters that encapsulate the different GE business strategies and initiatives (such as Work-Out, Six Sigma, and boundarylessness).

We call Book 2 "The GE Way: The CEO in the Field." In this section, we provide an in-depth look at Jack Welch in action: the author's interview with Welch of April 29, 1999, in its entirety, an interview that was conducted specifically for this book; a number of speeches by Welch, also provided in their entirety; the letter to shareholders from Jack Welch, which appears in the 1998 General Electric annual report; and a number of quotes from Welch on his various business strategies.

There is also a chapter on Jack Welch at Crotonville, GE's leadership institute, which explains how Welch interacts with GE executives taking courses there and why the institute is called the "Harvard of Corporate America." Finally, Book 2 contains chapters that showcase the primary strategic initiatives that have been the growth engines for GE.

Making sure that the book is as hands-on as possible, we have devised a step-by-step model for each chapter. The model features six icons that will help the reader to gain insight into how to implement the various GE strategies. The icons include:

The GE Refresher Course

Self-Assessment Exercise

Action Steps

The GE Way

What to Do Next

The GE Toolkit

The GE Refresher Course: Most chapters contain a refresher course that provides a context for the business strategies and the methods provided to implement those strategies.

Self-Assessment Exercise: Most chapters includes brief self-assessment exercises that aim at helping you to determine how closely you practice the GE Way. It goes without saying that the less you resemble GE, the more work you have to do.

Action Steps: This icon will appear when we wish to provide a series of steps or procedures that tell the reader how to implement a certain business strategy.

The GE Way: This icon will appear whenever we describe a specific GE practice or strategy.

What To Do Next: This icon will designate a series of how-to steps to follow to implement the strategy featured in that chapter. Most chapters end with this icon.

The GE Tool Kit: The GE Tool Kit appears at the end of some modules and features such training materials as charts and GE course descriptions.

How to Use the Fieldbook

This fieldbook is a companion volume to *Jack Welch and the GE Way.* However, we want to stress that that this book is intended as a stand-alone book. For those of you who have not read *Jack Welch and the GE Way,* and for those who would appreciate a review of Welch's strategies, we have provided a GE refresher course. Most of the chapters start with the GE refresher course (as indicated by an icon) that will provide an immediate context for the strategy or initiative highlighted in the chapter. We have boxed each of the courses for easy identification.

This book is also designed to be modular in approach. Readers are free to read or simply peruse the book in any order desired. In other words, each module can be read on its own.

Now let's take a brief look at the Jack Welch era at GE. That era covered nearly two decades (1981–1999). It was a period when Welch sensed that the company faced trouble, and when he mounted a revolution to stave off that trouble. We now recount the steps that Jack Welch took in bringing radical change to GE.

The GE Revolution

For Jack Welch, it was just another one of those days. A round of meetings at Fairfield headquarters in the morning. Back to his office to prepare the charts he would use for his lecture at Crotonville that afternoon. A private lunch in his small dining room off his office with the author and his VP for public relations, Beth Comstock. After lunch, a 15-minute helicopter flight to Crotonville where Welch would give a 3-hour lecture; then at dusk, a 10-minute chopper ride to White Plains, where he took the company plane to an unannounced destination. He was in a buoyant mood, pleased at GE's financial performance, expressing mixed feelings about his retirement (December 31, 2000), proud that thus far the succession race—one of the most widely watched races in American business—had gone smoothly.

It is widely watched, of course, because it will mean the end of the Jack Welch era—and what an era it has been. He has been around for so long as chairman and CEO of General Electric—nearly 20 years—that his concepts and strategies have become ingrained in the country's business fabric. No other American business figure has had such a major influence on the way we look at individual and corporate leadership.

It amuses Jack Welch that American companies are getting credit these days for downsizing their employee rolls and for rationalizing their businesses. It amuses him because such business strategies appear enlightened and timely and the CEOs who are implementing those strategies are acting as if they deserved badges of honor for moving so swiftly and aggressively. Welch knows better. That's why he's so amused.

He knows that the CEOs of today who engage in downsizing are late to the game. Downsizing is not a new business strategy. It's one that Jack Welch pretty much invented nearly 20 years ago. Indeed, many of the business strategies that CEOs are employing today—all designed to bring costs in line, to foster growth, to become more competitive—many of these strategies were pioneered by Welch over the past two decades.

Jack Welch dreamed of making GE the most competitive enterprise on earth.

Welch's dream when he became chairman and CEO of General Electric in April 1981 was to make GE the most competitive enterprise on earth. He had no idea whether he would succeed; the odds were certainly against him back then.

But over the next two decades Welch articulated a set of business strategies and succeeded beyond his wildest imagination. We have built *The GE Way Fieldbook* around the evolution of those business strategies and the cultural change that he has engendered at the company. We will be spending time delineating these strategies and showing how executives can work on implementing them in their own firms.

When he took over as chairman and CEO in April 1981, many thought GE was doing just fine: The previous year it had annual sales of $25 billion and earnings of $1.5 billion; with a $12 billion market value, it ranked tenth among American public companies. But Welch knew better. He believed that GE was heading for a fall, thanks to its undue emphasis on manufacturing, its bloated bureaucracy, and its failure to take into account mounting foreign competition.

What did the new chairman and CEO of GE do?

Exhibit R-1 shows just how much Jack Welch's General Electric has grown during his 18-year stewardship. He articulated and implemented three business strategies that at the time were

GE – A Brief Perspective

1981		($ in Billions)	Current
• Revenues	$27.2	• 20+% Avg. Annual Yield for Shareholders	$100.4
Net Income	1.6		9.3
• Businesses	– 45 SBUs – 350 Product Lines – 2 Global Businesses	• Divested 30% of '80 Sales • Invested $19B in Acquisitions • 2/3 Core —$→ 2/3 Tech/Svs	10 Unique Businesses – All Global
• Worldwide Employment	– 404,000	• Net Result of Acquisitions/ Divestitures/Rationalization	– 295,000
• Management Layers	– 9 to 11	• Reshaping the Decision Making Process	– 4 to 5
• Productivity	– 1 - 2%	Work-Out • Best Practices • Empowering People	– 4 - 5%
• Quality	– Zero Defects – Quality Circles	• Six Sigma Quality	Co. Wide Trng.
• Stock Options	– "Top 500"	• Recognize, Reward, Incent and Retain Best Talent	27,000

Exhibit R-1.

unheard of. He restructured his businesses, insisting that he would keep only those that were number one or number two in their markets. He downsized the GE payroll, ending the no-layoff policy that had characterized the company and many other large American ones. He sold $12 billion worth of businesses and purchased $26 billion worth of others. And he pared GE's workforce from 404,000 to a mere 229,000. Finally, he delayered GE's management tiers: each GE business had nine to eleven organizational layers when Welch took over; a decade later that figure had been cut to four to five.

Welch steered the company that Thomas Edison founded to $100.4 billion in sales (fifth highest in America) and $9.3 billion in earnings (second highest) in 1998. The company's growth that year alone was astonishing: revenues up 11 percent; earnings, 13 percent; earnings per share, 14 percent. During the Welch years GE has benefited investors enormously, consistently outperforming the stock market. Exhibit R-2 indicates that GE has brought in a total return of 2,026 percent over the 15-year period ending 1998, nearly double the return from the S&P 500 over the same period. In the fall of 1999, GE's market capitalization exceeded $400 billion. Since Welch became GE's leader in 1981, the company's market value has grown by over $300 billion.

GE's 1999 revenues should come in at the $110 to $115 billion level, and its earnings at $10 billion. Welch has produced double-

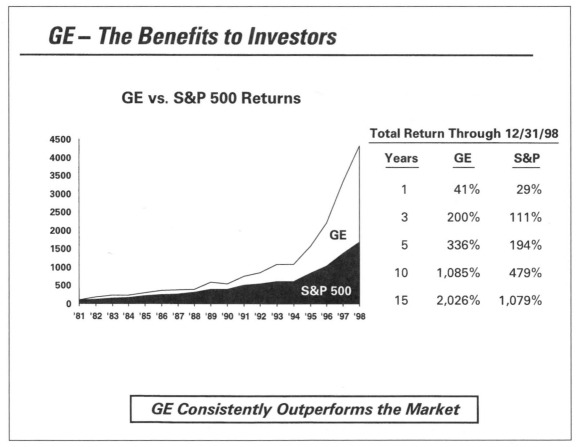

GE – The Benefits to Investors

GE vs. S&P 500 Returns

Total Return Through 12/31/98

Years	GE	S&P
1	41%	29%
3	200%	111%
5	336%	194%
10	1,085%	479%
15	2,026%	1,079%

GE Consistently Outperforms the Market

Exhibit R-2.

digit earnings growth since 1992—an astonishing rate for a company of GE's size and its complexity.

The Reshaping of GE

Jack Welch took the industrial giant, heavily dependent upon old-line manufacturing, and turned it into a highly competitive, global-thinking, service-oriented growth engine.

It was a revolution that he began as soon as he took over GE. If the revolution seemed topsy-turvy, it was because Welch began it not where most revolutions begin—at the bottom—but at the top. Applying a kind of "survival of the fittest" rule of thumb to his businesses and to his employees, he kept only those that were needed; all others were let go. He turned General Electric into a leaner, tougher, more competitive enterprise.

And Now, It's the Employees' Turn

By the latter part of the 1980s, once Jack Welch felt satisfied that he had restructured GE sufficiently—that the enterprise was in the best possible position to become a world-class competitor—he switched gears, turning his attention to GE employees.

He decided to let employees take part in company decision making. One major side benefit of this new plan was to make employees more productive as well. In 1989, he decided to empower GE employees through a new companywide vehicle he called Work-Out. This would be a program aimed at giving everyone down to the factory floor level a chance to propose ways of improving GE's day-to-day operations.

Welch believed that his employees should share in decision making.

As one can note in Exhibit R-3, Work-Out was the first step in a series of business strategies that Welch employed at GE over the next decade.

A decade later, during the late 1990s, Welch might have stepped back and decided that it was time to tread water, that he had established the most competitive enterprise on earth, and it was time to ease up. But Welch abhors complacency. He believes that the only way for a company like GE to survive is for its leaders to take a hard look at what they have done in the past few

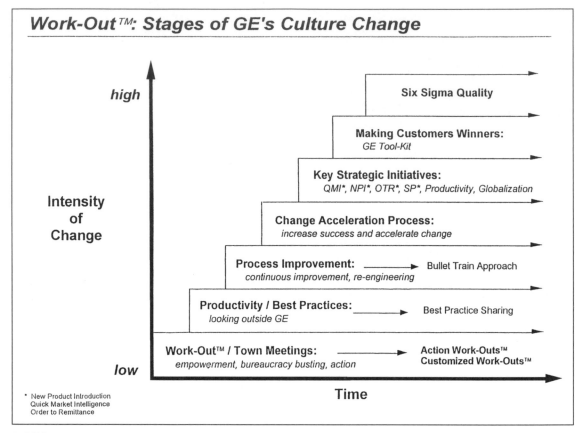

Exhibit R-3.

years, and then to change where necessary. He also believes fervently that GE must constantly look to the outside for ideas, rather than be held captive by its own modus operandi. Accordingly, in 1995, Welch became convinced that it was time for General Electric to embark on a massive campaign to improve the quality of its products and processes.

THE GE WAY

A Fieldbook
for Corporate Revolution

All of management is about self-confidence.
    —Jack Welch, March 1999

In this module you will learn what Jack Welch thinks are the basic ingredients of business leadership. You will also be given a series of exercises that will help you implement his strategies. We touch on the various models of business leadership that Welch has constructed and we go into detail on how the GE chairman seeks to hire and promote the best people.

In this module you'll learn four things that comprise Jack Welch's formula for successful business leadership:

- What Jack Welch thinks an ideal manager should be

- What are the five—and the only five—questions a business leader should ask

- Why Welch spends so much time on the people issues

- Why he is so fervent about rewarding good managers

CHAPTER 1

Leadership 1: Management Is Not Complicated

The command-and-control structures that were built after the war that practically sunk American business in the '70s and '80s had to be decimated.

A New Leadership Paradigm

The GE Refresher Course

American corporate life in the old days revolved around something akin to the military's command-and-control system. Not surprisingly, many business leaders, themselves products of the military, felt very comfortable in emulating that command-and-control model.

"Commanders" commanded and "sergeants" and "privates" implemented. Orders were issued from the top. The "grunts" listened and then did what they were told. There was no room for back talk. GE's corporate style was no exception. In fact, its command-and-control system proved a model for the American business community during the fifties, the sixties, and the seventies.

At GE and elsewhere, managers were expected to monitor, supervise, and control. They were supposed to manage—to make sure that all their subordinates did their jobs properly. They never actually talked to the factory-floor workers; they felt that they had no reason to as long as they were in touch with their direct reports. As a result, senior managers spent most of their time talking to direct reports, shooting memos back and forth, in effect closing themselves off from the reality of the trenches.

Drowning in their own flood of memos, managers were not expected to inspire or to give junior managers the opportunity to demonstrate their own leadership potential.

As late as the early 1980s, challenging such conventional wisdom was simply not done. After all, American corporations had served, seemingly forever, as the engines that drove the world's most powerful economy. Yet, the competitive landscape was changing. Too complacent, too content with their bottom lines, too arrogant to even notice the shifting winds, most business leaders thought they were handling their enterprises just fine and saw no reason to adjust.

With one notable exception.

To General Electric's Jack Welch, American corporations were inevitably headed for trouble (even if, as in the case of GE, those corporations were bringing in seemingly great bottom and top lines) and if the corporations were indeed going to weather the storm, they would need better, more sophisticated managers.

What was the best way of managing? Should one be a hands-on manager—or a hands-off one? In short, should a manager do as much managing as possible, or as little?

The less a manager manages, the better off a company is. That is Jack Welch's firm belief.

Welch takes a paradoxical view. The *less* managing someone does, the better off the company is.

He detests the very notion of management. Most managers, he insists, overmanage. Those who do so all too often help to create the bureaucratic sloth and sluggishness that large companies should avoid.

As soon as he became CEO of General Electric, Welch decided to establish an entire new management style. He vowed to end the military-style system of controlling and monitoring that most managers routinely followed. The only way to force GE to compete within a business environment that was increasingly competitive, and increasingly complex, he argued, would be to alter the behavior of GE's managers. No matter how alien the idea was to them, they would simply have to manage less.

Managing need not be overly complicated, Welch contends, because business is quite simple.

For Welch, the art of running a successful business is to assure that all important decision makers have access to precisely the same set of facts. If that happens, he is confident that they will reach roughly the same conclusion about how to deal with a business issue. That's why business is simple.

The problem, in Welch's view, is that people do *not* get the same information; they get different pieces of the entire information pie. Because they are cut off from the information they need, they cannot make a rational business decision.

Assessing Your Leadership Quotient

Now that you know what Jack Welch thinks about management, let's engage in a brief exercise that will help you determine whether you are one of those command-and-control types that Welch detests; or if your grades are good enough to get you into the Jack Welch School of Management. Circle either the Yes or the No.

**Self-Assessment
Exercise**

1. Do you think you hold more meetings than necessary?

   Yes   **No**

2. Do you believe that you issue too many memos?

   Yes   **No**

3. Do you find yourself approving most decisions made by direct reports?

   Yes   **No**

4. Do you sense that you are too hands-on in your direct reports' decision making?

   Yes   **No**

5. Do you feel that, in monitoring and supervising, you create more red tape than is needed, such as written approvals?

   Yes   **No**

If you have answered three or more in the affirmative, then it is likely that you have some work to do to become the kind of leader that gets an A+ at General Electric. If you've answered no to the majority of these questions, then you are hewing closer to Jack Welch's "managing less" leadership style.

However, to Jack Welch, managing less and avoiding bureaucracy is not enough. The ideal leader in his view is one who is able to energize and excite the troops. In order to figure out how you score on this scale, ask yourself the following key questions:

1. Do you come to work each morning filled with enthusiasm for the day ahead?

   Yes   **No**

2. Do you reach your desk each day with an open mind, fully prepared to rewrite your agenda, if necessary?

   Yes   **No**

3. Do you feel that you energize your staff?

   Yes   **No**

4. Do you feel that you have the drive, courage, and conviction of a truly effective leader?

   Yes   **No**

5. Do you feel that you execute well and deliver the results that you and your business strive for?

   Yes   **No**

If you've answered yes to the majority of the questions, then you fit an important aspect of the GE model for intelligent leadership. If, however, you have not answered yes to most of the questions, take heart: While there is much to be done, Jack Welch and GE have much to contribute to improve your leadership quotient.

The Key Leadership Ingredients

To Welch, lone wolves are not effective leaders even if they deliver on the numbers. A leader must be more than just a good businessperson. Some of the qualities of business leadership that Welch talks about really have nothing to do with the business

The GE Way

world per se. They have more to do with things like passion and energy and the ability to excite others. Business leaders who are passionate are models of excellence to Jack Welch.

Exhibit 1-1 lists the five qualities Welch feels an effective leader must possess. Welch committed these qualities to paper in mid-1997 when he was describing what constituted the ideal leaders for his new corporate initiative on six sigma quality. Six Sigma is Jack Welch's most important initiative of the 1990s. There will be much more on this subject in module 4.

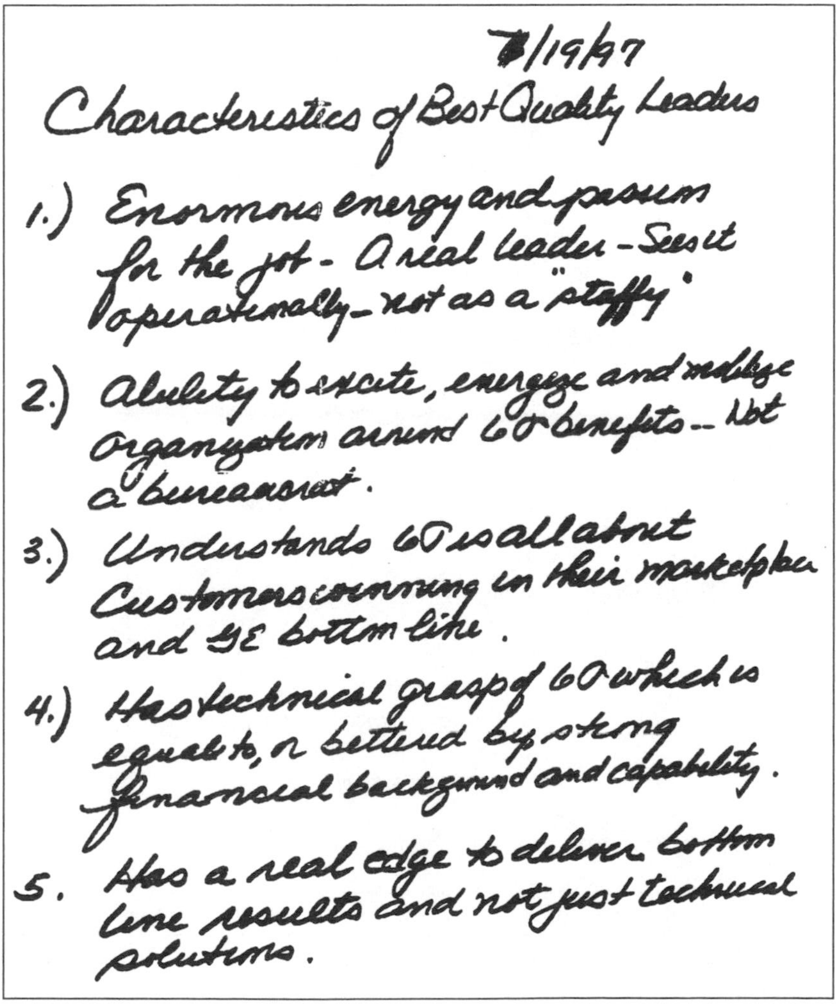

7/19/97

Characteristics of Best Quality Leaders

1.) Enormous energy and passion for the job - A real leader - Sees it operationally - not as a "staffy"

2.) Ability to excite, energize and mobilize organization around 6σ benefits -- Not a bureaucrat.

3.) Understands 6σ is all about Customers winning in their marketplace and GE bottom line.

4.) Has technical grasp of 6σ which is equal to, or bettered by strong financial background and capability.

5. Has a real edge to deliver bottom line results and not just technical solutions.

Exhibit 1-1

It is interesting to note that the top two characteristics involve energy, passion, and the ability to excite and energize others. To Welch, this is even more important than understanding the initiative itself, which he includes as the third priority. We'd like to draw the attention of the reader to item 5. Welch is widely known as a business leader who plays down the importance of attaining financial results (what he calls "bringing in the numbers"). But, realist that he is, he has designated delivering bottom results as a key characteristic of an effective leader. So, while energy and passion top the list, woe to the executive who forgets about the numbers completely.

Drawing on the five characteristics of effective leadership, Welch refined his views on leadership in 1999 by creating a scheme that wraps up leadership ingredients in four neatly bundled definitions, all starting with the letter E: He calls it E^4. The four are Energy, Energizer, Edge, and Execution (Exhibit 1-2).

Key GE Leadership Ingredients

"E^4"

Energy	Enormous Personal Energy – Strong Bias for Action
Energizer	Ability to Motivate and Energize Others ... Infectious Enthusiasm to Max Organization Potential
Edge	Competitive Spirit ... Instinctive Drive for Speed/Impact ... Strong Convictions and Courageous Advocacy
Execution	Deliver Results

Values and Performance Critical to Success

Exhibit 1-2.

The four E's are all the talk at GE. "This is real common terminology at GE," says William J. Conaty, GE's senior vice president for human resources. "If we're talking off the cuff about an individual, we'll say, 'Sure got the energy, pretty good energizer, not sure about the edge.'" While Welch's four phrases wrap into a nice E^4 package, there is really much more to effective leadership—and GE is the first to recognize that.

If the four E's represented the shorthand version of the ingredients that went into being a successful GE business leader, the authentic leadership model (Exhibit 1-3) is the longer version. Bill Conaty explains the Authentic Leadership Model:

"When I went around to businesses I asked myself: What are the real success factors here? There's boundarylessness, speed, and stretch. As for 'Self-Confidence with Humility—Sense of Humor,' we talk about how if somebody takes himself overly seriously in this company, they're going to have a long day. And they're probably going to have a shortened career. We used to

---

Authentic Leadership Model

- High Integrity – Trusted
- Business Acumen – a "Nose for Business" and How to Make Money
- Global Mindset
- Customer Touch – Understands and Anticipates Customer Needs
- Change Agent – Embraces Change – Hates Bureaucracy
- Self Confidence with Humility – Sense of Humor
- Open Communicator/Good Listener
- Team Builder
- Ability to Realign Organization Energies Around Business Objectives
- Mobilizes and Energizes – High Energy Level
- Infectious Enthusiasm – Strength to Tap Potential and Expand Capacity of Organization
- Delivers Bottom Line Results
- Has Fun Doing It!

> A **_Boundaryless_** Style – Actively Decisively with **_Speed_** and the Self Confidence to Set **_Stretch_** Targets

Exhibit 1-3.

have a fair share of folks who didn't fit this category. But I can tell you now, if you go to one of our CEC [Corporate Executive Council] meetings, you will see that they are two days a quarter of solid, hard-hitting business initiatives, and intense, but they're also a blast. We have fun with each other; there's always somebody in the doghouse businesswise and the other guys like to pile in a little bit; but then they're very quick to want to help that person because they know that their turn in the barrel is coming. It's just a great group."

The authentic leadership model expands upon Welch's original E^4 formula. These thirteen specific leadership traits describe GE's vision of the ideal business leader. Several things are noteworthy: first of all, for all of Welch's carefully thought-out business strategies, nothing is more important to him than making sure that business leaders are honest. Hence, high integrity tops the list. As we mentioned earlier, Welch, who often scorns the business executive who only brings in good financial results, still makes the earning of money his number two priority on this list. Moreover, Welch, through this list, makes it clear that a solid business leader is not someone who sits at a desk and pontificates day and night about how to run the business; rather, it is someone who gets down in the trenches, listens to employees and customers, communicates effectively with them, and stays in touch with all sorts of key constituencies. In short, a leader is simply someone who builds—and is a part of—a team.

One other aspect of the authentic leadership model needs explaining. The words "humor" and "fun" appear in different places. Humor? Fun? What do they have to do with effective leadership and bottom-line performance? Does the telling of a good joke mean that a leader will convince customers to buy more products? Will having fun on the job—and what kind of fun are we talking about here?—truly make a difference to the company's achievements? Clearly, the person is not talking about the ability to tell a good joke. What he has in mind is the fact that so many businesspeople are—and there's no other phrase for it— stuffed shirts. They don't smile. They don't laugh. They take themselves much too seriously. Such managers have difficulty igniting the performance of others. Managers who take themselves less seriously demonstrate greater self-confidence and are more capable of energizing and mobilizing their colleagues. In short, says Jack Welch, lighten up. It's good for business.

What to Do Next

1. Cut down on your meetings

2. Fire off fewer memos.

3. Delegate more decisions to your direct reports.

4. Require fewer approvals on routine matters.

5. Come to work tomorrow and come up with new ideas to energize those around you.

6. Lighten up!

CHAPTER 2

Leadership 2: Ask the Right Questions

An "A" leader has enormous personal energy and beyond that, the ability to energize others and draw out their best, usually on a global basis.

The GE Way

Developing a Leadership Mind-Set

Leadership, for Jack Welch, is at the core of his business strategies. He wants his executives to dwell day and night on what makes a good leader—and how they can become the best possible leaders.

Jack Welch likes to keep things simple. To him, there are only a handful of questions that a business leader should be asking of himself or herself. They are:

1. What does your global competitive environment look like?

2. In the last 3 years what have your competitors done?

3. In the same period what have you done to them?

4. How might they attack you in the future?

5. What are your plans to leapfrog them?

As these questions indicate, Welch feels that a strong leader must be aware both of the world at large and of one's immediate competitive environment; but at the same time that leader need not bog down in all sorts of irrelevant minutiae. Note how simple these questions are, yet how strategic in nature. They very elegantly cover the global arena, and the competitive environment, and at the same time provide a well laid out road map of the very few actions that managers should focus on. Business, as Jack Welch says time and again, need not be complicated.

1. Give three examples of what your global competitive environment looks like.

   _____

   _____

   _____

Self-Assessment Exercise

2. Name three moves that your competitors have made in the last three years.

   _____

   _____

   _____

3. Name three moves that you have done to your competitors during that same period.

   _____

   _____

   _____

4. Give two examples of how your competitors might attack you in the near future.

   _____

   _____

   _____

5. Give two examples of how you might put your competitors on the defensive in the next two years.

   _____

   _____

   _____

To Welch, leadership is not a destination, it's a journey. In other words, there is no one definition of leadership that will stand for all time. Leadership is an evolving concept. As for defining the ideal leader, Welch acknowledges that he does not have a monopoly on the best answer. Different people—especially, in Welch's view, GE people—can play a valuable role in defining the ideal leader.

Thus it was that in the early 1990s Welch's human resources team, led by GE's senior vice president for human resources, William J. Conaty, arranged for twenty GE vice presidents to assemble in one room at the company's headquarters in Fairfield, Connecticut.

The purpose of the gathering was to pick the brains of the executives—to get them to articulate their thoughts on what makes a good business leader—so that their ideas could be passed on to the next generation of GE executives. Each person in the room had the potential of becoming a CEO, a senior vice president, or the head of one of GE's businesses. In other words, these were leaders given the task of defining leadership. The seminar was truly extraordinary. Here were the best minds at GE, which had always prided itself on turning out the top business executives in the United States, studying and deciding upon the ideal ingredients of business leadership. As Bill Conaty recalled, "We said we want to pick your brains. We want you to give us your gems, your pearls of wisdom, to teach people down the line."

The results of that seminar have found their way into the written presentations that Jack Welch and his senior executives give to GE's senior and middle-level executives all around the world. In effect, this Advice from Successful Executives has become the raw material by which executives learn the GE way. It is Jack Welch's wisdom being passed on to the next generation of GE executives. Let's take an up-close look at the end product of these executives' ruminations.

This first piece of advice is: Do the job you own. "It's great to think about the future," says Conaty, "but it's a whole lot better to think about the future when you're hitting the ball out of the park on your current job. Do the job you are on better than anyone has ever done it. I tell people: If you treat the job you're on today like it's the last job you're ever going to be on, and you do it better than

---

Advice from Successful Executives

---

1. **Performance**

   Focus on Current Job Performance. Do Everything
   with a Sense of Urgency and Drive to Win. Make a
   Difference on Every Job. Develop a Reputation for
   Delivering Results Above and Beyond. It's OK to Think
   and Talk About Your Career, but Secondary to Job
   Performance and Better When You Are Hitting the
   Ball out of the Park in Your Current Job.

Exhibit 2-1.

anybody's ever done it before, I guarantee you won't stay on that
job. On the flip side of the coin, you don't want to get your head
out the window all the time, looking for a grass-is-greener situation, in or outside of GE. Be good at something; bring something
to the game; bring an area of expertise to the game."

In the second exhibit, one can see reflected in the language
one of Jack Welch's favorite business strategies: Face reality—
especially with regard to the exhortation to "become proficient
in one business/technical area."

Advice from Successful Executives

---

2. **Expertise**

   Become Proficient in One Business/Technical Area.
   Build a Strong Functional Competence. Look for
   Opportunities to Apply Your Expertise in a Broader
   Business Context: Multi-functional Teams, Process
   Initiatives, etc. Learn Finance ... It's the Language of
   Business. Manage Your Career so That You Can
   Evolve (Rather than Leap) into a Cross-Functional
   Assignment.

Exhibit 2-2.

The third advice sheet has a lot to do with Welch's insistence that leaders develop self-confidence. The person who whines about his career will not display self-confidence, nor will the person who fails to exhibit much interest in deepening his or her job skills.

Advice from Successful Executives

3. Ownership

Don't Whine About Your Career. Others Can Provide Advice but – in the End – You Are Responsible. Get in the Habit of Constantly Developing Yourself ... Like a Professional Athlete. Commit to Continuous Learning (Deeper/Broader). Develop Skills as Opposed to Accumulating Titles.

Exhibit 2-3.

The fourth piece of advice is very much along the lines of Jack Welch's dictum: Stretch yourself. By taking the difficult job, by playing offense with one's career, one goes beyond the ordinary and stretches one's skills and ambitions to the limit.

Advice from Successful Executives

4. Challenge and Visibility

Take the Hard Job. Err on the Side of the Bigger Challenge. Take on Work That the Business Considers Important. Seek out Assignments with Visibility Recognizing the Upside and Downside Potential. Play Offense with Your Career.

Exhibit 2-4.

The fifth dictum is to seek out those role models and mentors who can help your career. Jack Welch would say: Display as much energy as possible. It will pay off for you.

Advice from Successful Executives

5. **Mentors/Supporters/Role Models**

   Broaden Your Base of Support. Take Jobs with Different Managers/Clients. Work for People Who Will Challenge You. Seek Out Constructive Input on a Regular Basis and Don't Be Defensive When You Get It. Surround Yourself with Great People and Learn from Them. Be Persistent. When You Encounter the Imperfect Boss, Hang In ... Learn ... Make a Difference.

Exhibit 2-5.

Globalize—it's the wave of the future. That's the next piece of advice. The manager who is going to move forward at GE or anywhere else is the one who can truly move easily from one culture to another.

Advice from Successful Executives

6. **Global Experience/Cultural Breadth**

   Expose Yourself and Family to Different Cultures Early. Seek Out Positions Which Require Interaction Across Countries and Cultures. Consider Assignments Outside Your Home Country (Bubble or Longer Term), but Prepare by Becoming an Expert at Something, by Developing Teaching (as Well as Functional) Skills, and by Committing to Get a Specific Job Done.

Exhibit 2-6.

In Exhibit 2-7 GE defines what leadership is *not* about in order to clarify what leadership *is* about. For starters, the manager who constantly thinks about how to move on to the next job will not be rewarded with promotions very often. Nor will the manager who attempts to get singled out for praise all the time. There is no one catch-all formula for successful career management. That is why the motto at GE is: Successful careers are more like a marathon than a sprint.

Career Management in the Boundaryless Organization

A Few Concluding Thoughts

Successful Career Management ...

- Is Not About the Future, It's About Performance and Development Today
- Is Not About Outshining Others, It's About Energizing Others
- Is Not About Predictable Alternatives, It's About Possibilities
- Is Not About Definitive Answers, It's About Increasing the Odds
- Is Not About Structuring Long-Term Plans, It's About Iterating as You Go
- Is Not About Punching Tickets, It's About Self-Directed Personal/Professional Growth

Successful Careers Are More Like a Marathon than a Sprint!

Exhibit 2-7.

On another occasion, Welch and his team developed a separate chart (Exhibit 2-8) to explain why senior executives fail at GE. This exhibit's points apply more broadly to the top 500 executives of the company.

To Welch, executives fail, in simple terms, because by and large they do not subscribe to GE's highly defined set of business values. Their behavior runs counter to the corporate culture. And, whether they subscribe to the company's values or not, they fail to communicate or inspire a vision. They tend to build boundaries

Why Senior Executives Fail in GE

Bad Actor	Behavior Contrary to Corporate Culture/Values (e.g., Build Boundaries)
Flawed Organization Concept	Unnecessary Layer ... Drastically Underresourced ... Inherently Conflicting Expectations
Bad Selection	Missing Necessary 1Q Points ... Lacking Threshold Experience, Skills, or Behaviors
Insufficiently Heroic Objectives	Fails to Communicate and Inspire Around a Simple, Energizing Stretch Vision
Bad Beginning	Starts Behind and Never Catches Up
Bad Adapter	Skills Which Once Drove Success Begin to Drive Failure ... Not Open to Legitimate Criticism ... Unable to Fix Fatal Flaws
Can't Pull the Trigger	Talks a Good Game ... Great Analysis but Doesn't Get It Done
Out of Focus	Misses the Real Leverage Points ... Inability to Process Multiple Inputs
Bad Instincts	Can't Run with Scanty Data or Makes Wrong Conclusions off Insufficient Data
Self-Importance	Overly Critical and Sometimes Disdainful of Subordinates ... Lays Off Blame ... Soon Lacks Supporters
Pace	Moves at a Different Rate of Speed from Rest of Organization ... Time Management Issue ... Lacks Urgency

Exhibit 2-8.

when they should be knocking them down; they create management layers when they should be delayering. They have trouble organizing themselves for a maximum effort: they create too many management layers between themselves and their direct reports; they tend not to have the resources, financial or otherwise, to mount initiatives. Perhaps worst of all, they do not move at the fastest possible speed. They start behind and never seem to catch up. They lack urgency.

1. Try to speed up the work that you do—and certainly don't fall behind the pace of others.

What to Do Next

2. Diminish that ego of yours. You may think you know how to do things better in the workplace, but, remember, you're supposed to be a team player. Stop blaming others for your mistakes.

3. Stop analyzing so much. Just do your job.

4. Figure out how to remove boundaries, instead of creating them.

5. Polish up your communication skills. Even if you understand and agree with the company's values, you better be able to communicate them to your employees.

CHAPTER 3

Leadership 3: People Are Your Greatest Asset

What business leader worthy of the name would even consider fielding a team with anything other than the very best?

The People Priority

The GE Way

Hiring great people. And then making sure the truly effective people get promoted as fast and as far as possible. That's what Jack Welch says is the most important thing he does at GE.

How does he do it? What does he look for in someone?

How does he spend his time getting to know GE personnel well enough that he can evaluate them carefully and in depth?

How much actual time does Welch spend on the "human resources" side of his job? A great deal, as it turns out.

He likes to say that he spends more time on people issues than any other member of his staff or any other GE business leader.

Evaluating One's Managers

The GE Way

In April each year, you won't find Jack Welch at GE's Fairfield headquarters. He's out in the field, studying the talent, consulting with his top executives, then making quick decisions, all with the goal of promoting the best people and making sure they are rewarded. Welch undertakes an annual review of personnel that

For Jack Welch, there is nothing more important than hiring and then nurturing the right people.

constitutes a close look at the intellectual capital of General Electric. To conduct that review he heads right for the trenches.

This annual review is called—for reasons that no one at GE can quite identify—session C meetings. They run intermittently for 20 days or so and spill over into May. That may sound like a huge investment of the chairman's time, and it is, but he is convinced that it's time well spent. Nothing is more important to him than evaluating his managers and making sure that the best are properly encouraged and rewarded.

The session C process actually begins in February when every GE employee fills out a self-assessment review. He or she then discusses that review with a manager, and the manager sends an assessment up the management chain. The self-assessment review is clearly a tough assignment for the GE employee: Candor is expected, but how many of us are going to admit that we are not doing our jobs as well as management wants?

Welch, along with his vice chairmen and senior human resources personnel, meet with the business leaders at their respective headquarters, devoting a day for each business, two days for GE Capital. Welch and his senior colleagues also meet with senior human resources people at the business. The chairman could just as easily summon these executives to Fairfield, making the logistics far more simple for him; but he prefers to travel to the business sites and greet the executives on their own turf, so to speak.

All of the approximately 2,500 employees who are executive band and above are reviewed at these sessions. It's an exhausting experience for Welch, but often exhilarating. He often tells people that he doesn't know how to make an aircraft engine or create a *Seinfeld* show, but that flaw doesn't matter as long as he hires and promotes the best people.

There is no discussion of salaries at these meetings. That will come later. Right now, the key word is evaluation. Welch and his associates ask a number of questions of his business leaders:

Who is retiring?

Who do you want to promote?

Who should attend executive classes at Crotonville?

The session C process is so important to Welch that he spends far more than these 20 days on securing the best business leaders (see Exhibit 3-1). Indeed, he is thinking about the subject and making mental notes to himself all year round.

Sometimes Welch is directly involved in job placement. That's what happened in the case of George Jamison, who was working as a manager of global communications in Fairfield's public relations unit. Welch was attending a session C review at NBC when the subject of CNBC, the cable business station, came up. Someone at NBC said it was time to upgrade the communications function at CNBC. The cable station was doing well, but the world didn't know about it. Welch knew Jamison personally and suggested that NBC take a look at him. Within days Jamison visited NBC, and two weeks later he was at CNBC.

It is at the session C meetings that Jack Welch and his senior colleagues devote full attention to the human resources side of the business. To Welch, nothing is more important—not his business strategies, not his corporate initiatives—than making sure that the right people are hired and promoted. In effect, Welch makes the point that if he doesn't get the human resource side right—the people, the leadership—then none of his business strategies and values are going to be worth much.

Purpose of Session C

- To Review the Effectiveness of the Organization and Any Plans to Change

- To Review and Provide Feedback on the Performance, Promotability, and Developmental Needs of the Top Management

- To Review Plans and Suggestions for Backup Planning for Key Management Jobs

- Early Identification of High-Potential Talent to Ensure Appropriate Development

- To Focus Special Attention on Key Corporate or Business Messages

---

Exhibit 3-1.

The session C process is long and complicated—an indication of how important Welch and his colleagues feel about the human resources issue. The process carries on throughout the year. Exhibit 3-2 outlines the cycle. Some of the abbreviations in the exhibit need explaining: MDCC stands for Management Development and Compensation Committee of the GE board of directors, the five members of the board who are responsible for succession planning. The BOD stands for board of directors.

In earlier days, the session C process applied almost entirely to GE's American employees. That was not surprising, as the overseas staff was far smaller than it is today. But as time went

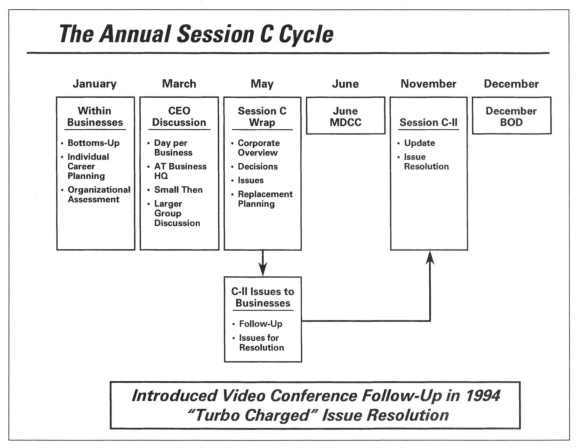

Exhibit 3-2.

on and the international staff grew, corporate executives back in Fairfield sensed that a way had to be found to include in the session C process all those people who had helped GE globalize, so a whole new review mechanism was introduced to make sure that the international side of the business was absorbed into that process. This is outlined in Exhibit 3-3. A decade earlier, someone on a global assignment could easily have been left out of the entire session C process—and not been given a deserved promotion. Today someone working abroad comes through the session C process via his or her business and internal GEI (GE International) reviews under the auspices of the area or country managers (who are termed NX in Exhibit 3-3). GE goes to great pains to make sure that no one is forgotten in this important process.

Everyone gets a very good look when it comes to promotions and the distribution of stock options.

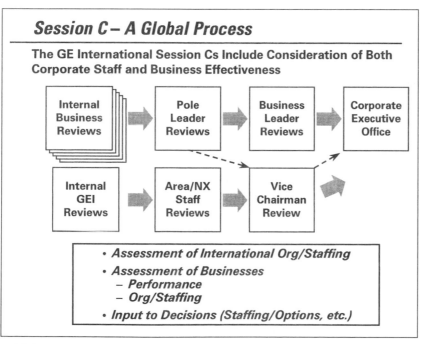

Exhibit 3-3.

Self-Assessment Exercise

How Do You Rate on the People Front?

1. Do you spend enough time evaluating people?

   Yes   **No**

2. Do you restrict your human resources activities to a small portion of the year?

   Yes   **No**

3. Do you make sure that the managers in your different businesses or sectors are reporting to you regularly on who is most worthy of promotion?

   Yes   **No**

4. Do you have a rewards incentive program in place to encourage employees whom you will want to promote one day?

   Yes   **No**

What to Do Next

1. Hire the best possible people, but don't let the human resources process stop there.

2. Establish a systematic effort for yourself and your managers to keep track of high-potential employees.

3. Reward those employees—not just once, but on a continuing basis.

4. Spend time with your human resources executives and encourage them to give you reports on high-potential staff on a regular basis.

5. Promote people on the basis of merit—avoid doing so for any other reason.

CHAPTER 4

Leadership 4: Reward
Your Best People

Rewarding your employees—that's what it's all about.
The most important thing I do as a leader is align the kind
of rewards I give out with the kind of behavior I want.

Only the Best Survive

As far as Jack Welch is concerned, middle managers have to be
team members and coaches. Their job is to facilitate, not control.
They should be able to excite and praise people and know when
to celebrate.

Managers should be energizers, not enervators.

In 1993, Welch began to speak candidly about the need to
take steps against those GE managers who failed to become
team players. He conceded that it would not be easy to change
the way GE managers think and behave. The compulsion to
manage, control, and direct was strong, he noted in the company's Annual Report, and was validated by GE's century-old tradition of measuring one's self-worth by how many people one
employed and whether or not one was a manager.

Jack Welch knew exactly what kind of manager he wanted at
GE. In spelling out the characteristics that managers must have,
Welch was suggesting that the *only* way to survive at General
Electric was to become a team player, to adapt oneself to the
company's values and culture.

**The GE Refresher
Course**

Back then, in the early 1990s, Welch talked about the four types of managers and explained which types were going to be successful and which were not:

Type 1   This type delivers on commitments—financial or otherwise—and shares GE's values. Welch regards type 1 as the ideal type.

Type 2   This type does not meet financial commitments and does not share GE's values. There is no place for type 2 managers at GE.

Type 3   This type misses financial commitments but shares in GE's value system. While many other business leaders could not forgive such a person, Welch is somewhat sympathetic. He cares more that the manager adheres to company values than meets the numbers. Thus, he is going to give this person every chance to succeed, perhaps at a different job within the company.

Type 4   This type delivers on financial commitments but does not subscribe to GE's values. It is this person who presents Welch with the greatest quandary.

Just who is the ideal business leader?

It may seem as if Welch has had a change of heart about the ideal manager, but he really hasn't. On a number of occasions he changed the language he used to distinguish good managers from bad ones. For example, by the late 1990s, Jack Welch spoke less of these four types of managers and more of three kinds of managers who will or will not do well at GE:

Type A's   Keep them. Promote them. Reward them.
Type B's   Nurture them in the hope that they may become A's.
Type C's   Dismiss them. Get rid of them as quickly as possible. Don't waste any time on trying to turn them into B's or A's.

Let's be clear here. In going from four types of managers to three, Welch didn't drop one by the wayside. He simply reduced the number by one in order to simplify things. Welch still feels that managers who share GE's values and meet their financial commitment are the ones that ought to be promoted.

Reward Your Best, Not Your Worst

The GE Way

During the late 1990s, Jack Welch was still focusing on what constituted the best business leader. But now he had shifted from concentrating on the ingredients—he felt he pretty much had that in harness—to figuring out how to make sure the best business leaders were rewarded properly. To help him in that endeavor, he began to rely upon what GE executives call the organization vitality chart (see Exhibit 4-1). The chart was used by senior GE executives during the session C process in 1999 to make sure that GE's best-performing employees are being rewarded and recognized and that the company is taking corrective action with regard to its least-effective performers. Being rewarded meant, in certain

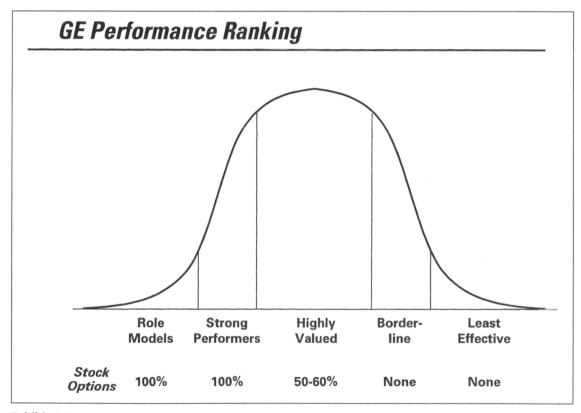

GE Performance Ranking

	Role Models	Strong Performers	Highly Valued	Border-line	Least Effective
Stock Options	100%	100%	50-60%	None	None

Exhibit 4-1.

cases, receiving stock options. There was a time when General Electric gave only 200 people stock options; by March 1999 that figure had grown to 27,000. Welch is convinced that apportioning stock options to the best performers is a sound management practice. He's also made a point of spreading those options throughout large segments of the company—including thousands of employees.

The chart also helped GE discover that too few of its people that were in the top 25 percent of the chart had had the chance to take Black Belt assignments as part of the Six Sigma quality initiative. Once that fact was discovered, GE moved quickly, deciding to offer 1½- to 2-year assignments over time to the top 25 percent on the vitality chart. Acceptance was voluntary, but Jack Welch made it clear that he and his senior colleagues count Six Sigma experience when it comes time for promotions.

Welch, asserts Bill Conaty, "doesn't want to micromanage to the point of name by name but he wants to force mechanisms every day that make sure that the most effective people are being treated the best; and that we've got our eyes on our least effective and are taking action on them."

So Welch and his colleagues combined the organization vitality chart with the submissions for stock options they received from the various business units.

The chart ranks people in the following manner: The top 10 percent are the role models; the next 15 percent are the strong performers; the middle 50 to 60 percent are the highly valued core; the next 15 percent are borderline; and the bottom 10 percent are the least effective. Welch wants to make sure that those who are role models or strong performers get the most stock options, while the high-performing core also gets its fair share. Welch wants no one in the borderline or least-effective categories to receive special perks, such as stock options. Recently, GE undertook a careful audit to discover just who was getting options with an eye toward checking whether low performers were being incorrectly rewarded. It was discovered that 8 percent of those people deemed least effective were getting stock options, as were 23 percent of those in the "caution" area.

As Conaty noted, "When you look at the organization vitality chart, you can say, 'Gee I did a pretty good job there, but I'm treating some of my people in the middle 50 percent better than some people I have in the top 10 percent.' In a lot of cases there'll be an answer that this individual, while in the middle 50 percent is the MVP of our business. Maybe not the most promotable, but a person that you couldn't go on without.

"The great part of this is that as we go forward nobody will do this exercise haphazardly; because they know that while we don't know all of the people on every list, the vitality chart will get us down into the organization, and we are going to look for trends. If a trend looks funny or your middle 50 percent got bigger increases than your top 10, why? So we'll continue to take different slices, different cuts. To make sure that we are constantly focusing on the extremes, from best to least-effective performers."

The 360-Degree Leadership Assessment Chart

The GE Way

Beyond Jack Welch's attempt to define ideal business leadership and GE's efforts to make sure that the most effective leaders are in place, the company makes an effort to help employees along in their personal quest to be better at their jobs. One tool that the company uses, not all that frequently, but on occasion, is the 360-degree leadership assessment chart (Exhibits 4-2 and 4-3).

The chart is put at the disposal of all GE businesses, and managers in those businesses are given the chance to use the chart to evaluate employees. Using the chart is optional for the managers, but most use it on a yearly basis as part of the annual management review. Some might use it every few years. Some business leaders require that every employee be examined via the chart, but that decision is left to the individual businesses.

The manager learns—sometimes from the employee—who are the person's peers and subordinates, and then sends the chart to them to fill out, assuring anonymity. Essentially, the chart allows executives to gauge how well employees are faring in adhering to the values of GE. The company's self-assessment exercise rates employees on ten different characteristics, from

GEIPS 360° Leadership Assessment

Characteristic	Performance Criteria	Mgr.	Peers	Subor-dinates	Other
Vision	• Has developed and communicated a clear, simple, customer-focused vision/direction for the organization. • Forward-thinking, stretches horizons, challenges imaginations. • Inspires and energizes others to commit to Vision. Captures minds. Leads by example. • As appropriate, updates Vision to reflect constant and accelerating change impacting the business.				
Customer/ Quality Focus	• Listens to customer and assigns the highest priority to customer satisfaction, including internal customers. • Inspires and demonstrates a passion for excellence in every aspect of work. • Strives to fulfill commitment to Quality in total product/service offering. • Lives Customer Service and creates service mind-set throughout organization.				
Integrity	• Maintains unequivocal commitment to honesty/truth in every facet of behavior. • Follows through on commitments; assumes responsibility for own mistakes. • Practices absolute conformance with company policies embodying GEI&PS commitment to ethical conduct. • Actions and behaviors are consistent with words. Absolutely trusted by others.				
Accountability /Commitment	• Sets and meets aggressive commitments to achieve business objectives. • Demonstrates courage/self-confidence to stand up for beliefs, ideas, co-workers. • Fair and compassionate yet willing to make difficult decisions. • Demonstrates uncompromising responsibility for preventing harm to the environment.				
Communica-tion/Influence	• Communicates in open, candid, clear, complete and consistent manner – invites response/dissent. • Listens effectively and probes for new ideas. • Uses facts and rational arguments to influence and persuade. • Breaks down barriers and develops influential relationships across teams, functions and layers.				

Exhibit 4-2.

vision to developing a global mind-set. After all evaluations are filled out and turned in, the manager then discusses the results with the employee.

The point of the exercise is to keep tabs on employees, not to let the deadwood—or the promising employees—go unnoticed. One assumes that when an employee comes under the scrutiny of peers and subordinates—even if the assessment is done rarely—the comments of those doing the judging will have a big impact on the employee. In short, the chart is one of GE's ways to assure that it has the best possible employees.

What to Do Next

1. Launch an initiative to judge the performance of your employees.

GEIPS 360° *Leadership Assessment (Continued)*

Characteristic	Performance Criteria	Mgr.	Peers	Subor-dinates	Other
Shared Ownership/ Boundaryless	• Self-confidence to share information across traditional boundaries and be open to new ideas. • Encourages/promotes shared ownership for Team Vision and goals. • Trusts others; encourages risk-taking and boundaryless behavior. • Champions Work-Out as a vehicle for everyone to be heard. Open to ideas from anywhere.				
Team Builder/ Empowerment	• Selects talented people; provides coaching and feedback to develop team members to fullest potential. • Delegates whole tasks; empowers team to maximize effectiveness. Is personally a Team Player. • Recognizes and rewards achievement. Creates positive/enjoyable work environment. • Fully utilizes diversity of team members (cultural, race, gender) to achieve business success.				
Knowledge/ Expertise/ Intellect	• Possesses and readily shares functional/technical knowledge and expertise. Constant interest in learning. • Demonstrates broad business knowledge/perspective with cross-functional/ multicultural awareness. • Makes good decisions with limited data. Applies intellect to the fullest. • Quickly sorts relevant from irrelevant information, grasps essentials of complex issues and initiates action.				
Initiative/ Speed	• Creates real and positive change. Sees change as an Opportunity. • Anticipates problems and initiates new and better ways of doing things. • Hates/avoids/eliminates "bureaucracy" and strives for brevity, simplicity, clarity. • Understands and uses speed as a competitive advantage.				
Global Mind-Set	• Demonstrates global awareness/sensitivity and is comfortable building diverse/global teams. • Values and promotes full utilization of global and work force diversity. • Considers the global consequences of every decision. Proactively seeks global knowledge. • Treats everyone with dignity, trust and respect.				

RATING SCALE: Significant Development Need ⌊ 1   2   3   4   5 ⌋ Outstanding Strength

Exhibit 4-2.

2. Select categories such as "Outstanding Performers," "Getting Along," "Weak Performers."

3. Place your employees into these three categories.

4. Determine which of your employees among the outstanding ones are not being rewarded sufficiently.

5. Determine which of your weak employees are being over-rewarded.

6. Adjust compensation plans accordingly.

THE EMPOWERMENT MODULE

Work-Out has made us faster and more open to ideas from anywhere, and, as a result, cracked the back of bureaucracy, got everyone involved, and made us a much better company.

—JACK WELCH, e-briefs, GE Intranet, June 7, 1999

In this module you will find out how GE carries out its highly respected Work-Out initiative. The module takes you back to the late 1980s when Jack Welch first came up with the idea, then moves you step-by-step through the Work-Out process. We also look at some of the situations that are particularly ripe for a Work-Out session.

In this module you'll learn why Jack Welch places so much emphasis on empowering employees. You'll learn about:

- His insistence on letting those closest to the work make day-to-day decisions

- His decision to launch Work-Out, one of the most innovative business tools of our era

CHAPTER 5

Work-Out 1: Using the Brains of All Your Workers

After a decade of Work-Out, most of the old bureaucracy and the boundaries among us have been demolished.

Involving Everyone in GE's Future

The GE Refresher Course

The early 1980s—these were the "hardware" years, when Jack Welch transformed GE, downsizing, restructuring. Though crucial for General Electric's balance sheet, the hardware phase unsettled remaining employees. Relieved to survive the cut, they still faced perilous futures as they confronted new plants, new bosses, new jobs. A cloud of uncertainty still hovered over all of their jobs. Were their futures truly safe? They doubted it. Not with Jack Welch in charge. Even as he downsized GE, Welch was determined to increase productivity, and as he cleared away the barriers to effective performance—the management layers, the useless employees, the paralyzing bureaucracy—employees continued to tremble in fear. They became disoriented. They badly needed to feel wanted, to develop some self-confidence, to believe that GE cared about them, what they were doing, what they were thinking.

Unwilling to promise his employees a job for life, convinced as he was that the job-for-life commitment that GE had made in the past had kept too much deadwood around, Welch understood that he had to provide new motivation to employees to work harder. The secret was giving workers a sense of empowerment, a feeling that they were "owners" of their businesses, not simply forgotten cogs in a faceless machine. This was the question Welch put to himself: How can I make my employees feel involved in the company?

The Work-Out program gets employees involved in helping to improve the productivity and efficiency of the company.

Welch came upon the solution, a companywide program he initiated called Work-Out, an effort that encouraged employees to speak their minds candidly to their bosses about what was wrong with their businesses. The Work-Out program made it more likely that employees would retain their jobs. Helping to improve their businesses would make for better financial results, and nothing guaranteed job security more than a strong business.

Welch recognized early on that those closest to the work and to the customer knew as much as their bosses, if not more, about how to improve the day-to-day operations of the business.

To Welch it was all very clear: The way to speed up business processes—a critical objective of his—was to unleash the energy and intelligence and self-confidence of workers, to turn them loose, to get management layers off their backs, to remove all the bureaucratic shackles.

Welch was quick to acknowledge that in former times, GE executives simply told employees what to do. And employees responded by doing precisely what they were told, nothing more. Now, through Work-Out, he expected employees to welcome their new freedom and to take advantage of it by using their minds creatively to figure out how to improve the company's operations—which was certainly more fulfilling than being told what to do all the time.

Welch, who became CEO at GE in 1981, felt badly waiting seven years to empower his employees. But he knew that launching such a massive initiative any earlier would have been a mistake: As long as Welch was downsizing people and reengineering businesses, it was hardly a time to seek the cooperation of employees who continued to fear for their own futures. How could he have convinced employees to become more productive and to take part in decision making amid so much disorienting and sweeping change?

The idea of Work-Out came to Welch one day in September 1988 during a visit to GE's Leadership Development Institute in Crotonville, New York. He showed up regularly to lecture to GE managers, who were taking courses there. Seated in his audience that day was management at all levels of the company. It turned out to be a frustrating day for Welch. The audience peppered him with questions. Some were the same ones he had heard for years. To many of the questioners, he replied simply that he did not know the answer. Other queries irked the GE boss even more; he was annoyed that the questions referred to problems that had not been solved by managers back home and seemed to have been festering for long periods of time.

Why were employers and employees within those businesses not engaging in dialogue? To his chagrin, Welch knew only too well that, despite the changes he had tried to make, the company remained essentially a rigid hierarchy—the bosses talked only to their direct reports, who in turn only talked to junior management, and only the junior managers spoke to factory-floor employees. More to the point, factory workers were expected to work, not offer their opinions to superiors about how to improve the place.

But perhaps, Welch thought, by harnessing the talent and energy of those lower-level employees, by forcing the bosses to answer questions that day, it might be possible to end this chain-of-command rigidity. It just might be possible to get employees and managers aboard Jack Welch's corporate revolution.

Indeed, Welch imagined Work-Out to be a broad effort that would at once cut back on bureaucracy and encourage employees to communicate with one another more openly and candidly.

Jack Welch couldn't solve all the issues raised by the Crotonville audience. But in urging GE personnel to bring work-related issues to their managers back home—rather than to the GE chairman—he could, he hoped, make vast headway.

Through the Work-Out program, Welch would insist that GE's business leaders take the unprecedented step of standing in front of their employees—and listening to what they had to say. It might be rough going at first, for such a dialogue was hardly natural. Managers were unlikely to be thrilled at turning over the "managing" of the business to foot soldiers.

Convinced that managers had no monopoly on good ideas or quick solutions to day-to-day problems, Welch thought the effort worth the risk. He had a strong conviction that it was the men and women closest to the actual work who possessed much of the creativity and innovation that could spark productivity.

It was not some altruistic impulse that encouraged Jack Welch to advocate the greater involvement of his employees in company affairs; nor was it in the belief that employees were smarter than their bosses. Welch had simply come around to the view that employees had to be treated as an integral part of the business. Allow them to take part, he argued, and you will discover employees becoming a good deal more conscientious. And conscientious employees automatically become more productive.

Self-Assessment Exercise

Assessing Your Response Quotient

In a truly open company, bosses do not hide behind their desks when more junior employees or managers present good ideas to them. These bosses are willing to stand before their colleagues, listen to their ideas, and act upon those ideas if they are good ones. What type of a leader are you? Here are a series of questions to help you assess your Response Quotient.

1. Do you feel that you give your employees sufficient opportunity to speak their minds?

   Yes   No

2. Can you honestly say that if confronted with a good idea, you would be willing to implement it on the spot?

   Yes   No

3. Have you ever, when confronted by an employee with a reasonable-sounding proposal, given the go-ahead to implement the proposal right there and then?

   Yes   No

4. Do you think less of an idea that comes from the shop-floor supervisor than one that is raised by your boss?

   Yes   No

5. Do you routinely engage in give-and-take dialogue with your employees?

   Yes   **No**

6. Do you truly believe that those closest to the work—and the customer—know as much about the business as you do?

   Yes   **No**

If you answered yes to the majority of these questions, you probably already have the rudiments of a Work-Out session in your workplace. But you can still benefit from learning more about the Jack Welch Work-Out model because it has become a finely tuned management forum that has proven its worth time and time again.

The Purpose of Work-Out

Most businesses contain practices that are, upon reflection, hard to explain, and harder to justify. Just as an example: All companies have at least one incredibly complicated form that was dreamed up years ago by someone with a hyperactive imagination. You know the one: It seems to be written in a different language and requires something like a dozen signatures of approval before it can be processed. Such routines are more annoying than productive, and remain in existence only because no one can figure out how to get the boss to dump them. They make no sense, they slow up the organization, and they create bureaucracy. In short, they are stiflers of progress, but no one has the guts or the savvy to figure out how to get rid of them. This is a tailor-made situation for a Work-Out session.

The GE Way

One of the main objectives of Work-Out is to force people to expose those routines to the light, in effect to put those routines out on the table for discussion and action—and then to eradicate them, at once, if possible.

As you see in Exhibit 5-1, Work-Out, as practiced at GE, had six basic objectives. These objectives fell into two distinct categories: the first four have to do with improving internal systems; and the latter two, with improving GE's external relationships.

> ### *Potential Objectives & Purposes of Work-Out*
>
> - **Reducing Bureaucracy**
>   e.g. reports, approvals, meetings, policies, practices, measures
>
> - **Improving Organizational Processes**
>
> - **Empowering Employees; Reducing Vertical Boundaries**
>
> - **Breaking Down Intra-Organizational Walls**
>   e.g. Between Departments or Functions, Union and Management
>
> - **Developing Formal Alliances or Informal Relationships with Customers**
>
> - **Developing Other Extra-Organizational Relationships**
>   e.g. with Vendors or Regulators

Exhibit 5-1.

When GE began its Work-Out sessions, it focused exclusively on improving the company's internal operations. Eventually, it occurred to organizers of Work-Out that the entire experience could be applied to helping GE enhance their customer and vendor relationships. After all, it was not only within GE that certain long-standing stiflers of progress existed; on various occasions, GE knew all too well that such stiflers were preventing GE from getting more out of its customers.

What to Do Next

1. Reduce the number of approvals required on routine matters.

2. Respond quickly and, where possible, immediately, to good ideas—no matter where they come from.

3. Create an atmosphere where underlings feel free to speak their minds.

4. Come to grips with the fact that you don't have all the answers.

CHAPTER 6

Work-Out 2: A Work-Out Instruction Guide

People closest to the work know, more than anyone, how it could be done better.

The Goal of Work-Out

The idea of Work-Out, Jack Welch's companywide program that started in 1989, was to push cultural change through GE. The program had a number of objectives:

The GE Refresher Course

1. Broaden debate throughout the company.

2. Take the "boss element" (Jack Welch's phrase) out of General Electric.

3. Redefine the notion of management. Managers now had to listen to employees. Employees had the right—indeed, the responsibility—to devise their own ideas for resolving issues; bosses no longer had a monopoly over decision making.

4. Clean up GE. Put it in better working order, make workers more productive, make processes simpler, more clear-cut.

5. Get rid of the wasted hours, the wasted energy, the wasted effort—all that unwanted, unnecessary baggage that a

large company like GE had been forced to carry for so long.

Work-Out was unique. It marked the first time that an entire company sought to empower its employees.

The Work-Out program at GE was unique; it was the first empowerment effort to include all employees in the company. Work-Out, in the GE chairman's view, was meant to encourage employees to stop wrestling with the kinds of absurdities that were a by-product of large organizations—too many approvals, duplication, and waste.

Such views from Jack Welch were ironic. Here was one of the nation's toughest, most aggressive bosses acknowledging to his workers that they had been bossed around far too much. Yet Work-Out was a sacred venture for Welch, and he could handle a little irony. For Work-Out was meant to promote Jack Welch's corporate revolution, setting forth a new business culture.

One that was boundaryless.

One that encouraged employees to behave with speed, simplicity, and self-confidence.

One that was informal and open—and expected everyone to share ideas and learn from one another.

Work-Out had two defining aspects:

- Employees would make suggestions to their bosses face-to-face.

- Employees would get a response—on the spot, if possible.

This was Work-Out in general terms. Now let's look at the specifics.

The GE Way

How GE Implements Work-Out

The model that appeared most suitable for bridging the walls of hostility between employees and workers at General Electric was the New England town meeting, which provided local citizens with a forum for dialogue with city leaders. GE's own version of these town meetings—Work-Out—began in March 1989.

Jack Welch wanted everyone at GE to have a taste of Work-Out by the end of its first year, so the program was *not* optional. But to diminish fears that the program was just a GE ruse for downsizing, Welch let only volunteers take part at first.

GE businesses were encouraged to hold Work-Out meetings as quickly as possible and not worry about heavy planning in advance of the meetings. The idea: get as many bodies through the program as possible.

Early workshops in Work-Out were not focused on specific workplace topics. Any issue at all could be discussed. (Later on, as Work-Out participants grew less suspicious of the program, workshops were held to determine specific goals for the meetings.)

Business leaders urged future participants to probe fellow employees for ideas that could become workshop discussion subjects. Work-Out organizers reminded those attending to feel free to raise any topic.

How GE Organized Its Work-Out Program

Exhibit 6-1 describes the three phases of Work-Out: the premeeting stage; the "town meeting" effort; and the postmeeting steps that need to be taken.

The GE Way

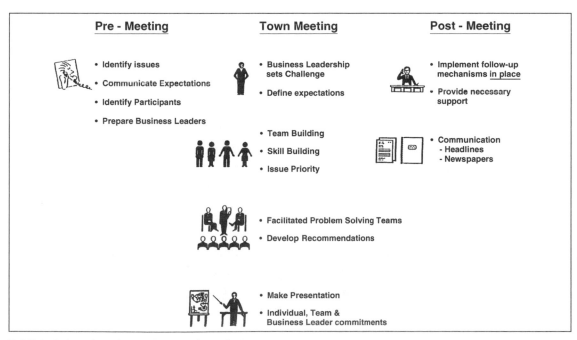

Exhibit 6-1. The three phases of Work-Out

What is clear from Exhibit 6-1 is that problem solving is a key focus of the Work-Out format—and that much planning and thought need to be put into the effort.

Preparations

Here's how Work-Out is done at GE.

1. Designate the department or business unit that will do Work-Out.

2. Send out letters to those pinpointed by organizers. The letters explains what Work-Out is all about. An invitation is issued. Candidates are told the planned dates and asked to hold those dates open. Prospective participants are told explicitly that they are not required to attend. They are asked to note whether they are interested in attending.

3. Send out a second round of letters. A second letter is mailed to those who have expressed interest in the program with details about where the opening session will be held.

4. Decide on dress code for meetings. Employees and managers alike are asked to dress casually at the workshops— chinos, T-shirts—in order to erase distinctions between managers and workers.

The Workshop Begins

Workshops usually last three days. They are always held off-site, usually at a hotel. If they are held at the office, say GE organizers, attendees will exploit their coffee breaks to drop in on their offices, return phone calls, and the like. Coffee breaks during the meetings are fine. Visits to the hotel's fitness center are a definite no! (The purpose of these sessions is to improve GE's operations, not to improve muscle tone.)

Organizers also suggest the following:

- Assign someone full-time to sit outside a Work-Out session and pass on emergency work messages. Save the nonemergency messages for a session break. (No one at GE wants to do serious damage to a GE business during these Work-Out sessions.)

- Don't have the Work-Out site too distant from the office. Perhaps a participant will need to consult a work colleague on some point raised at the Work-Out session. Encourage participants, however, to phone the office and only visit it if absolutely necessary.

- Arrange for someone back at the home office to visit the Work-Out session for a half-day. Place work manuals on a table in the back of the workshop room. (Being close to the office will allow a participant to retrieve some papers from the home office if the papers are crucial for the workshop discussion.)

The Work-Out session usually consists of forty to fifty invitees, though some sessions may have only twenty. They are a cross-section of GE personnel and range from senior and junior managers to salaried and hourly workers.

On hand is a person called the facilitator, usually an academic with expertise in how businesses function at the macro level. The facilitator is there to break the ice, if necessary; to keep the Work-Out session moving along; especially, to encourage people in the audience to speak out freely and frankly.

DAY 1

Day 1 of Work-Out.

The business leader or some other senior member of the business starts the session by describing the particular business and its strengths and weaknesses and explaining how that business fits into General Electric's overall strategy. Then the business leader leaves, and remains away from the sessions for some time. Not only does the "boss" *have* to leave. It is made clear to the boss that interfering with the session can jeopardize his or her career.

The facilitator then breaks the group into four smaller groups. These break-out groups of eight to twelve people meet in separate but adjacent conference rooms. (Facilitators recommend that the "break-out rooms" be close together, not on separate hotel floors. In that way, the facilitator can move quickly and easily from one room to another.)

Participants are asked to evaluate four aspects of their businesses:

- Reports

- Meetings

- Measurements

- Approvals

Which reports or meetings make sense, and which do not? What kinds of measurements and approvals can be eliminated? This phase is designed to get people talking.

The job of the facilitator at this stage is to keep the discussions on topic and to make sure two or more of the break-out groups are not discussing the same subject matter. It is not necessarily a problem if more than one group discusses the same topic. The facilitator simply wants to let each group know when the discussions overlap. Facilitators enjoy no veto power over what topics can be deliberated. But they are like baseball umpires. They are there to keep one employee or another from dominating a conversation—or bullying others. Like a good umpire, the facilitators are doing their job best when they are interfering the least.

From the start, organizers realized that the amount of time devoted to a Work-Out session might not be enough to deal with all the critical problems that need solving. So they decided to prioritize the problems, making sure that the most important ones were dealt with at the meetings.

Exhibit 6-2 provides a technique for prioritizing ideas that arise at a Work-Out session. Facilitators tell participants to consider how easy or hard an idea would be to implement (the "easy-hard" effort axis). If the idea were implemented, would there be a high or a low payoff for the company (the "high-low" payoff axis)? Assume that twenty-five ideas are raised during the brainstorming phase of the Work-Out; those ideas are then placed in one of the four quadrants on a chalkboard, using the easy-hard, high-low payoff axes. In this way we end up with four categories of a problem:

1. *Low-hanging fruit.* These are the most obvious ideas that are the easiest to solve. Therefore the effort is easy and the payoff is low.

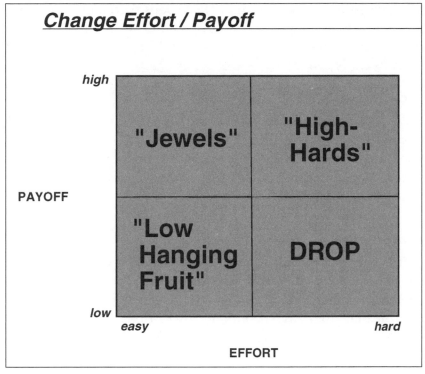

Exhibit 6-2.

2. *Jewels.* These are also problems that are easy to identify, but if they are implemented, they will have a bigger payoff to the company than the low-hanging fruit.

3. *High-hards.* These are the problems that are hard to identify but also have a big payoff to the company.

4. *Drop.* The "drops" are those issues hard to identify that have a low payoff to the company. Work-Out rules call for these issues to be dropped entirely. Better to deal with the issues that aren't so complicated or have a bigger payoff to the company.

DAY 2   **Day 2 of Work-Out.**

If it is a two-day Work-Out, the facilitator asks the break-out groups to join forces in the morning so that everyone can learn what the others are discussing. The groups then make their presentations to the boss. No one takes notes during the first two days of these sessions. It's just wasteful bureaucracy, as far as Jack Welch is concerned.

The facilitators suggest that a hot line to the home office be set up. Arrange for experts from the business's various departments (legal, finance, etc.) to be available by phone from 9 to 11 A.M. on the second day of the Work-Out gathering. The expert should not take other meetings or phone calls during that time. If someone at the session has a question, use the hot line to get hold of an expert for the answer.

Day 3 of Work-Out.

DAY 3

If it is a three-day Work-Out, the small groups converge on the morning of day 3. Only in the last few hours of the third day does the boss reappear. Work-Out reaches its peak of drama and tension in that final-day encounter between boss and employees. For two days the boss has been isolated from the employees who have been dissecting the business. This time the employees are the ones who have something to say to the boss.

The boss has to feel pressure, taking a position at the front of the room. The idea is for the boss to respond positively to as many of their proposals as possible—immediately. In the past, the boss gained authority and respect by moving to the front of the room. Now, standing before the employees, the boss may feel the ground shifting under his or her feet—an unpleasant feeling. Still, the boss must listen.

The boss remains in the dark, unaware of what has gone on in these rooms in the past few days. Soon everything becomes clear. Some facilitators encourage a different person to read out each proposal. In some Work-Out sessions the same person reads all the proposals. An important point: the facilitator should not bring up the proposals. This must come from the employees themselves.

Someone reads the proposals, and the boss gives one of three responses:

1. Agree on the spot to implement a proposal from the Work-Out attendees.

2. Say no to the proposal.

3. Ask for more information, in effect postponing a decision. The boss must then authorize a team to get that information and respond within a month.

It is a testament to the great success of Work-Out that four out of five proposals are routinely approved on the spot by the boss. That the boss is so forthcoming so quickly is also proof positive that the company has been filled with wasteful and irrelevant procedures.

Take a moment to think about your own business. Think about all the forms, reports, e-mails, and unduly long memos that are part of your company's practice—all the time-wasters. Imagine now that you could eliminate 80 percent of those energy-sapping activities once and for all. Now you appreciate the relevance of a Work-Out session, and how much immediate impact it can have on your productivity. With just about every employee at GE passing through the Work-Out program, is it any wonder that Jack Welch has been getting such high productivity rates and bottom-line results?

The Follow-up

1. Someone is asked to put together a memo on all proposals, sometimes numbering as many as twenty-five, along with steps to be taken by the management as part of checking whether a proposal can be implemented.

2. The memo, often four pages in length, is then quickly distributed to Work-Out participants, who have to certify that it accurately reflects what transpired at the final Work-Out session with the boss.

3. The memo is then circulated to everyone in the business.

4. Next to each recommendation is the name of a Work-Out participant, known as the "champion." That person takes responsibility for following up on the recommendation. He or she informs the attendees, through their Work-Out leader, of what progress has been made in getting the proposal implemented.

5. Participants are asked to avoid vague language in the memo. Sentences such as "We want to have this new policy" are discouraged.

6. Each recommendation contains action items, sometimes as many as three, and each action item has to be accompanied by a date.

7. The Work-Out leader assigned to each business, dubbed the "road-block buster," has the task of following up to make sure that each deadline is met.

Action Steps

A Work-Out Primer

Here are the seven steps required to implement Work-Out:

1. Choose issues to discuss.

2. Select a cross-functional team appropriate for the problem.

The 7 critical steps in a Work-Out program.

3. Choose a "champion" who will see any Work-Out recommendations through to implementation.

4. Let the team meet for 3 days (or 2½), drawing up recommendations to improve your company's processes.

5. Meet with managers who can say on the spot "Yes," "No," or "I'll get on to that" (with further study time specified) to each recommendation.

6. Hold more meetings as required to pursue the implementation of the recommendations.

7. Keep the process going, with these and other issues.

The whole notion of Work-Out seems counterintuitive. For decades bosses made decisions without consulting with their employees. Indeed, employees who offered suggestions for improvements were scorned and made to feel that their ideas were unwelcome. But with Work-Out, employees are encouraged—in fact, they are urged—to speak out to bosses and seek solutions to long-standing business problems. And bosses are required to take a back seat to employees who systematically critique the business, without any worry of being punished or fired. No matter how counterintuitive the program seemed, Jack Welch was determined to give the idea a chance. If Work-Out succeeded, GE would have a whole new method for improving the company. GE would benefit from all that candor that had been bottled up for so long.

The premises of Work-Out are quite simple:

- Those closest to the work are more knowledgeable about it than their bosses.

- The single best way of getting these workers to pass on that knowledge to their superiors is to give them more power.

- In exchange for that power, an employee is expected to assume more responsibility for his or her job.

With the success of Work-Out, GE reported three important benefits:

1. Productivity was higher

2. Needless tasks were jettisoned.

3. Workers felt liberated and satisfied at having those tasks done away with.

In June 1999, it was clear to Jack Welch that Work-Out still had its uses at GE. While the great burst of Work-Out sessions had occurred in the earlier part of the 1990s, the GE chairman felt it was time for a revival of the business technique, given the fact that bureaucracy seemed to be creeping back into parts of the company. "Our organizational 'attics' have probably gotten a bit cluttered again," he suggested, "and now is the time to go back, with the Internet as a tool, and clean out and simplify our organization and processes once again." Accordingly, GE Corporate was to begin a fresh Work-Out program with what Welch called a 90-day blitz beginning in September 1999.

Exhibit 6-3 illustrates the three phases of Work-Out, plotting the evolutionary process over time. It shows that as the easier quick hits were solved, ideas would gain momentum and inculcate themselves into the fabric of the GE culture. Over time, the

Work-Out initiative led to a greater sense of confidence and the new practice eventually became a part of the GE culture. As it turned out, Work-Out provided the bedrock foundation that allowed Jack Welch to create a learning organization and to launch the Six Sigma quality program.

Exhibit 6-3 presents Work-Out as an evolutionary process. In the early phase of Work-Out unnecessary work should be eliminated; confidence should be built. There should be no attempt to undertake a massive cultural change at the outset. That should come later. "You walk before you run," according to Steven Kerr, vice president of leadership development.

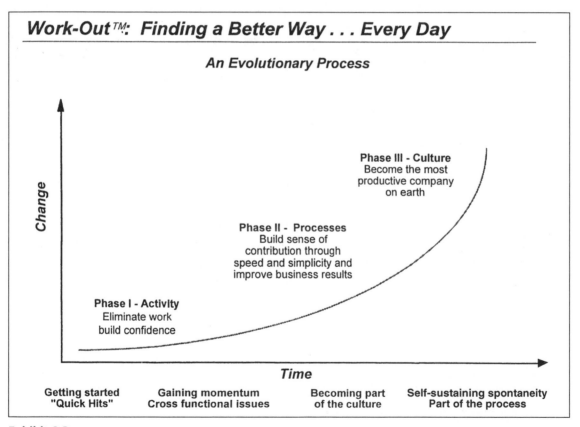

Work-Out™: Finding a Better Way . . . Every Day

An Evolutionary Process

Change (y-axis) / Time (x-axis)

Phase III - Culture
Become the most productive company on earth

Phase II - Processes
Build sense of contribution through speed and simplicity and improve business results

Phase I - Activity
Eliminate work build confidence

| Getting started "Quick Hits" | Gaining momentum Cross functional issues | Becoming part of the culture | Self-sustaining spontaneity Part of the process |

Exhibit 6-3.

1. Take a few minutes to think about the most time-wasting and ludicrous activities that exist in your company. Jot down three of them here.

    _____

    _____

    _____

Self-Assessment Exercise

2. Find out from colleagues why those three activities were thought important in the first place and put down the answers here.

    _____

    _____

    _____

3. Ask a colleague to name the three most illogical activities in the company—as a way of finding out if you and your colleagues agree on what are the most time-wasting activities. Jot down your colleague's three choices here.

    _____

    _____

    _____

In Search of Time-Wasters

Here are ten situations that lend themselves to a Work-Out session. We offer them as examples in order to stimulate your thinking about how to get rid of these annoyances and other similar daunting problems.

The GE Refresher Course

1. A young woman puts out a popular and well-received plant newspaper. But she must obtain seven signatures each month to get the newspaper published. Why does she need all those signatures?

Situations that lend themselves to Work-Out.

2. A factory worker operates a valuable piece of equipment that requires him to wear gloves. The gloves wear out several times a month. To acquire another pair he has to call in a relief operator or, if none is available, shut his machine down. He then has to walk to another building, go to the supply room, and fill out a form. He then has to walk around the plant tracking down a supervisor of sufficient authority to cosign his request. Only after he has returned the signed form to the supply room is he given a new pair of gloves. Frequently he loses as much as an hour of work. Isn't there some easy solution for him?

3. Managers at one factory are provided with special parking places. No one can think of a good reason. Are those special parking spots really necessary?

4. A secretary asks why she has to interrupt her own work to empty the out tray on her boss's desk. Why, on his next trip out of his office, can he not drop the material off on her desk? Isn't there some quick solution for this secretary?

5. At one factory the purchasing department chooses certain products without consulting with fellow employees who know those products best and who actually use the equipment. Wouldn't it make sense to have that department confer with its own employees in advance of buying the products?

6. People in the field often wonder why they have to write long reports that hardly get read and take up valuable time. Perhaps there is a way to condense the reports so that people actually do read them.

7. Workers at a plant complain that the machines they work around make the work environment steamy in the summer. But the vents are all closed on the company's orders. Why can't those vents be opened? What about buying some fans?

8. The number of forms that supervisors have to write up can be amazing. Are they all necessary? Could fewer forms be used in order to save valuable time?

9. A manager calls a meeting once a week to discuss ongoing problems. Each meeting lasts an hour and a half—often because it's someone's birthday or just because the boss wants to celebrate some achievement. Couldn't those meetings last less time? Perhaps the celebrations could be held after hours?

10. Each time a guest comes to visit a factory the manager chooses the same people to show off a new piece of equipment. Couldn't the boss train two or three people on that equipment and share the burden?

What to Do Next

1. Walk around your plant or office and look carefully at the way people do their jobs.

2. Set aside ten minutes and ask each of your direct reports to come up with a list of the biggest time-wasters.

3. Having demonstrated that your office needs some help, organize a Work-Out session along the lines of GE's format.

4. Try to implement as many of the proposals on the spot as possible.

5. For those proposals that require more time to implement, make sure they are dealt with as quickly as possible.

THE ORGANIZATION MODULE

We want people who get up every morning with a passion about finding a better way: finding from their associate in the office, finding from another company. We're constantly on the search.
—JACK WELCH, January 1999

In the following chapters we look at the way GE's Jack Welch has gone about building the best possible business organization. That organization's two main features, in his view, are what he calls boundarylessness—which we describe at great length in the opening chapter of this section—and the learning culture—referred to in the next three chapters of the section. We provide a series of questionnaires and other self-assessment exercises to help you better understand how to implement Welch's organizational strategies.

In this module you'll learn about that clumsy, but powerful word "boundarylessness" and why it's crucial to turn your company into a learning organization. You'll find Jack Welch's thoughts on:

- Learning to be as comfortable making a business deal in some foreign land as in the good old United States

- Why you need feel no shame about "stealing" someone else's ideas

- Why it's crucial to take advantage of a great source of information about your company—your very own employees!

CHAPTER 7

The Boundaryless Enterprise

We described our emerging culture by an awkward but descriptive name: "boundaryless." It is the soul of our integrated diversity and at the heart of everything we do well.

As Comfortable in Tokyo as in Toledo

General Electric had boundaries. Lots of them. And Jack Welch didn't like it, not at all. Those boundaries kept the company from functioning smoothly; they weakened the links between GE and its customers and between GE and its suppliers. Because they kept GE people from communicating with one another, because they kept GE personnel from conversing with customers and suppliers with ease and without interruption, the boundaries might as well have been barbed wire.

The GE Refresher Course

When Jack Welch took over as chairman and CEO at GE in 1981, it did not take him long to locate all the damaging boundaries within GE. Even if they were harder to spot than actual barbed wire, the boundaries existed within management where senior managers would never think of talking to anyone except their immediate direct reports. They existed between General Electric and the outside world thanks in large measure to what was commonly called NIH—a not-invented-here attitude that convinced GE employees that there was little to learn from anyone outside the corporation.

Welch couldn't understand why GE personnel automatically closed themselves off from good ideas on the outside, why they had erected boundaries. But he didn't have to understand the reasoning. All he needed to do was figure out how to get rid of the boundaries. He knew that if he could eliminate most, if not all, of the boundaries within the company, he would go far toward creating the open, informal business environment that he believed was essential to making GE as competitive as possible.

Welch could have said: "We're going to tear down the walls." Instead, he insisted that GE become boundaryless . . . a very awkward, but descriptive word.

In deciding on this new policy, Welch might have declared simply that: "We're going to tear down the walls." Or he might have decreed, "We're going to get rid of those boundaries." Instead, he called upon GE to become boundaryless. The adjective—certainly not to be found in any dictionary—was an awkward, clumsy word, and Jack Welch was the first to acknowledge it. But the word stuck and became part of the Welch lexicon, and without the GE chairman defining the word too elaborately, everyone more or less got the idea.

When he first defined the term—usually in speeches he gave in the early 1990s—Welch argued that the business strategies he had employed in the 1980s—restructuring, reducing the number of management layers, and the like—were no longer practical. They took too long to really affect the company; in short, they were too incremental.

To survive and flourish in the 1990s, he argued, GE would have to get faster, it would have to communicate to its employees more effectively, and it would have to get everyone in the company involved in improving relationships with customers. In order for all that to occur, GE had to become boundaryless. GE, said Welch, could no longer afford the luxury of scaling barriers that existed, say, between engineering and marketing, or between employees, some of whom were managers, some salaried workers, some on hourly pay. Nor, if GE was going to become a truly global company, and that was what Jack Welch wanted very badly, could it allow geographic barriers to stand in its way. In a phrase that Welch used time and time again, GE people would have to become as comfortable in New Delhi and Seoul as they already were in Louisville and Schenectady.

Boundarylessness became a key Jack Welch strategy at GE.

Exhibit 7-1 indicates how such aspects of GE's corporate culture—including its town meetings, which are part of the Work-Out program, and its productivity best-practices workshops—all contribute to the creation of a boundaryless corporation. The exhibit uses the Work-Out program to suggest that boundarylessness is a multistep process. In the case of Work-Out it begins with town meetings, expands to include customers, and only succeeds when the systems (or structure of the Work-Out program) and measurements are in place.

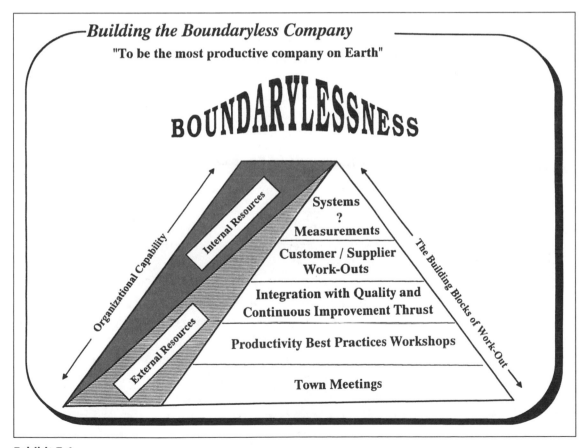

Exhibit 7-1.

The goal of boundarylessness is to make GE "the most productive company on earth." The more barriers are brought down, the more productive a company will become.

How boundaryless is your company?

One of Jack Welch's great dreams was for GE to run as if it were a small company. Of course, it was anything but small. Yet having worked in sprawling, bureaucratic GE all of his career, Welch at times yearned for the simplicity that characterized the corner grocery store. Grocery stores had no boundaries. If he could make GE boundaryless, he was certain that productivity would be enhanced, if only because there would be less bureaucratic waste. But most important to Welch, if he could make GE boundaryless, he would at the same time give his employees a new sense of empowerment, he would give them a greater degree of involvement in the day-to-day operations of the company. Tearing down the walls would finally make it possible for employees to think and speak out for themselves—and for someone above them to listen. Welch liked that. He thought the liberating of the worker held out great promise. In time, Jack Welch came to view boundaryless behavior as his most important business strategy.

Self-Assessment Exercise

How Boundaryless Is Your Company?

How boundaryless is your company? To find out, take the questionnaire shown in Exhibit 7-2. This questionnaire was drawn up by former GE consultants in the early 1990s.

Complete this exercise by assessing the extent to which each statement characterizes your company, circling a number from 1 (not true at all) to 5 (very true) for each of the sixteen entries.

To score the questionnaire, total your scores across the rows and down the columns. Each row and column score ought to be a number between 4 and 20.

Column scores reflect your organization's relative achievement of the new success factors. If you obtained a score of 12 or less on any single factor, this indicates work may be needed, particularly if the factor is critical to your industry or kind of organization. If you obtained a score of 16 or more, this suggests that

Questionnaire #1

Stepping Up to the Line: How Boundaryless Is Your Organization?

Instructions: The following sixteen statements describe the behavior of boundaryless organizations. Assess the extent to which each statement characterizes your current organization, circling a number from 1 (not true at all) to 5 (very true).

	Speed	Flexibility	Integration	Innovation	Total Score
Vertical Boundary	Most decisions are made on the spot by those closest to the work, and they are acted on in hours rather than weeks. 1 2 3 4 5	Managers at all levels routinely take on frontline responsibilities as well as broad strategic assignments. 1 2 3 4 5	Key problems are tackled by multilevel teams whose members operate with little regard to formal rank in the organization. 1 2 3 4 5	New ideas are screened and decided on without fancy overheads and multiple rounds of approvals. 1 2 3 4 5	
Horizontal Boundary	New products or services are getting to market at an increasingly fast pace. 1 2 3 4 5	Resources quickly, frequently, and effortlessly shift between centers of expertise and operating units. 1 2 3 4 5	Routine work gets done through end-to-end process teams; other work is handled by project teams drawn from shared centers of experience. 1 2 3 4 5	Ad hoc teams representing various stakeholders spontaneously form to explore new ideas. 1 2 3 4 5	
External Boundary	Customer requests, complaints, and needs are anticipated and responded to in real time. 1 2 3 4 5	Strategic resources and key managers are often "on loan" to customers and suppliers. 1 2 3 4 5	Supplier and customer reps are key players in teams tackling strategic initiatives. 1 2 3 4 5	Suppliers and customers are regular and prolific contributors of new product and process ideas. 1 2 3 4 5	
Geographic Boundary	Best practices are disseminated and leveraged quickly across country operations. 1 2 3 4 5	Business leaders rotate regularly between country operations. 1 2 3 4 5	There are standard product platforms, common practices, and shared centers of experience across countries. 1 2 3 4 5	New product ideas are evaluated for viability beyond the country where they emerged. 1 2 3 4 5	
Total Score					

Exhibit 7-2.

your organization has already acquired significant strength in the factor, but building on that strength is still important.

Row scores indicate your organization's relative success in achieving permeability of the four boundaries. A score of 12 or less on any one boundary indicates a chance for significant improvement, and a score of 16 or more indicates an area of strength.

Self-Assessment Exercise

How Healthy Is Your Organization's Hierarchy?

A second exercise related to boundaryless behavior asks: "How healthy is your organization's hierarchy?" The GE consultants who created this exercise, shown in Exhibit 7-3, suggest the following approach to this questionnaire: Have someone complete the questionnaire first; then ask colleagues to complete it. Later, hold a group forum to compare the answers and discuss the following questions:

- How important is it to our organization's success that we loosen our vertical boundaries? In other words, do we really need to operate faster and more flexibly?

- Are the red flags serious and recurrent? Which ones are most worrisome?

- To what extent is our current vertical profile dragging us down and causing us problems?

- In the current profile of our hierarchy, which dimensions are strongest? Where do we most need to change in order to be more successful?

- What is our desired profile of vertical boundaries? Where would we like to be on each of the four dimensions in the next year or so—that is, what profile do we need to complete successfully now and into the future?

Self-Assessment Exercise

How Congruent Are Your Organization's Horizontal Boundaries?

The next exercise relates to horizontal boundaries (Exhibit 7-4). Part 1 asks the person to map their organizational functions according to importance to key customers and the degree of collaboration with other functions. Part 2 asks the person to identify warning signs in the organization. And Part 3 asks the person to identify the extent of horizontal harmony in the organization. In the space provided below, the person is supposed to identify ten or more functional disciplines or specialties that exist as different units in his or her organization and then use the table to

Questionnaire #2

Stepping Up to the Line: How Healthy Is Your Organization's Hierarchy?

Part 1: Success Factors

Instructions: Determine how critical the four new paradigm success factors are in your organization, circling High, Medium, or Low for each factor.

1. Speed	High	Medium	Low
2. Flexibility	High	Medium	Low
3. Integration	High	Medium	Low
4. Innovation	High	Medium	Low

Part 2: Red Flags

Instructions: Evaluate how often the following five danger signs appear in your organization, circling a number from 1 (too often) to 10 (seldom).

	Too often	Sometimes	Seldom
1. Slow response time	1 2 3 4 5 6 7 8 9 10		
2. Rigidity to change	1 2 3 4 5 6 7 8 9 10		
3. Underground activity	1 2 3 4 5 6 7 8 9 10		
4. Internal employee frustration	1 2 3 4 5 6 7 8 9 10		
5. Customer alienation	1 2 3 4 5 6 7 8 9 10		

Part 3: Profile of Vertical Boundaries

Instructions: Assess where your company stands today on the four dimensions of information, authority, competence, and rewards, circling a number from 1 (traditional) to 10 (healthy).

Traditional Hierarchy		Healthy Hierarchy
Information closely held at top	1 2 3 4 5 6 7 8 9 10	Information widely shared
Authority to make decisions centralized at top	1 2 3 4 5 6 7 8 9 10	Authority to make decisions distributed to wherever appropriate
Competence specialized and focused—people do one job	1 2 3 4 5 6 7 8 9 10	Competence widespread—people do multiple tasks as needed
Rewards based on position	1 2 3 4 5 6 7 8 9 10	Rewards based on skills and accomplishments

Exhibit 7-3.

Questionnaire #3

Stepping Up to the Line: How Congruent Are Your Organization's Horizontal Boundaries?

PART 1: Map Relationships

Instructions: In the space below, identify ten or more functional disciplines or specialties that exist as different units in your organization.

Now use the following table to note the ways in which these units contribute to key customers and collaborate with each other. This will produce an informal map of the horizontal groups in your organization.

Organizational Unit	Professional Disciplines in the Unit	Extent of Collaboration with Other Functions (High, Medium, Low)	Contributions to Customers	Effectiveness of the Function as Viewed by the Customer (High, Medium, Low)

PART 2: Identify Warning Signs

Instructions: Assess your organization on the following warning signs of haywire horizontal boundaries. Use the scale next to each statement to indicate the extent to which the statement characterizes your organization's behavior, circling a number from 1 (not true at all) to 5 (very true). Also, make a note of an example that supports your assessment.

	Not true at all				Very true
	1	2	3	4	5

1. Organizational processes tend to be slow and sequential instead of fast and parallel.

    1   2   3   4   5

2. Functional groups are more concerned with protecting their turf than with serving the customer.

    1   2   3   4   5

3. Functional groups and disciplines place greater priority on meeting their own functional goals than on contributing to overall organizational achievements.

    1   2   3   4   5

4. Functional groups and disciplines regard each other with suspicion, blame each other for problems, and operate as though the enemy is within the organization.

    1   2   3   4   5

5. The customer needs to integrate our products and services.

    1   2   3   4   5

6. Our organization tends to swing back and forth between centralization and decentralization every few years.

    1   2   3   4   5

PART 3: Assess Horizontal Harmony

Instructions: Identify the extent to which your organization applies the five principles for creating horizontal harmony. Use the scale next to each statement to indicate the extent to which the statement characterizes your organization's behavior, circling a number from 1 (not true at all) to 5 (very true).

	Not true at all				Very true
1. The focus of attention is always on the customer.	1	2	3	4	5
2. The customer has a single point of contact with our organization.	1	2	3	4	5
3. We form and reform teams to serve the customer.	1	2	3	4	5
4. We have an extensive pool of competence that we can draw upon for customer teams—and we keep that pool refreshed.	1	2	3	4	5
5. We have active and robust processes for sharing learnings across customer teams and across functions.	1	2	3	4	5

Exhibit 7-4.

note the ways that these units contribute to important customers and collaborate with each other.

The point of this questionnaire is to get you to focus on the nature of your organization's horizontal boundaries. By filling out the questionnaire, you can assess the degree to which these boundaries may be harming the organization.

Self-Assessment Exercise

Are You a Boundaryless Leader?

In this exercise (Exhibit 7-5) you are asked to decide whether you are a boundaryless leader. Where do you think you need or want to be to move the organization forward into the twenty-first century? And where are you currently on the same scale?

The difference between the two scores is called your gap score. Since different organizations and situations require different degrees of boundarylessness, the questionnaire is built as a gap analysis. It defines the distance between where someone is currently on each dimension of the questionnaire and where that person wants to be. The person measures himself or herself against his or her own needs, not against an abstract standard.

To find one's overall score, add your eighteen individual gap scores. The results can be interpreted in the following way:

1. *A gap of 25 or less:* Either your expectations are very low or you have already achieved a remarkable level of boundaryless leadership. If your O scores are already over on the right-hand side, that's great; you could be a model of the leadership needed for the next century.

2. *A gap of 26 to 75:* You have a long way to go to become a boundaryless leader.

3. *A gap of 76 or more.* You are just getting started in your quest to achieve boundaryless leadership.

Boundarylessness in Action: The CEC in Action

There is no better example of boundarylessness at GE than the Corporate Executive Council, created in 1986 and comprising the top twenty-five to thirty executives of the company. It meets every three months—mid-March, mid-June, mid-September, and

The GE Way

mid-December—always a few weeks before the end of each business quarter.

Welch believes that a large part of what makes GE unique—and what makes GE achieve such great numbers—is the exchange of ideas that goes on among the leaders of the company's ten major businesses. The CEC meets from a Monday to Wednesday.

Welch gleefully explains the difference between the way the old conglomerates functioned and the way GE works in the late 1990s: The old conglomerate had a divisional manager and a finance manager who never met or shared ideas. Each business quarter, the divisional manager phoned the finance person to report the numbers. That was the extent of synergy in that organization. GE is different, Welch boasts. Via the CEC, its business leaders don't merely discuss numbers. They swap ideas and information from inventory turnovers to new products. Apart from the board of directors, the CEC is the most senior forum.

From time to time junior executives will be asked to give presentations to the CEC. Welch likes to keep the CEC sessions loose: There is no formal agenda put before the group. A senior GE official may distribute a brief memo to participants in advance of the get-together to alert them that Welch will want to focus at the next meeting on, say, the quality initiative. The whole purpose of the CEC is to spread ideas across the organization, to learn what problems exist in other businesses, to pick up good ideas that might work in one's own business.

In the 1980s, Welch held the CEC meetings at Fairfield headquarters. But that location seemed too formal and stuffy to him. He searched for a more comfortable site. Thus it was that in the early nineties he switched the CEC's locale to the company's leadership institute at Crotonville, New York, in the belief that the informality which pervades the campus-like setting would encourage better exchanges among the business leaders. In short, he wanted to encourage more boundaryless behavior. The change of venue worked like a charm. Welch believes that the best CEC meetings have been the more recent ones at Crotonville.

GE's great model of boundaryless behavior— the Corporate Executive Council.

Questionnaire #6

Stepping Up to the Line: Are You a Boundaryless Leader?

Instructions: On each 1 to 10 scale, place an O where you think you need to be, or want to be, to move your organization forward into the twenty-first century. Then place an X where you think you currently are on the scale. The difference between the two scores (O – X) is your gap score.

Gap Score (O – X)

1. Leadership to break down vertical boundaries

	Scale	
You and your senior management team make most decisions.	1 2 3 4 5 6 7 8 9 10	Most decisions are made close to the action.
You hold information close to the vest—and promote a need-to-know approach to information sharing.	1 2 3 4 5 6 7 8 9 10	You share information about overall performance and business strategy with as broad a base of constituents as possible.
Your recognition and reward system is based solely on individual contributions.	1 2 3 4 5 6 7 8 9 10	Your recognition and reward system is primarily team-based.

2. Leadership to break down horizontal boundaries

	Scale	
Your people have narrowly defined roles, responsibilities, and skills.	1 2 3 4 5 6 7 8 9 10	You encourage people to develop multiple skills—so everyone feels ready to do what it takes to get the job done.
You have clear functional agendas that determine the way things get done and the pace of implementation.	1 2 3 4 5 6 7 8 9 10	You ensure everyone is focused on shared goals, across functions.
You have put in place strong controls—with multiple hand-offs and sign-offs—to get work done effectively.	1 2 3 4 5 6 7 8 9 10	You push for integrated end-to-end processes with a single point of accountability to get work done—streamlined, efficient, and value-added every step of the way.

3. Leadership to break down internal boundaries

	Scale	
You and your senior management team focus most of your attention on your own company's current performance.	1 2 3 4 5 6 7 8 9 10	You are focused primarily on maximizing value to the end user.
You encourage a tough negotiating approach to interacting with customers and suppliers.	1 2 3 4 5 6 7 8 9 10	You actively seek partnership and relationships of trust with customers and suppliers.
You spend a significant portion of your time in internal meetings and in running in-house committees.	1 2 3 4 5 6 7 8 9 10	You spend most of your time with customers, suppliers, and other outside constituents.
You look for new business opportunities solely on the basis of your company's capabilities.	1 2 3 4 5 6 7 8 9 10	You formulate new business in partnership with your customers—based on their needs and changes in their markets.

4. Leadership to break down geographic boundaries

	1	2	3	4	5	6	7	8	9	10	
You promote a look-alike culture—hiring and promoting people who look like you.	1	2	3	4	5	6	7	8	9	10	You seek diversity in the people you hire and promote.
To get a shot at the top positions, executives need to "punch their ticket" in a series of domestic positions.	1	2	3	4	5	6	7	8	9	10	Significant international experience is a prerequisite for top positions.
You try to apply the domestic model for doing business to each international market you are involved in.	1	2	3	4	5	6	7	8	9	10	You always start from the local market conditions and build your business practices around these—taking very little for granted.

5. Overall leadership to make it happen

	1	2	3	4	5	6	7	8	9	10	
You are preoccupied with task management—constantly trying to explain to your subordinates the steps they need to take.	1	2	3	4	5	6	7	8	9	10	You are focused on results—you clarify expectations about the desired end results and let your people figure out how to get there.
You exercise a command-and-control model of leadership.	1	2	3	4	5	6	7	8	9	10	You lead through articulating clear goals, then coaching, counseling, and cheerleading people to achieve them.
You prefer to wait for all the analyses, reports, and studies to come in before staking a position about the issues facing the organization.	1	2	3	4	5	6	7	8	9	10	You are comfortable sketching out a rough-and-ready vision of where the organization needs to go and using actions as a way to test and refine the vision and the overall direction.
You are constantly worried about giving people more than they can handle—considering everything else on their plate.	1	2	3	4	5	6	7	8	9	10	You are comfortable putting out exceptional challenges to people—even if you have no clue how people will deliver on them.
You promote a keep-your-head-down policy—one mistake can derail a career.	1	2	3	4	5	6	7	8	9	10	You create an environment in which coming up with and exploring new ideas is encouraged and rewarded.

Exhibit 7-5.

What to Do Next

1. Pick up the phone to someone way down the organization chart when you need some information quickly.

2. Invite customers to share their problems with you openly and honestly.

3. Call a meeting of people from different functional departments in your business to tackle a thorny problem.

4. Eliminate forms that require multiple approvals; instead empower someone close to the work to make the decision.

5. Host a half-day meeting with your top customers; ask them to rate your company on the quality of your products and the speed with which you deliver them.

CHAPTER 8

Learning Culture 1: Creating the Learning Culture

It's a badge of honor to say you found something from somebody and then spread it.

No Shame in Stealing Ideas

General Electric has long been one of the great multibusiness institutions in the United States and in the world. It makes power generators and lightbulbs, aircraft engines and locomotives. In GE Capital, it has one of the most successful financial service businesses in the country; and in NBC, one of the major U.S. television networks. GE is complex and varied, and plenty of analysts—before Jack Welch came along—thought its complexity and size made it unmanageable.

The GE Refresher Course

Welch didn't agree. He was convinced that GE's diversity and complexity could be turned into an asset by creating what he called a learning culture.

How, some asked, could someone in one GE business learn something from another one if those businesses are so different?

Wasn't GE simply a conglomerate with no real coherence?

For years critics of such large organizations assailed these so-called messy conglomerates for lacking the kind of coherence that Wall Street always loved. Welch was emphatic in thinking that a concept like integrated diversity could help GE become more coherent—or at least give the impression that there was some value to being so large and diverse. Still, many wondered how such a business giant, replete with 350 businesses, could exchange ideas profitably.

Welch's reply was that the businesses were not all that different. That business was really simple. He urged employees not to make things complicated. In the mid- and late 1990s, Jack Welch began to focus on the need for GE employees to learn from one another—and to learn from outsiders.

The GE chairman understood that large, diverse corporations were potentially problematic. They needed both strong integration and strong diversity to work most effectively. Then, and only then, might the whole organization outperform the sum of its parts.

First Welch called it "Integrated Diversity"; then, the learning culture. It was all the same thing.

Welch liked to say that GE's uniqueness was based on it being a multibusiness enterprise *with a learning culture*. He explained that openness was essential. When an organization learned, and then translated that learning into action, it gained a big competitive advantage.

What Welch was driving at was the need to create a learning culture at General Electric. In an earlier era—during the 1980s—he called it "integrated diversity." The idea was that GE businesses should share knowledge and learn from one another. Out of that shared knowledge came GE's special competitive advantage. The biggest benefit would be the boost in annual growth rates.

He observed that integrated diversity could only work when the elements of that diversity, GE's businesses, were strong in their own right. That was why, he asserted, it had been so important to create strong, stand-alone businesses in the 1980s. He contends that some companies are very good at diversity, some are great at integration, but very few understand or recognize the true value of integrated diversity, of building a true learning culture.

Welch credits GE's learning culture with improving the company's performance in several ways:

- *Operating margins,* under 10 percent for the last 100 years, have risen to 16.7 percent in 1998.

- *Inventory turns,* a key measure of the use of assets, had run in the 3 to 4 range for a century, but are now 9.2.

- *Company earnings,* showing single-digit increases throughout the 1980s, have been reaching double-digit growth levels since 1992.

Assess Your Learning Culture Quotient

1. Do you find that the senior managers in your company have little sympathy for ideas they did not come up with?

   Yes   **No**

2. Do you personally feel that there is little to learn from the other parts of your businesses?

   Yes   **No**

3. Have you made a conscious effort in the last year to pick the brains of other colleagues to find out what they know that might be applied in your own work?

   Yes   **No**

4. Do you automatically assume that the way you and your company have been doing things is the best way, and there's no point in trying to learn what others are doing?

   Yes   **No**

5. Does your company offer any opportunity, formal or informal, for various divisions to share ideas?

   Yes   **No**

Self-Assessment Exercise

If you answered two or more of these questions in the affirmative, it is likely that you are part of the old way of doing business, and that there is much for you to learn from GE's attitude toward the need for a true learning culture within a business.

Self-Assessment Exercise

Let's take the learning culture assessment one step further. Please take a few minutes to jot down your answers to the following questions:

1. Write down three ideas that are in practice in your division or company that originated from an outside source.

   _____

   _____

   _____

2. Name the three most likely places you would turn for new ideas.

   _____

   _____

   _____

3. What specific plans do you have to learn from other organizations (e.g., upcoming conferences, meeting with industry colleagues, etc.)?

   _____

   _____

   _____

If you had difficulty in coming up with answers to these three straightforward questions, there is a good chance that you suffer from the not-invented-here syndrome. But take heart. In short order, we are going to provide a road map for you so that you can acquire the tools that will enable you to eliminate the NIH malady.

The GE Way

How Does a Learning Culture Work?

In GE's case, it has adapted new product introduction techniques from Chrysler and Canon; effective sourcing techniques from GM and Toyota; and quality initiatives from Motorola and Ford. Jack Welch is very proud that GE didn't invent the quality initiative—Motorola did, and Allied followed up with it; only then did GE adapt it. It's a true badge of honor, says Welch, to grab good ideas and run with them, regardless of where they originate. There's nothing intrinsically wrong with that. Indeed, it's a virtue.

Welch takes further pride in the fact that GE businesses share many things—technology, design, personnel compensation and evaluation systems, manufacturing processes, and customer and country knowledge: Gas Turbines shares manufacturing technology with Aircraft Engines. Motors and Transportation Systems work together on new locomotive propulsion systems. Lighting and Medical Systems collaborate to improve x-ray tube processes. GE Capital provides innovative financing packages that help all GE businesses.

For example, GE Capital is able to obtain solid market intelligence from GE Power Systems, which, because it builds power plants, is well acquainted with the utility industry.

GE Capital is able to generate new business after it learns that Power Systems is having problems with some of its backroom operations. Evidently Power is looking for a way to outsource some of its more troubling backroom activities, such as billing and collection. When GE Capital's retailer financial services group, which handles billing and collections for 75 million store-brand credit cards, learns of this, it springs into action to secure the account—and new business opportunity for GE Capital.

1. Search aggressively for new ideas inside and outside your organization.

2. Attend industry events in order to rub shoulders with other industry colleagues who just may have that next groundbreaking idea.

3. Make a point of phoning ten of your closest business allies and asking them what recent ideas they have implemented in their businesses.

What to Do Next

4. Spend an hour or two on the Internet each week scanning your competitors' Web sites with an eye to figuring out if they are doing anything you might learn from.

5. Look for magazine cover stories that are particularly focused on innovative business ideas.

6. Keep yourself abreast of the latest business books, particularly those on innovation and state-of-the-art technologies.

CHAPTER 9

Learning Culture 2: Stealing Shamelessly

The ultimate competitive advantage lies in an organization's ability to learn and to rapidly transform that learning into action.

Implementing the Learning Culture—An Unlikely Tool

In the last chapter you learned the background for the emergence of a learning organization within GE. Now let's shift our focus and look at some specific examples of the learning organization at work.

Action Steps

Identifying Best Practices

Lloyd Trotter, head of Electrical Distribution and Control, devised his Trotter matrix, a performance-measurement tool that he introduced in the early 1990s to describe various aspects of their businesses (Exhibit 9-1). It was quickly adopted as a way of identifying best practices in a certain business and spreading those best practices through that business. In essence, Trotter created a benchmarking tool that would win the hearts and minds of the whole company. He listed all his manufacturing plants on a vertical axis and listed a number of attributes on the horizontal axis. He then ranked all the plants on all the attri-

The GE Way

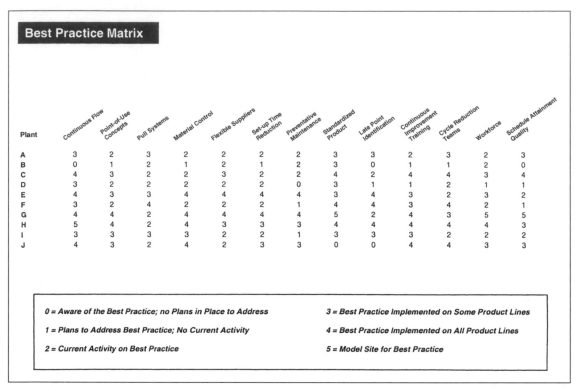

Best Practice Matrix

Plant	Continuous Flow	Point-of-Use Concepts	Pull Systems	Material Control	Flexible Suppliers	Set-up Time Reduction	Preventative Maintenance	Standardized Product	Late Point Identification	Continuous Improvement Training	Cycle Reduction Teams	Workforce	Schedule Attainment Quality
A	3	2	3	2	2	2	2	3	3	2	3	2	3
B	0	1	2	1	2	1	2	3	0	1	1	2	0
C	4	3	2	2	3	2	2	4	2	4	4	3	4
D	3	2	2	2	2	2	0	3	1	1	2	1	1
E	4	3	3	4	4	4	4	3	4	3	2	3	2
F	3	2	4	2	2	2	1	4	3	4	3	2	1
G	4	4	2	4	4	4	4	5	2	4	3	5	5
H	5	4	2	4	3	3	3	4	4	4	4	4	3
I	3	3	3	3	2	2	1	3	3	3	2	2	2
J	4	3	2	4	2	3	3	0	0	4	4	3	3

0 = Aware of the Best Practice; no Plans in Place to Address

1 = Plans to Address Best Practice; No Current Activity

2 = Current Activity on Best Practice

3 = Best Practice Implemented on Some Product Lines

4 = Best Practice Implemented on All Product Lines

5 = Model Site for Best Practice

Exhibit 9-1.

GE's Trotter Matrix—a way to identify best practices.

butes. Such a matrix could be used for many kinds of evaluations within GE, but Trotter used his to identify the plants that were performing at the highest levels.

Trotter got the idea for the matrix when he was vice president and general manager of manufacturing for Electrical Distribution and Control. He had been traveling from plant to plant and began to realize that some plants had something constructive to offer the other plants by way of "best practices." After a trip to look at GE's plants in Puerto Rico, he came to the conclusion that "we had to take some of these best practices and move them around. We had to figure out how to get into what I call institutional learning; we have to figure out how to get the plants out of the NIH mode. In the matrix that I came up with there are going to be some heroes who will be teachers and some who will be recipients of those lessons. We started in the area of inventory turns. We said we want everyone to do a 30 to 50 percent improvement over a period of time."

The truly remarkable thing about the Trotter matrix was its universal application. The matrix was straightforward and required no formal training, so any business could use it as a benchmarking tool with the minimum of fuss.

Applying the Trotter Matrix

To apply the Trotter matrix to your business, follow these steps.

Action Steps

1. Designate a business process (e.g., improved inventory turns) that you would like to assess. List it at the top of the matrix.

2. Along the vertical axis of the matrix, list the items or areas (departments, factories, etc.) to be assessed.

3. Along the horizontal axis, list the various criteria by which you judge the performance of the business process being assessed.

4. Using a simple scoring system, such as the one shown in Exhibit 9-2, rate each area or item listed on the vertical axis by each criterion listed on the horizontal axis.

5. Compile a total score for each area/item in the vertical column and for each business process in the horizontal column.

The Trotter Matrix in Action

The best-practice matrix and the scoring system were sent to every plant. The plant manager and his or her team—roughly 20 percent of the plant—then rated their plant on each of the criteria listed.

The GE Way

Trotter also devised operating rules for the matrix based on the ratings achieved—a 5 is a best-practice model site and a 0 is the lowest score, with the most ground to cover (Exhibit 9-3). Trotter's action plan for each plant is as follows:

```
GE ED&C                    Executive Development Course
─────────────────────────────────────────────────────────
Translating Needs Into Action ...


            ┌─────────────────┐
            │ Scoring System  │
            └─────────────────┘
                 0  =  Aware of Best Practice

                 1  =  Plans in Place

                 2  =  Current Implementation Activity

                 3  =  Best Practice Partially Implemented

                 4  =  Best Practice Fully Implemented

                 5  =  Best Practice Model Site
```

Exhibit 9-2.

Category 1   Those plants with a score of 0–1 were urged to visit a best-practice model site, and to devise a plan for moving toward best-practice status.

Category 2   Those scoring 2–3 were expected to step up their performance.

Category 3   The stars who ranked the highest—4–5—were asked to serve as mentors for the underachievers.

```
GE ED&C                    Executive Development Course
─────────────────────────────────────────────────────────
Translating Needs Into Action ...



            ┌─────────────────┐
            │ Operating Rules │
            └─────────────────┘
              0–1  =   Visit a 5 ... Develop a Plan

              2–3  =   Accelerate Progress ... Raise the Bar

              4–5  =   Share Strengths ... Continuous Improvement
```

Exhibit 9-3.

Lloyd Trotter explained what was expected of each of the plant managers after they received their rating: "If you are a category 1 plant you go to visit a category 3 (best-practice model site) right away. The task of the category 3 plant is to visit a weaker plant, either individually or as a team, and help it solve a specific problem. Their task is to get the 1 to a 5 quickly.

For those Trotter matrix junkies out there, here are two additional examples. Exhibit 9-4 applies the Trotter matrix to five plants that were asked to evaluate various tasks. The list of "Advantages" on the right side of the exhibit suggests the various benefits that accrue from adhering to the "Best Practice" program.

Exhibit 9-5 shows how the Trotter matrix is applied to the GE quality initiative. It asks GE businesses for evaluations on such

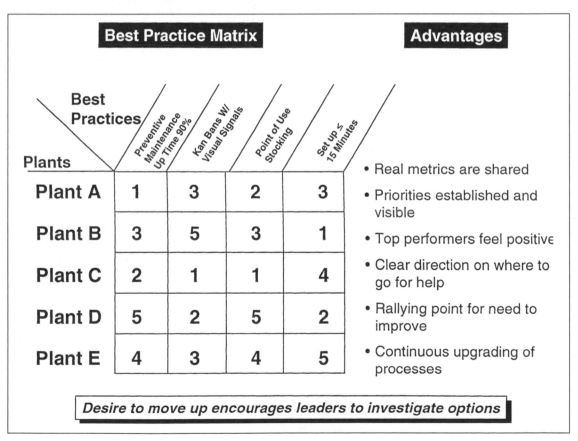

Plants	Preventive Maintenance Up Time 90%	Kan Bans w/ Visual Signals	Point of Use Stocking	Set up ≤ 15 Minutes
Plant A	1	3	2	3
Plant B	3	5	3	1
Plant C	2	1	1	4
Plant D	5	2	5	2
Plant E	4	3	4	5

Best Practice Matrix — **Advantages**

Advantages:
- Real metrics are shared
- Priorities established and visible
- Top performers feel positive
- Clear direction on where to go for help
- Rallying point for need to improve
- Continuous upgrading of processes

Desire to move up encourages leaders to investigate options

Exhibit 9-4.

QUALITY MATRIX

	GEA	D &	GEL	EMI	GEP	GEAE	GEMS	GEPS	GETS	apita	GEIS	NBC	uppl	External
QUALITY LEADERSHIP														
SUPPLIER MANAGEMENT														
PROCESS OPERATION CONTROL & IMPROVEMENT														
QUALITY INFORMATION MANAGEMENT														
PROBLEM SOLVING TECHNIQUES														
PEOPLE COMMITMENT														
CUSTOMER SATISFACTION														
NEW PRODUCT/TECHNOLOGY/ SERVICE INTRODUCTION														
CHANGE CAPABILITY														

Rating Scale: 1 = No Current Activity
2 = Ongoing Efforts
3 = Competent
4 = Best Practice
5 = Confirmed Best Practice

Exhibit 9-5.

quality-related topics as supplier management, quality information management, and customer satisfaction.

Trotter admits that the whole purpose of his matrix is "shamelessly stealing other people's ideas to make the outcome better. If you've got everybody trying to one-up each other, the creativity is enormous."

Jack Welch learned of the Trotter matrix at a company meeting where GE business leaders had gathered to discuss their specific plans for the next year. At the meeting, Trotter mentioned that he had begun using the matrix as a best-practice tool, specifically with respect to improving productivity turns. Welch was so impressed that he immediately asked Trotter to make a presentation on his Matrix at the forthcoming operating managers meeting in January 1992 in Boca Raton, Florida.

"Now it's used across the company," Trotter said proudly, "because it's so generic. You can pretty much put anything in across the top and bottom. The key is getting people to mobilize their efforts and begin to understand what to do."

Here's another example that shows how GE businesses learn from one another.

The service people in the Medical Systems business have learned how to remotely monitor a GE CT scanner as it operates in a hospital, at times detecting and repairing an impending malfunction on-line, sometimes before the customer even knows a problem exists.

Medical Systems shared this technique with other GE businesses—in jet engines, locomotives, Motors and Industrial Systems, and Power Systems—bringing overall improvement to GE businesses as a whole. Now GE businesses can monitor the performance of jet engines in flight, locomotives pulling freight, paper mills in operation, and turbines in customer power plants. This capability gives GE the opportunity to create a multibillion dollar service business by upgrading installed GE equipment.

Sharing Ideas at the Top

If executives want to figure out how to create and implement a learning action, there's no better way than studying the GE Corporate Executive Council.

It is the forum that Jack Welch has set up to ensure that knowledge is shared between and among various GE businesses.

The GE Way

Sharing ideas among GE's leaders.

Gary Wendt, the former head of GE Capital, mentioned at one of the CEC meetings that his employee orientation program was devoting a full day to Six Sigma quality training. Welch loved the idea. A few business leaders liked the idea too and said they would adapt it to their businesses; others said they saw no need to change their current employee orientation programs. Welch didn't care. The important thing was that his business leaders were exchanging ideas, learning from one another.

Welch put no pressure on the leaders to adapt every new best practice that aired at these sessions. All Welch wanted his top staff to do was generate ideas and adopt any they liked.

The CEC is meant to produce ideas. But that's not enough for Welch. So he devotes much of his energies to assuring that good ideas are implemented quickly. To Jack Welch, ideas are valuable, but they matter little unless implemented.

At the September 1997 CEC meeting, Jeff Immelt, the head of GE Medical Systems, observed to the group that another GE business, GE Transportation, performed the "dashboard" customer service tracking process better than his business did. When Immelt returned to his headquarters he called John Rice, the CEO of GE Transportation, and said he wanted to send a team over to see how Rice's business did dashboards. In a few weeks, Immelt's team descended on Rice's people.

David L. Calhoun, the head of GE Lighting, mentioned at the CEC meeting in September 1997 that he had decreed that Black Belts—the name given to project team leaders in GE's quality program—must work full-time as Black Belts for two years. Calhoun proposed the idea as a best practice for the other business leaders. Welch thought it was a great idea. But no one else did. The chairman wasn't upset. The idea has been tossed around. Some learning has been done.

What to Do Next

1. Assume that there is much to be gained from studying the business practices of your colleagues in your company. Don't overlook their efforts.

2. Pick up the phone to a manager or senior executive in your neighborhood. Explain that you want to pick his or her brain on business practices over a cup of coffee. During the get-together, listen carefully to each and every idea thrown your way, selecting the best ones. Implement those as quickly as possible.

3. Take every opportunity to find out how others in your company perform business functions—from something as simple as how they run a meeting to the more complicated tasks such as performance reviews and establishing budget goals.

CHAPTER 10

Learning Culture 3: Learning from Your Employees

We poll 10,000 employees every year. In 1995 they came back and said, 'We desperately need a quality issue.' So Six Sigma was something we adopted then.

Do You Know What Your Employees Are Thinking?

Before we learn about how GE gets inside the minds of its company employees, let's spend a few moments engaged in some thinking of our own.

Self-Assessment Exercise

1. Do you feel that your employees have anything to teach you about the future direction of your business?

   Yes   **No**

2. Have you in the past year undertaken any general surveys of what your employees think on any issue?

   Yes   **No**

3. Do you honestly know how your employees feel about the company's most important initiatives?

   Yes   **No**

4. Do you feel that the vast majority of your employees are happy to be working at your firm?

   Yes   **No**

5. Do you feel that the overwhelming majority of your employees have confidence in the senior management team?

   Yes　　　　　　**No**

If you answered a majority of the questions yes, then it's clear
that you're on the right track—you have confidence in the judgment of your employees and you rely upon that judgment for
your decision making. But if you did not answer most questions
in the affirmative, then you can benefit enormously from the way
GE's Jack Welch uses the wisdom of his employees.

The Search Within

The GE Way

GE relies heavily on employee surveys as part of its learning culture.

In a true learning culture no stone is left unturned in the quest for
knowledge. Frequently, however, CEOs who thirst for knowledge
disparage one very important source—their own employees.
Employees, they feel—incorrectly—are the last people to be offer-
ing advice on the direction a company should take. Jack Welch
has learned just the opposite. His faith in the collective wisdom of
his employees has brought him to the point where he relies upon
their judgment often, and sometimes above all others.

We don't want to give the impression that Welch wanders the
corridors of his factories and offices and buttonholes just any
employee, seeking information at random. He is far more systematic than that. He has learned to rely upon professional survey techniques that allow him to canvas a sizable portion of his
worker population, giving him on a yearly basis a broad-gauged
look at what his employees worry about and what satisfies them.
To Welch, they are the very fount of wisdom. From the moment
that his employees identified the improvement of quality as an
urgent GE need in an employee survey, Welch has come to trust
the judgment of his employees implicitly. He genuinely believes
that they have their fingers on the pulse of both the company and
broader business trends.

For all these reasons, Welch has focused on employee surveys
as a key to GE's learning culture. Such surveys are a fairly
unusual corporate practice. Companies going through the same
turmoil today that GE went through in the early and mid-1980s

feel that they have no incentive to undertake such surveys. After all, who would want to ask employees how satisfied they feel with their company when downsizing is rampant and the fear of losing one's job is a predominant concern? Executives would be afraid of getting their head handed to them if they carried out a survey like that.

But not in Jack Welch's General Electric.

Each year since 1994 in the first week of April, Welch has sent out questionnaires—known as the CEO survey—to get a sense of how employees feel about a whole variety of business issues. Jack Welch uses the surveys to test how successfully his corporatewide initiatives are permeating the entire rank-and-file; he also uses the surveys to learn whether the company should be devoting more resources and effort to certain issues.

How the employee survey works.

He started to conduct the survey with the aim of making sure that his own initiatives and rhetoric were consistent with the reality, as seen by his businesses. He realized in time that the survey had far more value than simply serving as a reality check: It could indeed become part of the learning culture that Welch was so keen on promoting. By taking advantage of the survey, Welch's GE could adjust its strategic directions. The classic example Welch always points to, of course, was the first survey in which employees noted that quality had been neglected at GE.

Past employee responses have also encouraged the company to upgrade its information technology capability; and to devote more resources to the service initiative. Employees, perhaps encouraged by the fact that their responses are anonymous, have also prodded Welch to deal more decisively with poor performers within the company.

Who gets surveyed?

All GE vice presidents, the entire senior executive band, and all executive bands—some 3,500 employees. Beyond that, another 7,000 professional employees are randomly surveyed, including the newest hires. Welch sends everyone surveyed a letter, but not to his or her office; instead GE sends these surveys to the employee's home.

Those surveyed are given a month to answer. Because a certain number do not respond—they mislay the letter or discard it or they may have moved—a second letter is sent out two weeks later. Out of the 10,000 surveys issued, GE gets a very impressive 80 percent return. Not all questionnaires are the same: for example, employees in businesses that have a heavy service element are asked a few questions about services. The questions posed are based upon those business topics that are highlighted in Jack Welch's most recent letter in the GE annual report. William J. Conaty noted: "We continue to win all these great awards for having the best annual report. The analysts love it, but do our employees really believe all this stuff?" Welch uses the survey to tell whether he is going too fast or too slow in advancing such programs as Six Sigma.

There are roughly fifty questions in the survey. Most of the questions—80 to 85 percent—have not changed in the five years of the survey. The other 15 to 20 percent are tailored to GE's current initiatives and business strategies, e.g., services, information technology, or quality. "We know we're going to get some negative comments to these questions," observed Conaty. "That's what we want. We want to see what it feels like down in the organization so then we can address it. We can then do a better job of explaining why, for instance, we have a rationale for outsourcing." The respondents are asked to grade the questions 1 through 5, where 1 is "strongly disagree," 2 is "disagree," 3 is "neither agree or disagree," 4 is "agree," and 5 is "strongly agree." Here are a few sample questions taken from GE's survey:

1. I see a clear Internet strategy emerging in my business.

2. The impact that the Internet will have on the future of this business has been clearly explained to me.

3. My business leaders have explained the reasons for sourcing products, components, and intellectual work from low-cost countries.

4. In many cases my business is better off sourcing from lower-cost global suppliers.

"We don't want the survey to be stale," said Conaty. Then he added: "We know from these new questions that we're not going to get overwhelmingly positive answers because the questions are new. These are initiatives that we're pushing. On the Internet questions, you're going to find a lot of people who say, 'No way, no one's ever explained the Internet to me.' Or you'll find a lot of people in the neutral category who feel: 'I don't have a clue.'"

Three senior GE executives decided on the original questions (the 80 to 85 percent that remain from year to year): Jack Welch, Bill Conaty, and Conaty's assistant, statistician John Hollenbach, who is manager for employee research. Welch thought this important enough to devote two days to thrashing out the best questions with Conaty and Hollenbach.

Exhibit 10-1 is the letter that Conaty sends to GE business leaders to make sure that GE employees respond to the survey. Jack Welch himself also pens a letter to those being asked to participate in the survey.

Once the surveys are collected, the results are tabulated by machine. (You may wish to tabulate the results by hand if the

---

TO: GE Business Leaders
          Business HR Managers

FROM   Bill Conaty

DATE   March 29, 1999

     In the first week of April, the CEO will be sending the attached letter and survey to a sample of exempt employees. Similar surveys have provided useful insights into GE's progress toward the goals that Jack outlines in his Annual Report letter.

     This year's survey will be sent to all Vice Presidents, SEBs, and EBs, and 7,000 exempt employees below EB. The survey will go to people's homes with a request that it be returned in two weeks.

     Please use your normal business meetings and other opportunities to encourage exempt employees to participate if they happen to receive the survey. Your endorsement and support have a big impact on the success of this effort to provide direct feedback to the CEO.

     Thanks very much for your help.

Bill

Exhibit 10-1. William J. Conaty Letter to Business Leaders

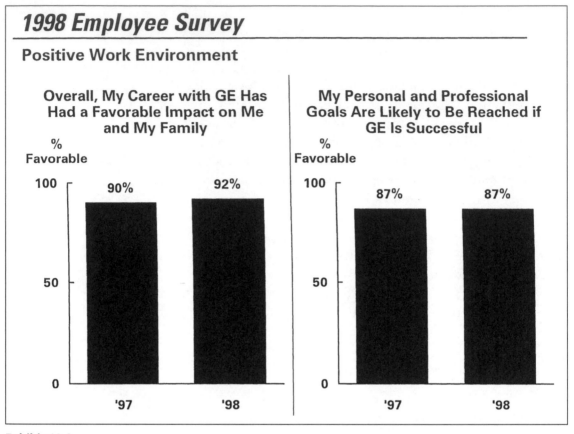

1998 Employee Survey

Positive Work Environment

Overall, My Career with GE Has Had a Favorable Impact on Me and My Family

My Personal and Professional Goals Are Likely to Be Reached if GE Is Successful

Exhibit 10-2.

number of participants in your survey are fewer than those in GE.) Exhibit 10-2 shows a graphic tabulation of two questions from the 1998 questionnaire. The overwhelming majority of GE employees—87 percent—say that their personal and professional goals are likely to be attained if GE is successful.

What to Do Next

1. Start to give your employees the feeling that you respect their opinions. Send a companywide e-mail indicating that you are planning to launch a survey and need their help.

2. If you haven't done so in the past year, work with your human resource manager to develop an in-depth employee survey.

3. Tailor the survey to the most pressing topics related to your latest initiatives.

4. Once the results of your survey are in, pay close attention to what your employees are telling you.

5. Make sure to follow up with an e-mail to all employees that lays out your plans for addressing their concerns.

THE CUSTOMER MODULE

Six Sigma is the most important management training thing we've ever had. It's better than going to Harvard Business School. It's better than going to Crotonville. It teaches you how to think differently.
—JACK WELCH, Interview, April 1999

The Six Sigma quality initiative is unquestionably the most important corporate initiative ever launched by Jack Welch. It has had a tremendous impact on the company since its inception in 1996 and it will continue to do so. In the following section we present a complete picture of GE's Six Sigma program, how it began, how it works, what impact it has had on the company, and what Jack Welch thinks about it.

In this module we'll take you through a step-by-step primer on how to implement a Six Sigma quality program. You will learn:

- Why Jack Welch dismissed quality programs at first as ineffective and meaningless

- How Jack Welch came to realize that GE had to have a major quality initiative

- How Welch spread the Six Sigma quality effort through GE at lightning speed and with remarkable results

- Just what Six Sigma quality is and how it can be employed in many business situations

CHAPTER 11

Six Sigma 1: Setting the Stage

Six Sigma training is the breeding ground of the GE business leadership of the next century.

Why Opt for Six Sigma?

When Jack Welch decides that the time has come for GE to tackle a problem, he does not care if he is late in suggesting the idea, nor does he care if others have been toying with the idea for years. He only cares whether the idea can help General Electric. If it can, he acts without hesitation, quickly, decisively, without concern for what others might think or say.

The GE Refresher Course

Case in point: In the mid-1990s he became convinced that the time had come for a sweeping corporate initiative on quality.

At first it seemed an odd choice for Welch to make. He had never really been a big fan of quality programs. Past GE efforts at improving quality never quite got off the ground. Sure, the brass was always ready to put up banners and slogans urging employees to improve quality, but most understood that the company's heart was hardly in the endeavor. Most glanced at the slogans, then promptly forgot them.

Moreover, no one had really questioned the level of quality at GE. The company had certainly made a big point about having quality products and processes in the past, and its reputation on the whole had been a good one. So why was Welch so certain that GE had to take on quality as if its very survival depended on it?

One explanation: GE's products and processes had not yet attained world-class quality. Other companies like Motorola, Toyota, and Hewlett-Packard enjoyed glowing reputations, but not GE.

Furthermore, Jack Welch had made a mistake and later admitted it: He had taken for granted that his business strategies alone would in and of themselves generate higher quality throughout the organization. As long as Welch improved the speed with which GE employees operated, as long as he improved their productivity, as long as he raised their level of involvement in company decision making, he would get quality. He was sure of it. But the expected level of quality never materialized.

It was only when GE employees argued forcefully that there was a big problem with the company's quality that the GE chairman decided to act.

Welch learned from his employees that they were spending too much time fixing and reworking a product before it got out of the factory. The wasted time was costly, but no one seemed to mind. Indeed, the wasted time was simply chalked up to the cost of doing business or the cost of attaining quality. But all was not well; one of the key goals of any quality initiative is pleasing the customer. Lengthy product delays that result from reworking and retesting only fuel customer dismay. With so much reworking and retesting going on, quality suffered.

GE's inertia over quality could be traced to one of Welch's pet programs, Work-Out, which had been one of his core business strategies. Welch simply assumed that he would get quality in his products and processes by promoting Work-Out. After all, many of Welch's values were promoted through that program—informality and openness, boundarylessness, high involvement, creating a learning culture, and the three Welch S's: self-confidence, simplicity, and speed. If those values were spread throughout the company, quality would emerge—at least that was Welch's theory.

Beyond disseminating these values, the entire Crotonville experience was designed, among other things, to improve quality.

Eventually, Jack Welch realizes that GE must do something to improve its quality—both of its products and of its processes.

The fact was, there was little incentive to worry about quality, for as long as GE's top-line and bottom-line kept growing, few questioned whether GE's quality was at a sufficiently high level. Yet Welch got a real comeuppance from reading employee surveys. He had seen the slogans and banners touting quality at GE, but had paid little attention to them. Now, reading the complaints of his own employees, he knew that his theory was simply wrong. He realized that he had no other choice but to act, and to act decisively.

Welch knew that only a broad-based, companywide initiative would have a chance of helping him reach his goal: substantially improving the quality of GE's products and processes. Everyone would have to get involved. He had no objection to more slogans and banners, but this time there would have to be meaningful follow-up and close monitoring of the situation. The extent of the new initiative would be more akin to a comprehensive battle plan, as opposed to an ill-defined set of exhortations. In Welch's world, there was simply no room for failure.

How Does Your Company Rate on the Quality Issue?

Self-Assessment Exercise

1. Are you confident that your customers would rank your product among the industry's best?

   Yes   **No**

2. Have you given much thought to improving quality in your products and processes in the past?

   Yes   **No**

3. In the past year have you sent reminders to employees—whether in the form of banners or e-mails or company-wide memos—urging them to improve the quality of your products and processes?

   Yes   **No**

4. In the past year have you done any benchmarking at other companies to find out what they are doing to improve quality?

   Yes   **No**

5. In the last year have you undertaken a specific program to improve quality?

   Yes   **No**

6. Have you given thought to starting a companywide initiative that would strive to improve quality throughout your company?

   Yes   **No**

How does your company rate on quality?

If you answered a majority of these questions in the affirmative, it is clear that you have felt a need to promote the idea of quality around your company. But what you have undertaken may not be enough. We would like to argue that much more could be done.

Let's take a moment to assess how far along your company is in implementing a companywide quality initiative.

Self-Assessment Exercise

1. Please note the products you feel would benefit from an improvement in quality.

   _____

   _____

   _____

2. Please note the processes you feel would benefit from a quality improvement program.

   _____

   _____

   _____

3. What are the three largest barriers to your company's ability to launch a companywide quality initiative?

   _____

   _____

   _____

4. What can be done to overcome these barriers?

_____

_____

_____

How Jack Welch Attacked the Quality Problem

Once Welch decided to confront GE's problem with quality, he attacked the matter like a bulldog, and GE has not been the same company since. He found the answer in two words: Six Sigma.

The GE Way

Before going on, we would like to warn you that the stuff that comes next could make math haters cringe. After all, a lengthy discussion of mathematics and statistics is hardly beach reading. Don't be put off. This discussion is vital to understanding what Jack Welch and GE did to improve quality. We'll try to make this as painless as possible.

Six Sigma is the statistical measure that expresses how close a product comes to its quality goal. Six Sigma became GE's yardstick. If a GE product or process reached Six Sigma levels, it signified the attainment of high quality.

You've probably figured out by now that the number before the word "Sigma" carries great significance. You're right.

If the 6 is equal to high quality, it makes sense that lower numbers indicate lower quality.

One Sigma = 68 percent of one's products are acceptable
Three Sigma = 99.7 percent
Six Sigma = 99.999997 percent

Six Sigma means there are only 3.4 defects per million parts. This has emerged as the benchmark for high quality—fewer than 3.5 defects per million.

In effect then, Six Sigma is a mathematical measure of faulty parts per million pieces manufactured, with Six Sigma being perfection—or pretty close to it.

It is this statistical standard—Six Sigma—against which figures can be multiplied: the greater the figure, the higher the precision; the higher the precision, the higher the quality. In short,

Six Sigma suggests far more quality than Three Sigma. At Six Sigma, only 3.4 defects per million operations occur. At Three and a Half Sigma, average for most companies, there are an astounding 35,000 defects per million.

It was the Japanese who for decades had been placing great emphasis on quality; their products, like televisions and watches, routinely reached Six Sigma standards. In the hope of rivaling the increasingly competitive Japanese, certain American companies led by Motorola—whose quality standards were only Four Sigma—decided to make quality a top priority. This was long before GE got into the act.

The American companies had one advantage in their quest for higher quality. Japan's high standards applied only to products such as precision instruments, cars, and electric equipment, that is, only to manufacturing. Japan had not focused its quality programs on improving business processes. If American companies such as GE could improve not only their products but their processes, it might defeat the Japanese on the quality front.

Motorola became the first American company to put in place a Six Sigma effort. This was in the late 1980s and early 1990s. The results were impressive: reducing the number of defects in Motorola's products, moving from Four Sigma to Five and a Half Sigma, saving $2.2 billion in the process. Allied Signal and Texas Instruments adopted the program as well.

By 1994 and early 1995, word of the Six Sigma programs spread to GE. At first, Jack Welch was concerned that Six Sigma ran counter to his business strategies for the following three reasons:

1. It was centrally managed.

2. With its reports and standard nomenclature, it appeared too bureaucratic.

3. It required specifically agreed-upon measures.

Welch was hesitant, not yet willing to throw his hat into the Six Sigma ring. The Six Sigma initiative simply didn't feel like a GE program in the way that Work-Out did, with its stress on breaking down bureaucratic boundaries, pushing for openness, and encouraging employees to learn from one another. The goal of Work-Out had been to cut down, if not eliminate entirely, all those meetings and measures, all those reports and approvals. And now here was Six Sigma appearing to welcome back measurements and monitoring.

That his own workers—in particular the manufacturing and engineering people—had recognized and spoken up in favor of GE getting behind a solid quality initiative finally convinced Welch to adopt the Six Sigma approach.

April 1995: It is one month before Jack Welch enters the hospital for ten days for triple-bypass heart surgery. GE sends around an employment survey and the results come back showing that GE employees are not content with the quality of the company's products and processes. Peering at the results of that survey, Welch is beginning to come around. But he's not quite there yet.

The decisive moment comes in the spring. Larry Bossidy, the chairman of Allied Signal, provides the spark. Welch has the greatest respect for Bossidy who until July 1991, when he took his current job at Allied Signal, had been a vice chairman at GE and one of Welch's closest friends. In 1994, Bossidy began his own Six Sigma effort at Allied Signal. One day he phoned Welch to tell him what he thought of the concept: "Jack, this ain't b.s. This is really great stuff."

Welch then asked Bossidy to appear before GE's Corporate Executive Council where Bossidy suggested that Six Sigma could have an enormous impact for the good on GE. "GE is a great company," he told the CEC. "I know. I worked there for thirty-four years. But there is a lot you can do to become greater. If GE decides to engage in Six Sigma, you'll write the book on quality." Welch was getting close to making a decision on Six Sigma. If Larry Bossidy was that high on the idea, GE could only benefit, Welch believed.

Soon after that CEC meeting, Welch, putting Gary M. Reiner, senior vice president and chief information officer, in charge of the new program, ordered him to do some research on how other companies (including Motorola and Allied Signal) had been handling their Six Sigma programs.

By the fall of 1995, Welch was ready to move ahead with Six Sigma. He was determined to give the idea of quality his full attention. The entire company would be involved. From what he had heard, he was now convinced that quality improvement could be the breakthrough business strategy that would make GE the most competitive company on earth.

It was estimated that the cost of *not* implementing Six Sigma (i.e., staying at Three Sigma or Four Sigma) could be as much as 10 to 15 percent of GE's annual revenues—an astronomical $8 to $12 billion. GE hoped to save that money within five to seven years via the quality initiative.

What to Do Next

1. Don't believe that quality will just happen.

2. Use your banners and slogans if you must, but don't put too much trust in them.

3. Understand that quality won't come simply from a speech, a slogan, or an isolated effort on your part.

4. Piecemeal quality efforts are doomed to fail; launch your quality effort only on a companywide basis.

5. Don't launch a quality effort on a shoestring; make sure you have the necessary resources before you launch the drive.

CHAPTER 12

Six Sigma 2: Designing a Six Sigma Program

We're basically changing every process we have in the company.

Early in January 1996 Jack Welch announced to his top 500 managers at a meeting in Boca Raton, Florida, that he was launching a path-breaking program that he hoped would transform the company. The new effort would be "the biggest opportunity for growth, increased profitability, and individual employee satisfaction in the history of our company," said Welch.

The GE Refresher Course

At this same meeting Welch set forth the time line he envisioned for the Six Sigma effort, predicting that GE would become a Six Sigma company in four years. He realized that such a prediction might seem overly ambitious, but four years, he was convinced, was doable. It had taken pioneer Motorola an entire decade to reach Five and a Half Sigma. Yet, Motorola, he knew, had had to start from scratch and develop the tools. GE would benefit from all of Motorola's testing and hard work. In addition, GE, with its open, informal Work-Out culture, would be more likely to find its employees eager to embrace the quality initiative.

Until early 1996, GE's level of quality was no higher than Three and a Half Sigma, about average for most American corporations. This sigma level generated as many as 35,000 defects per million operations. Jack Welch and GE certainly had their work cut out for them. For GE to attain Six Sigma quality, it would have to cut down its defect rate by 10,000 times. Using the year 2000 as its target goal, that represented an average reduction in defect levels of 84 percent a year.

GE, and most other American firms, were far from perfect. But there was one notable exception—and thank God for that!—the airlines. They can't afford to perform at anything less than Six Sigma standards—any lower would mean crashing planes and lives lost. So it's not at all surprising to find that airlines take this Six Sigma business quite seriously—and their safety record has been calculated at less than 0.5 failures per million operations; that puts their quality rating at Seven Sigma plus. Now that's safety. (Of course, their baggage operations are another matter. These operations are in the 35,000 to 50,000 defect range, no better or worse than the quality levels attained in other business areas.)

Action Steps

How to Get Started in Six Sigma

The first step in implementing the Six Sigma initiative is to set up teams that will take on projects that aim for a Six Sigma level of precision. Each team can have as many members as needed, as few as one, even.

These teams move along a four-step process known as MAIC:

1. Measurement

2. Analysis

3. Improvement

4. Control

The Six Sigma program at GE called for the creation of a whole new "warrior class," consisting of:

• Green Belts

• Black Belts

• Master Black Belts

To get "belted," GE managers undergo the complex statistical training of Six Sigma.

On May 22, 1997, Jack Welch issued an order to his 500 senior managers linking Six Sigma training to promotion (Exhibit 12-1). This memo from Welch, cosigned by his two vice chairmen, underscores the importance top management placed on the Six Sigma initiative.

May 22, 1997

TO: All Boca Attendees

FROM: J. F. Welch, P. Fresco and J. D. Opie

RE: **Clarification of Promotion Requirements
            Associated with 6σ Quality**

- Effective 1/1/98, one must have <u>begun</u> Green Belt or Black Belt training in order to be promoted to an EB or SEB position.

- Effective 7/1/98, one must have <u>completed</u> Green Belt or Black Belt training in order to be promoted to an EB or SEB position.

- Effective 1/1/99, all exempt employees including Officers, must have begun Green Belt or Black Belt training.

- To ensure consistency of Green Belt definition:

    - for all but Sales personnel .... very similar or identical to Black Belt training but part time project work

    - Sales personnel ... business discretion on magnitude of training with minimum of five days.

Exhibit 12-1.

At the heart of Welch's memo is a not-so-subtle threat: Get a belt, get promoted. Don't get a belt, get left behind, or perhaps even fired! That threat was proof-positive that Welch was not only serious, he was also willing to bet his employees' future on the success of the program. To further underscore his commitment, Welch tied 40 percent of his 120 vice presidents' bonuses to exhibiting progress in the quality program.

At the start of its quality effort, GE focused on cutting down on time-wasting and effort-expending tasks that cost the company money. For example:

1. Billing a customer

2. Making the base of an incandescent lightbulb

3. Approving a credit card application

4. Installing a turbine

5. Lending money

6. Servicing an aircraft engine

7. Answering a service call for an appliance

8. Underwriting an insurance policy

9. Developing software for a new CT product

10. Overhauling a locomotive

11. Invoicing an industrial distributor

The GE Way

Six Sigma: Assuring Early Success

In its first year or so, GE's Six Sigma initiative was considered just another management fad, and it was difficult for employees to gauge how serious senior leadership was about pushing it aggressively. The real lowdown on the program trickled through the ranks at a snail's pace. This was not what top management had in mind for Six Sigma. So Welch took it upon himself to make sure that GE employees knew precisely what the program was all about. More to the point, Welch wanted to convey to employees what their roles would be in the effort. Hence, he stepped up his personal promotion of the plan, talking about it in speeches, and, in the spring of 1996, distributing a pamphlet entitled "The Goal and the Journey." This pamphlet, only six pages in length, told succinctly what Six Sigma was all about. GE employees weren't expected to memorize the whole thing, but they were certainly supposed to digest the main message, which was that the company would be devoting a significant percentage of its resources and time to this initiative. What Welch was saying in so many words was, Get aboard or get out.

Six Sigma quality was taught and implemented throughout the company. At Crotonville, courses were taught. Responding to Welch's warnings that GE personnel were expected to "volunteer" for Six Sigma training—or face some form of punishment—not surprisingly, the list of applicants for training programs grew and grew.

Implementing the Six Sigma program.

Anyone visiting GE sites was bound to sense the excitement. Those sites evoked a feeling of one large boot camp where the "troops" rallied around the quality program to the point of becoming obsessive. By the end of 1998, GE's ranks had swelled to 293,000, owing to an important degree to the quality initiative's need for extra personnel:

1. When launching a quality initiative, spread the word as fast as possible.

2. Don't rely on the company grapevine to get the message out.

Action Steps

3. To insure early buy-in, senior management should play an active role in rallying the troops.

4. Provide a true monetary incentive that will reward people for getting on board the quality program quickly.

5. Punish the laggards, even to the point of threatening them with dismissal.

CHAPTER 13

Six Sigma 3: Putting It into Practice

Six Sigma has spread like wildfire across the company, and it is transforming everything we do.

Action Steps

Getting Started in Six Sigma

General Electric built its quality program on the Motorola model and divided its Six Sigma process into four basic steps:

1. Measuring every process and transaction

2. Analyzing each of them

3. Painstakingly improving every process and transaction

4. Rigorously controlling them for consistency once they have been improved

GE probes, measures, and analyzes in order to get at the root causes of a quality-inhibiting problem.

It then tries to keep the problem from recurring.

This control phase is the most important. Until Six Sigma began at GE, products and processes were fixed—but they didn't stay fixed. There were just not enough controls. That's where Six Sigma comes to the rescue; the control phase insures that whatever gets fixed stays fixed. GE quality initiative projects are audited for 6 to 12 months—and then every 6 months there-after—to keep quality standards high at all times.

Implementing the Six Sigma Program

Here are the steps for implementing Six Sigma.

Action Steps

1. Designate a project for Six Sigma.

2. Define critical-to-quality characteristics. (CTQs are those items that are essential for customer satisfaction in a product or a business process.)

3. Start the Six Sigma process. Master Black Belts (defined below) mentor Black Belts following the four-phase Six Sigma MAIC technique:

*   *Measure* Start by identifying the crucial internal process that influences CTQs and then measure the defects generated relative to identified CTQs. A defect is an out-of-tolerance CTQ. The phase is complete when the Black Belt can successfully measure the defects generated for a key process affecting the CTQ.

*   *Analyze* Try to understand the reasons why defects are generated. This phase calls for brainstorming, using statistical tools and other means to find out what are the key variables (X) that cause the defects. The phase ends when there is a clear-cut sense of those variables that are likely to drive process variation the most.

*   *Improve* Confirm the key variables, then quantify the effect of these variables on the CTQs. Identify the maximum acceptable ranges of the key variables to assure that the measurement systems can measure the variation in the key variables. Finally, modify the process so that it stays within the acceptable ranges.

*   *Control* Ensure that the modified process now permits the key variables (X) to stay within the maximum acceptable ranges using tools such as statistical process control (SPC) or basic checklists.

Let's stop here and give a thumbnail sketch of the different players in the Six Sigma effort as described at GE:

Champions, Master Black Belts, Black Belts, Green Belts—the players in Six Sigma.

Champions   These are the senior managers who define the projects and lead the Six Sigma efforts. They approve and fund projects and do whatever troubleshooting is required. At the outset of the program some business leaders were Champions. A GE business routinely has seven to ten Champions. Champions are not required to work full-time in the quality program, but they are supposed to devote as much time as necessary to making sure the program succeeds. Length of time that Champions train: 1 week. The quality program began with some 200 Champions. By the spring of 1999 every officer and every senior executive had become a Champion—some 800 people altogether.

Master Black Belts   Full-time teachers with a good deal of quantitative skills and teaching and leadership ability, these Master Black Belts review and mentor Black Belts. Length of training: at least 2 weeks. In the spring of 1999 there were 700 Master Black Belts. A Master Black Belt gets certified after overseeing at least ten Black Belts who become certified, and is approved by the business Champion team.

Black Belts   Black Belts are full-time quality executives who lead teams, focus on key processes, and report the results back to the Champions. These team leaders are responsible for measuring, analyzing, improving, and controlling key processes that influence customer satisfaction and/or productivity growth. Black Belts work full-time in the Six Sigma program. In the spring of 1999 there were 4,500 Black Belts, compared to 2,600 at the end of 1997. To become certified, a Black Belt must be approved by the business Champion team.

Green Belts   These are GE personnel who take part in Black Belt projects on a part-time basis. Upon completing the Black Belt project, team members must continue to use Six Sigma tools in their regular job. By the spring of 1999 GE had trained almost all of those intended for Green Belt training.

Here are key elements of the Six Sigma time line:

- Length of time for each phase of MAIC is 1 month.

- Each phase starts with 3 days of training.

- Next step includes 3 weeks of "doing."

- Then there is a 1-day formal review by the Master Black Belts and Champions.

After a Black Belt completes the first project under the aegis of a Master Black Belt, he or she takes on further projects, which are only reviewed by a Master Black Belt. Both Masters and Black Belts are supposed to work full-time in their roles for at least 2 years. A Black Belt is certified after completing two projects, the first under the aegis of a Master Black Belt, the second one more independently.

GE measures the success of Six Sigma quality projects in very exact terms: If the process began at less than Three Sigma (66,000 defects per million operations), the defects must be reduced ten times in order for the quality project to be deemed a success. If the process began at greater than Three Sigma, success occurs when there is a 50 percent reduction in defects.

The Five Measures of Six Sigma Progress

When the program got underway, GE decided on five criteria to help participants determine progress made in striving for Six Sigma:

Action Steps

Customer satisfaction   Each business performs customer surveys, in which it asks customers to grade GE and the best-in-category on critical-to-quality issues. A defect is considered any score that is either less than best in a category or, even if best in a category, less than 4 (on a scale of 1 to 5). GE measures defects per million survey responses. As with all measures in the project, the results are reported quarterly. (By the spring of 1999, GE had made customer satisfaction a focus of the quality program.)

Cost of poor quality There are three components: appraisal, which is largely inspection; internal costs, largely scrap and rework; and external costs, mostly warranties and concessions. GE keeps track of the total as a percent of revenues quarterly.

Supplier quality GE keeps track of defects per million units purchased, where the defective part has either one or more CTQs out of tolerance and thus must be returned or reworked or the part is received outside the schedule.

Internal performance GE measures the defects generated by its processes. That measure is the total of all defects in relation to the sum of all opportunities (CTQs) for defects.

Design for manufacturability GE measures the percent of drawings reviewed for CTQs and the percent of CTQs designed to Six Sigma. All new products are now designed for Six Sigma. This measure is very important since the design approach often drives the defect levels.

The GE Way

The Results of Six Sigma

Since the Six Sigma initiative began, the results have exceeded even Jack Welch's ambitious hopes and expectations.

GE began the quality initiative in late 1995 with 200 projects and massive training. In 1996, it finished 3,000 projects, each averaging 7 months, and trained 30,000 employees in various aspects of the Six Sigma program. Although the company invested heavily in that first year of the initiative—$200 million—nearly all of it came back—$170 million—in quality-related savings.

Cost savings were not the only benefit to GE. In 1998, GE's operating margin was a record 16.7 percent, up a full percentage point from the previous year and up over 4 percentage points from the early '90s level (see Exhibit 13-1). GE continued to expand its Six Sigma quality initiatives in 1998 by investing $450 million in training thousands of GE employees. Benefits from Six Sigma exceeded an impressive $1.5 billion in 1998.

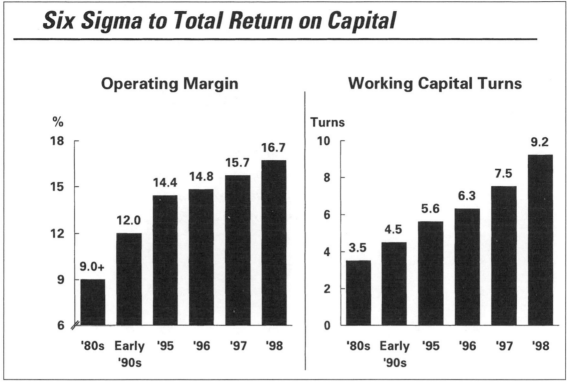

Six Sigma to Total Return on Capital

Operating Margin

Working Capital Turns

Exhibit 13-1.

GE's Rules for Implementing Six Sigma

1. Become an aggressive team member of a quality project and show your bosses that you care deeply about quality.

2. Probe, measure, improve, and analyze to get your products and processes up to Six Sigma standards.

3. To ensure the long-range success of Six Sigma, you must monitor all aspects of the quality program well into the future.

4. Designate team members for specific roles in the quality effort, and then reward those players generously for their involvement.

Action Steps

CHAPTER 14

Six Sigma 4:
How Six Sigma Has Worked at GE

*So it's become an enormous training ground. It's really
gone from a quality program to a productivity program
to a customer satisfaction program to changing
the fundamental DNA of the company.*

The GE Way

Just how has Six Sigma worked at GE over its first three and a
half years?

In April 1999, Jack Welch noted that during the first two
years of the program GE had invested some $500 million in
training its workforce. It had also diverted its best talent, thousands of employees, to full-time duty on Six Sigma projects.

Nearly every professional worker at GE had become a Green
Belt—with 3 weeks of training and one Six Sigma project under
his or her belt. Another 5,000 full-time Black Belts and Master
Black Belts were starting and supervising GE Six Sigma projects.
A number of those Master Black Belts and Black Belts had
already been promoted into key leadership posts at GE.

As for the financial returns from Six Sigma, they were better
than expected. Savings in 1998 from Six Sigma projects
amounted to $750 million over and above GE's investment. In
1999 that figure was expected to rise to $1 billion. Welch pre-
dicted that billions more would be saved in increased volume
and market share.

The year 1998 marked a time when GE's first major products designed for Six Sigma production came into existence. Those products have been designed by customers and incorporated every feature the customer deemed critical to quality.

Building Six Sigma into products at the outset.

The first such product was the LightSpeed, a multislice CT scanner that revolutionized medical diagnostics: a chest scan that once took 3 minutes to perform now takes only 17 seconds, thanks to LightSpeed. A full body scan for a trauma patient that once took 10 minutes or longer now takes a mere 32 seconds and can truly be lifesaving. GE, Welch suggested, was looking forward to the day when *all* its products were designed for Six Sigma. The Light-Speed system cost over $60 million to develop and aimed at the $1.7 billion global CT market. It is the world's first scanner that permits physicians to capture multiple images of a patient's anatomy simultaneously. With the new advanced technology, doctors will have more diagnostic information; its improved speed will save valuable time in life-or-death trauma situations. GE happily discovered that the new LightSpeed systems were being ordered at faster rates than any of its previous introductions.

Here are some other examples of how Six Sigma has worked at GE: GE's lighting business had a billing system that didn't mesh very well electronically with the purchasing system of Wal-Mart, one of GE's better customers. This caused disruptions, payments had to be postponed, time was wasted for Wal-Mart. Enter a GE Black Belt team with a $30,000 budget. Four months later: defects dropped by 98 percent. Wal-Mart's productivity improved.

Employees at GE's Capital Mortgage Corporation were handling 300,000 telephone calls a year from customers. When not available, they relied on voice-mail. Though GE personnel always called back, sometimes it was too late: customers had already shifted to another company. Enter the GE Master Black Belt team. Research showed that one of the corporation's forty-two branches seemed to be able to answer its phone calls the first time around. Why was that happening? The team found the answer, then spread it throughout the other forty-one branches. GE was soon attracting millions of dollars of business thanks to those quick callbacks.

One GE business that has embraced Six Sigma aggressively has been Aircraft Engines, located in Evendale, Ohio. In 1997 and 1998, it has invested $83 million in the program, with net benefits of $36 million in 1997 and a whopping $275 million in 1998.

GEAE officials note that GE engines had already attained the Six Sigma level even before the program began. But to reach that level, GEAE personnel were spending a great deal of time on rework and retesting. The Six Sigma effort was designed to eliminate that wasteful effort by getting it right the first time.

Green Belts were getting 10 days of training in using the statistical tools needed to measure a process—anything from distributing engine manuals to drilling holes in metal. To complete the training, a Green Belt had to complete a project. In 1997, GEAE completed 2,279 projects, and in 1998 the figure jumped to 6,000. Some examples:

1. The business was able to reduce the time it took to prepare CFM56 engines for shipment from 2 days to about 10 hours by deploying so-called parallel work teams.

2. The business cut assembly time on CFM56 engines from 5.8 days to just under 3 days by implementing a transfer bridge that moved engines between workstations, thus created a smoother work flow.

3. The business cut the faults by a robot used to assemble engine cores from sixteen to under two per engine through a series of hardware and process changes identified by a Black Belt project.

GEAE officials were insistent that its statistics measured only those things that had an impact on customers. Hence, it has been using customer "dashboards," devices that measure GEAE's performance on issues that each airline customer agrees are important: that is, critical-to-quality.

By the spring of 1999 GEAE had come up with forty-two large commercial customer dashboards; each contained different dials that measured various performance characteristics with some of its largest commercial airline customers around the world. The color-coded dials, maintained in a computer data base, are updated monthly with information supplied by the customers. Some customers have more than one dashboard, bringing the total number of dashboards to seventy. The value of dashboards is that GEAE and the airline can now closely track several key trends in evaluating the performance and financial impact the engines are having on the airline operation, as opposed to having to rely on anecdotal incidents.

As engines become more reliable every year, customer expectations increase along with them. A measurement that might be considered unacceptable today, for example, a particular in-flight shutdown rate, would have been most welcome just 15 years ago.

Each dial is linked to a specific Six Sigma project through Microsoft computer software, so that with a couple of clicks of a computer mouse GEAE managers and their customers can see how a specific project contributes to their operation. The data on the dashboards tracked includes:

- Average time on-wing. This is key because when an engine is taken off-wing for an overhaul, it requires more than $200,000 in shop costs sometimes. The longer an airline can keep engines on-wing, the more dramatic the reduction in maintenance costs. Time on-wing, which for a typical GE engine doubled since the mid-1980s, is a huge selling point for GE and CFM56 engines.

- Engine gas temperatures. As an engine gets older, it runs at increasingly higher temperatures, ultimately resulting in a full engine overhaul. GEAE has put an increased focus on improving engine gas temperature margins for its fleet—to increase the time an engine is on-wing, thus saving the airline money.

Sometime late in 1998 Jack Welch and his senior colleagues became aware of a very important problem related to the Six Sigma initiative: the company was saving a great deal of money by raising the quality of its products and processes; but somehow customers did not feel that GE had done anything that represented a substantial improvement for them. In short, the customers did not feel any difference. They were reading about GE's great new quality initiative in the newspapers, but when they dealt with the company, they did not sense any great improvement. The reason had to do with the notion of variance.

Resolving the customer issue in Six Sigma.

The problem can best be illustrated by a hypothetical example, order delivery time (see Exhibit 14-1). Looking just at the performance mean, it appears that there have been substantial improvements in customer service: the mean delivery time has been cut from 17 to 12 days. GE certainly felt good about that "improvement," but how did the customers feel? As it turned out, not nearly as good. Why? Well, if we study the exhibit more closely, it becomes clear that the customer may not feel any real improvement because even with Six Sigma analysis, there were wide variances in the order delivery times: from as little as 4 days to as much as 20 days. When GE pointed to its Six Sigma initiative, and asserted that the mean average performance had dipped from 17 to 12 days, the customer, recalling the 20-day and the 13-day delivery times, wondered why GE thought it had improved matters. In time, GE concluded that it was vital to give the customer a sense that deliveries would always be made in a very narrow time frame. That would represent true quality.

The issue came to a head at the operating managers meeting in January 1999 in Boca Raton, Florida, where executives from various GE businesses focused on the "variance" issue. Denis J. Nayden, president and CEO of GE Capital, summed up the feelings of many at the meeting. "Our customers' own voices tell us we have a long way to go before they start feeling quality."

In his annual report, issued in the early spring of 1999, Welch portrayed the problem with his usual candor. He urged GE employees to focus on helping customers to feel the benefits of GE's Six Sigma program.

Using the hypothetical example in Exhibit 14-1, Welch noted that GE had repeated this kind of improvement in thousands of GE processes, yielding less rework and more cash flow. But the customer still sees variances. The customers, whose lives remain the same, whose profitability hasn't increased at all, "hear the sounds of celebration coming from within GE walls and ask,

Example

Customer Dashboard: Customer XYZ
Dashboard Dial: Order to Delivery Time

Order by Order Delivery Times

	Starting Point	After Project	
	28 Days	29 Days	**Mean Aspect**
	18	6	
	6	10	**Big Change**
	23	12	
	5	4	
	8	10	
	16	13	**Variance Aspect**
	19	10	
	33	20	
	11	13	**No Change**
Average Performance	**17 Days**	**12 Days**	

Customers Feel Variance!

Exhibit 14-1.

'What's the big event? What did we miss?' The customer only feels the variance that we have not yet removed."

The challenge he laid out to his top managers was to turn the company's outlook "outside in"—to begin to measure the parameters of customer needs and processes and work toward zero variability. Assigned to solve the problem that Welch had identified at the operating managers meeting was Piet C. van Abeelen, GE's vice president for Six Sigma quality. Van Abeelen devised a one-and-a-half-day training event for all business CEOs and their staffs. When he delivered the presentation, he noted: "The lesson learned is that solutions for reducing variance are very, very different from our historical beliefs and experience. Leaders need to grasp this change in order to allow and encourage the new solutions. The purpose is to transfer this new knowledge base to our leaders, provide them with a new set of leadership skills and insights that allows them to apply Six Sigma to business-process issues. These business-process issues are approached from an 'outside-in' perspective, forcing us to understand how process variability impacts customers and what we need to change in the way we work. To put this learning into our behavior, the CEOs lead customer impact projects. The roll out within the individual business is done through the business Six Sigma quality leaders and follows the same format."

We have selected a sample of the charts van Abeelen used in his presentation. Exhibit 14-2 encourages GE employees to look at situations as the customer sees them. Van Abeelen's points emphasize that it is crucial to find out what the customer wants and how to make him or her happy.

Exhibit 14-3 draws a performance continuum, showing where the gap resides between customer expectations and GE's performance. Again, the overriding theme of van Abeelen's presentation, as reflected in this exhibit, is to figure out what the customer wants, and then try to satisfy the customer. If this

---

Roadmap to Customer Impact   *Introduction*

Start with the Customer

1. Measure the Same as the Customer Does

2. Determine Your Capability as the Customer Sees It

3. Understand the Variance in the Output Signal

4. Find the In-Process Keys to Impact the Customer

Exhibit 14-2.

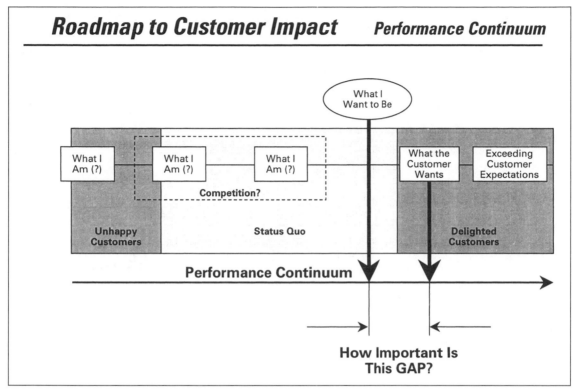

Roadmap to Customer Impact *Performance Continuum*

What I Want to Be

What I Am (?)

What I Am (?)

What I Am (?)

Competition?

What the Customer Wants

Exceeding Customer Expectations

Unhappy Customers

Status Quo

Delighted Customers

Performance Continuum

How Important Is This GAP?

Exhibit 14-3.

exhibit seems complicated, the message is simple: Figure out how to please the customer!

Exhibit 14-4 presents another way of looking at the situation: the trajectory AB shows GE's view of its performance, and contrasts with the customer's view (AC). This exhibit shows that GE and the customer often do not see eye to eye on the impact of the Six Sigma initiative.

When General Electric began the Six Sigma initiative almost all of its manufacturing and engineering processes appeared to be Three to Four Sigma. By 1998 it was operating at Four and a Half to Five and a Half Sigma in critical-to-quality areas. This was also the case for the transactional processes and new products and services. In April 1999, Piet van Abeelen concluded:

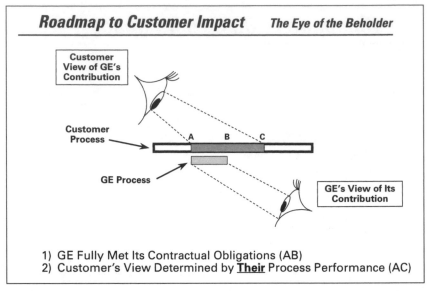

Roadmap to Customer Impact *The Eye of the Beholder*

Customer View of GE's Contribution

Customer Process

GE Process

GE's View of Its Contribution

1) GE Fully Met Its Contractual Obligations (AB)
2) Customer's View Determined by **Their** Process Performance (AC)

Exhibit 14-4.

"Now we have come to a phase where people see that Six Sigma is not just a numerical goal in itself but 'the way we work.'"

What to Do Next

1. Learn the valuable lesson that GE is now learning: When launching any initiative, make sure that the customer is being taken into account.

2. Bring the customer into discussions on your initiative at a fairly early stage.

3. Don't start the initiative and assume that customers are going to be thrilled with it.

4. Monitor customer reaction to the initiative on a continuing basis.

5. Make sure that your employees are aware that they have to satisfy customers as part of the new initiative—and not just attain the company's stated objectives for the initiative itself.

CHAPTER 15

The GE Tool Kit

The GE Way

An invaluable tool for businesses wishing to improve quality is GE's Six Sigma Quality Coach, a Web-based mentoring program that provides support for those who wish to learn Six Sigma methodologies and associated tools. The software for the Quality Coach is sold to other companies. When people log in their Six Sigma projects, the software will run computations for them as part of its training and tracking features. The GE Six Sigma Quality Coach is found at *http://www.gelearningsolutions.com/Quality-Coach*. Exhibit 15-1 shows some of the pages from the Quality Coach Web site.

GE Learning Solutions

GE Six Sigma Quality Coach

Home

GELS services

Learn more
about GELS

GE Six Sigma
Quality Coach

Contact us

The GE Six Sigma Quality Coach is the most innovative web-based mentoring program available in the marketplace today. To learn more about the initiative behind the GE Quality Coach, and what makes this exciting quality management tool so special, choose any of the topics listed below.

• What is the GE Six Sigma Quality Coach
• How the GE Six Sigma Quality Coach can help you
• Features and benefits
• How the GE Six Sigma Quality Coach is structured
• Set up an account on the GE Quality Coach
• See a demonstration of the GE Quality Coach
• About Six Sigma
• Six Sigma at GE

GE home page   *GE Learning Solutions*

| GE home page | GE Learning Solutions |
| GE news | GE business finder | GE products & services |

Exhibit 15-1.

GE Learning Solutions

GE Six Sigma Quality Coach

Home

GELS services

Learn more
about GELS

GE Six Sigma
Quality Coach

• What it is
• How it can help you
• Features and benefits
• How it is structured
• Set up an account
• See a demonstration
• About Six Sigma
• Six Sigma at GE

Contact us

What is the GE Six Sigma Quality Coach?

The GE Six Sigma Quality Coach is a web-based performance
support system for the Six Sigma methodologies and
associated tools.

Whether your goal is to

• Improve an existing product or service
• Build Six Sigma quality into new designs
• Get training in the Six Sigma approach to quality

*The GE Six Sigma Quality Coach provides the mechanism to
achieve Six Sigma quality.*

The GE Quality Coach was created from the collective
experience of GE's Six Sigma program involving more than
55,000 projects and 4,000 quality leaders. In addition to
serving as a knowledge management '"warehouse" for Six
Sigma, the GE Quality Coach provides a common language
and ensures standardized delivery of the Six Sigma quality
initiative throughout the worldwide GE organization.

*Personalization capabilities enable content to be customized
to individual user and project profiles.*

Use the GE Quality Coach to

• Engage in self-directed training
• Obtain project support
• Browse through content at will

This valuable resource–accessible at all times and from even
the most remote locations–provides an easy way to integrate
Six Sigma methodologies into all aspects of how you conduct
business.

At GE, it's the way we work.

GE home page   *GE Learning Solutions*

| GE home page | GE Learning Solutions |

Exhibit 15-1. *(Continued)*

GE Learning Solutions

GE Six Sigma Quality Coach

How can the GE Six Sigma Quality Coach help you?

The GE Quality Coach can play a strategic role in helping your company:

- Increase profits
- Improve operational efficiency
- Enhance your competitive position
- Reduce waste
- Eliminate costly rework
- Enhance productivity and yield
- Reduce cycle times
- Monitor performance against customer-defined factors that are critical to quality
- Reduce the cost of poor quality
- Increase market share
- Maintain customer loyalty

Your customers will notice the difference:

- Higher levels of satisfaction
- Increased product consistency
- Better response to their needs
- Faster new product introductions at substantially higher levels of quality than have been available historically

The GE Quality Coach supports employees:

- Allows more time for performing value-added tasks and enhancing skills and talents
- Facilitates understanding of Six Sigma concepts–key to career advancement and professional growth
- Promotes pride in a job well done

GE home page   *GE Learning Solutions*

| GE home page | GE Learning Solutions |
| GE news | GE business finder | GE products & services |

Navigation panel (left sidebar):

Home

GELS services

Learn more about GELS

GE Six Sigma Quality Coach

- What it is
- How it can help you
- Features and benefits
- How it is structured
- Set up an account
- See a demonstration
- About Six Sigma
- Six Sigma at GE

Contact us

Exhibit 15-1. *(Continued)*

GE Learning Solutions

GE Six Sigma Quality Coach

Home

GELS services

Learn more
about GELS

GE Six Sigma
Quality Coach

• What it is
• How it can help you
• Features and benefits
• How it is structured
• Set up an account
• See a demonstration
• About Six Sigma
• Six Sigma at GE

Contact us

How the GE Six Sigma Quality Coach is structured

The GE Six Sigma Quality Coach consists of two methodologies and a variety of associated tools.

- **DMAIC** improves existing products and processes. The acronym DMAIC represents the five phases in the methodology: Define, Measure, Analyze, Improve, and Control.

- **DMADV**, also known as Designs for Six Sigma (DFSS), builds defect prevention into new designs. DMADV stands for the five phases in the methodology: Define, Measure, Analyze, Design, and Verify.

Each phase consists of one or more deliverables. Each deliverable contains a series of steps that provide explicit instruction on how to achieve the intended output. Whether at the phase, deliverable, or step level, the GE Quality Coach includes an introductory Overview module to give the user the big picture and to forecast what's to come. Also included are sections for completing the step, using the appropriate tools, and more.

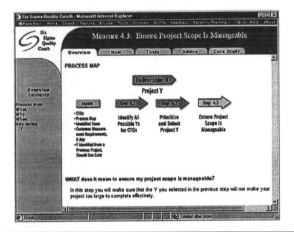

Exhibit 15-1. *(Continued)*

In addition, the GE Quality Coach includes more than 50 tools that are used in the course of completing a DMAIC or DMADV project. These tools include explanations for an assortment of statistical software packages and group process exercises. The GE Quality Coach provides direction for using the tools and interpreting their outputs.

| GE home page | GE Learning Solutions |

| GE home page | GE Learning Solutions |
| GE news | GE business finder | GE products & services |

Exhibit 15-1. *(Continued)*

THE GE WAY: THE CEO IN THE FIELD

*I think of Crotonville as the most important thing
in the transformation*
> —JACK WELCH, April 1999

In the chapter in this section, we focus on GE's leadership institute in Crotonville. It is the place where GE discusses and debates its business strategies and corporate initiatives.

In this module you will learn:

- What Jack Welch is like when he's teaching a course at Crotonville

- Why Jack Welch decided not to shut the place down

- How Crotonville works

CHAPTER 16

Professor Welch Takes a Class

It is at Crotonville that Jack Welch comes alive. He feels more at home at Crotonville than at any other locale of GE, even more than at Fairfield headquarters. Crotonville is perfect for Welch, the ideal vehicle for him to get through to GE executives, and to find out what's going on in his company. Walter Wriston, a former member of GE's board, once said that the chairman and CEO would always be the last to know when something was going on in the company. Welch has always thought of Crotonville as providing him with a chance to show Wriston that he was wrong.

Jack Welch visits Crotonville twice a month, lecturing to GE executives, and mingling at receptions for more informal, one-on-one conversation. He speaks to some 1,000 GE executives a year through his teaching.

Jack Welch visits Crotonville twice a month.

While journalists and authors have had access to many parts of GE, Welch has kept Crotonville largely out of bounds, in the belief that the presence of writers would discourage GE personnel from speaking openly and honestly to him. Welch, however, has permitted me to attend his Crotonville sessions in 1991, 1997, and in 1999. The first two times Welch asked me not to use a tape recorder, but to rely on notes alone. He clearly wanted me to be as unobtrusive as possible. Assuming that the same rules applied when I attended class with Welch in 1999, I quietly took a seat in the back row of the lecture hall, notebook in hand. I was once again prepared to be as inconspicuous as the proverbial fly on the wall. To my utter surprise, Welch began his remarks by introducing me to the audience. He was obviously getting comfortable with the notion of visitors attending Crotonville sessions.

A visit to Crotonville with Welch begins at GE headquarters in Fairfield, Connecticut. Beth Comstock, the vice president for public relations, and I wait for Welch in the lobby of the main building. When Welch appears, he is carrying a small briefcase that he's been using since 1977. Inside are the charts he plans to use for his Crotonville lecture. He prepares for the lectures carefully, pulling together charts he has used at a recent talk to financial analysts or the board of directors, thinking about what he wants to say. He will use no notes. It's all in his head.

The three of us get into a car waiting outside the front lobby and drive a few minutes to a nearby helipad where we board a helicopter. Welch takes this 15-minute chopper ride to Crotonville often. He uses the ride to take one last look at his charts. Though sometimes the scenery is breathtaking, he barely looks out the window. Because of the noise of the helicopter's engine, conversation is nearly impossible. When we land, a van takes us on a 2-minute drive to a building where the classroom is located. Welch heads straight for the classroom—he can't wait to get started. The audience consists of mid-level GE executives who have been with the company for roughly 8 to 10 years, less for those from firms more recently acquired. They have been attending the 3-week manager development course, where they learned skills that would enable them to run one of GE's businesses. According to the syllabus, "participants develop executive skills in relation to key business issues, such as developing business strategy, competing globally, diversity and globalization, leading teams and change, and advancing customer satisfaction." It is the third week of the course and, while other senior GE executives have addressed the students, Welch is clearly the highlight, and a celebrity in his own right, so the audience is hushed in anticipation of this big moment.

Welch has budgeted 3 hours for his talk, but he will only stand up in front of the class for part of that time. One of his objectives during this visit is to get to know the people in the class. There are sixty or seventy in attendance, and getting to know them all would be out of the question. Still, he wants to make the effort. The room he walks into is known as the Pit. GE likes to refer to it as one of the most famous business classrooms in the world. The cavernous lecture hall contains five horseshoe-shaped elevated rows of seats that force the lecturer to look up to the audience. Therefore, the lecturer feels as if he or she was at the bottom of a pit.

It is a spare room. There are no photographs of Jack Welch. No photographs of GE founder Tom Edison. No GE logos either. The American map and clock on the wall are the only adornment to the room. In front of each member of the audience is the obligatory name card. Jack Welch enters the room and to make a point, rather than head right for stage center, he grabs a second-row seat, making sure to face everyone. He takes off his suit jacket, looks around the room, as if trying to get a quick first impression of the group. He hopes to have some interaction with everyone there. So he begins each visit asking each person to introduce himself or herself and to mention the GE business for which each works. For almost everyone making an introduction, Welch has some comment or question. He will listen to the person mention a certain GE business and that will trigger a thought:

Welch spends hours in a classroom, lecturing to GE executives.

"How's the labor environment?"
"Congratulations on last year's performance."
"Your business is coming back?"
"Nice pitch you gave the other day."
"How much business are you doing?"
"How's that unit doing? Are they broke yet?"

To a member of an NBC television station, Welch quips, "You guys own the market up there. What does the sales manager do there?"

After certain Welch comments or questions, the audience laughs self-consciously, a nervous kind of laugh, and no wonder. Some of the boss's observations are hard to read. Is he praising me or making fun of me? He seems to be praising me, but does he have something else in mind? Meeting with the chairman and CEO in this setting, the audience has every reason to be nervous.

But they have been trained—during their work experience and here at Crotonville—to be confrontational, not to be afraid to take the speaker on. When they meet Welch or any other senior GE executive at Crotonville, they are supposed to practice—in a favorite GE phrase—"pushback." As GE defines it, pushback is not merely obeying a directive or carrying out an assignment that you regard as inefficient, pointless, or counterproductive; but rather, stating to your boss why you think there's a better way. GE wants executives who can display self-confidence, who can be assertive. And so, even in this, the chairman's ice-breaking segment, there is a surprising amount of candor coming from the group.

Welch has by now spoken to each member of the audience. The chairman has been neither patronizing nor antagonistic. He shows much patience. As for the audience, few seem really intimidated. He gets their respect, but not their adulation. Welch has created an informal feeling among the group. They pick up on that. No one calls him Mr. Welch. It's always Jack.

Welch rises from his seat in the audience, moves quickly to the front, and stands near an overhead projector. He begins his presentation, but quickly gets into a conversation with members of the audience. He seems genuinely interested in what they have to say, and they respond positively to that. But they understand that he has not come to listen to them give lectures. Their comments are brief, to the point.

After a few moments, one member of the audience comes to the front of the room and runs through a series of questions that the group has prepared for Welch to answer. It is "pushback" time. The questions have to do with personal development and job satisfaction and how those things can be improved. Welch has thought long and hard about the proper ingredients of business leadership during his 18 years as General Electric's chairman and CEO. But today, as in recent weeks and months, he bears down on one theme over and over again: the importance of a manager, including those in the audience, rewarding performance. "Rewarding your employees—that's what it's all about," he tells the audience. "The most important thing I do as a leader is align the kind of rewards I give out with the kind of behavior I want." His reward of choice has been the stock option. He reveals to the group that when he became the head of GE, he had options for 4,750 shares of GE stock, then quickly observes: "There are people in this room with that amount today."

Welch has come to Crotonville to transmit his, and the company's, business values, but he is also there to listen to what this batch of GE executives has to say about how the place is being run. He's a zealot about listening to his executives—not just the handful of senior executives whose spacious offices are near his. And few American CEOs have opened up the channels of communication with employees as much as Welch has, focused around the Work-Out companywide initiative. Welch genuinely believes that what his employees think matters. He began the 1995 quality initiative in large measure because his employees responded to a CEO survey by indicating that GE must do something immediately to improve the quality of its products and processes. But for all of his insistence that GE employees be candid with him, Welch is the boss. More than that, he has been touted as the most successful U.S. CEO for a decade or more. He has his own ideas of how the company should be run, and it's clear that anyone with an idea for the chairman had better make it a good one.

Thus it was both intriguing and revealing to watch as the group prodded Welch to give middle-level executives like themselves more decision-making power by creating a new forum that would meet just prior to Welch's annual meeting with the 500 top operating managers at Boca Raton, Florida. The group even had a name for the new forum—a "mini-Boca." Welch listened politely to the idea, but then his body language took over. He remained silent for what seemed like an interminably long time, as if he were trying to figure out how to break the bad news to the group as gently as possible. At first he said only, "It's an interesting thought." Some in the group took heart. The chairman seemed indeed to be listening. But then he unveiled some of his own candor. "I'm not so sure about this one. We could be meeting forever. We've got plenty of meetings already. We've got a rhythm going here." Then, trying to soften the blow: "This might be a good one for my successor to take up."

When at Crotonville, Welch does as much listening as lecturing. It's his way of finding out what's going on at GE.

The audience didn't let up. A few kept after Welch to adopt the idea. Welch wouldn't budge. Someone mentioned that perhaps a gathering of old Crotonville classes would do the trick. Welch thought that idea sounded more reasonable. Finally, he said, "OK, I got the message." He didn't need to say, "Let's move on." The audience got the point.

Listening to Welch, one could sense his dilemma: here he was, 18 years at the helm—in short, he'd been around and had heard thousands of ideas before, and rejected many of them. Many observers of the business scene had called him the greatest CEO around. It was not so easy to adopt every idea that he heard. Still, as the man who preached openness, candor, and the need to face reality, he couldn't just reject every single thought that came along. It was a dilemma indeed. In the end, Welch listened, nodded politely, but there was never any doubt about who was in charge, about who would make the ultimate decision.

One suggestion that someone in the audience raised was to take the mentoring program that GE employed to boost its minority population and spread it throughout the organization. He quickly dismissed that idea, saying in effect that they as managers were already supposed to be mentoring their staffs, especially the better ones. "We don't need to mentor the top 10 percent of our employees. They should already be mentored by everyone, every day. They should be loved, hugged, nurtured, rewarded. One of your jobs as managers is to totally love your team. You should be excited about their promotions and about their options."

The mentoring issue gave Welch the chance to talk about the topic that is closest to his heart—the need for GE executives to nurture only the best and to get rid of the deadwood. It was not an easy message to get across to managers, some of whom clearly had trouble with dismissing colleagues. But Welch argued: "If the flower grows, be proud of your beautiful garden. But if it doesn't, cut the plant out. This is really your job. Managing is all about hugging and trusting and believing only the best. You don't have to shoot the bad ones. Find them a job elsewhere."

The conversation turns to another favorite topic of Welch: the GE Six Sigma quality program. Welch talks about the new road map course that his vice president for Six Sigma, Piet C. van Abeelen, has designed and is disseminating through GE. That course is intended to improve customer awareness of GE's quality initiative. Some in the audience profess that they had only heard about van Abeelen's efforts and the new focus on customers in the quality initiative when they saw a videotape recently of the January 1999 operating managers meeting. Welch is upset to hear such things, but he tries to give the class some comfort: "What you're really saying is that communicating in an organization with 300,000 people is difficult." Someone suggests that Piet van Abeelen make a videotape about the customer issue and Welch should then distribute the tape around the company. The chairman instantly likes the idea. "Done," he says with finality. "You got a deal."

It is 5:30 P.M. Time for Welch to leave. Often he stays on for a reception with the class, then dinner. Not this time. He has to get on the company plane for some unspecified destination that evening, so he begs off. He's been lecturing for over 3 hours. He has trouble separating himself from the audience. The "students" gather around him. One last chance to hear the chairman's view on things, one last chance to register a favorable impression with the boss. Finally, Welch emerges from the Pit, a smile on his face. He's been in his element for 3 hours, and he's relished every minute of it. He's gotten out of the office. He's learned something about his company He's imparted his values to another group of GE executives. He's done his job. It's no wonder that he loves the place so much.

GE's Leadership Academy

Welch loves the fact that Crotonville exists. He is delighted to point out that all throughout the difficult period of the early 1980s, even when he was downsizing GE, he was investing in his leadership institute. He could have treated Crotonville as an unnecessary luxury in the downsizing age. Yet he poured money into the place, to make sure that it continued to serve as the intellectual engine of the company, as the catalyst for the teaching and disseminating of GE's core business values.

In his early days as CEO, Welch could have closed Crotonville. He could have deemed it irrelevant, a relic of the past that was too costly. But he understood that it had the same potential for transmitting his business values that his predecessors had seen. (GE spends $1 billion a year on its various training and educational programs at Crotonville and elsewhere.)

Crotonville is located in New York state's Hudson Valley and rests on a 50-acre campus that feels more like a New England college than the leadership institute of one of the world's largest corporations. The place has quite a reputation. *Fortune* magazine described Crotonville as "the Harvard of Corporate America." It was the world's first major corporate business school—created in 1956. General Electric purchased the property in the early 1950s. First it was a farm, then an artist's colony. There is something unique about Crotonville. Other businesses summon senior executives to seminars or retreats, but no other company labors so systematically to provide junior executives with extensive course work and exposure to the brass over so long a period as does Crotonville.

Just how does Crotonville work?

The GE leadership institute is not meant simply to inform GE executives about what is going on in the company. It also provides a forum for lively debates about what constitutes good management, and for exchanging information about the external business environment.

Courses are taught at Crotonville, but in place of the old-style education where teachers teach and students do little more than listen, confrontation is a cornerstone of the institute; students are encouraged to challenge their teachers, to question what they are doing, to offer fresh ways of looking at business issues.

There are three types of courses taught at Crotonville:

1. Those that make GE personnel more expert in a technical specialty, e.g., finance, human resources, information technology. These courses, which run, for the most part, less than a week, are not a large part of the Crotonville curriculum.

2. Those tied to specific career stages. One such course, being developed now, will be called Influence without

Authority. Or Peer Leadership. Another course is called New Manager.

3. Those that help GE executives implement a corporate priority or initiative, such as Six Sigma, deflation, and the CAP (change acceleration process) tool. In the case of the deflation course, Jack Welch himself insisted on the course and decided who should attend (the finance person and the head of sourcing for each GE business). For manufacturing businesses, he insisted that the head engineer of each business attend; for nonmanufacturing businesses, the head of information technology. For the CAP course, Welch said he wanted every business leader, every officer of the company, every senior executive to bring their staff and attend.

Who decides which GE executives get to attend Crotonville courses?

At first, Welch didn't play much of a role in determining who would attend the senior courses—management development course and higher—but he assumed control of the selection process once he realized that going to Crotonville had come to be regarded as a consolation prize. "These are courses for winners, not for the pass-overs," he argued. Welch decreed also that only those who had been deemed worthy of getting stock options could attend the senior courses. Today some 5,000 to 6,000 GE managers attend Crotonville classes each year.

Who makes the decision on what courses to teach?

In the specialty courses, the decision is made by the personnel in charge of that specialty in a GE business; information technology personnel in a GE business decide on the content and frequency of an information technology course, and so on. In the career stage courses, the director of Crotonville, Steve Kerr, and his staff decide on what courses to run.

In 1997, Kerr commissioned a one-year curriculum revision study. A course training GE executives to become Black Belts was piloted in 1998 and is now part of the general curriculum. Half its content is linked to the Six Sigma quality initiative; the other half, Kerr hopes, will be prototype material for the peer leadership course.

When Kerr began at Crotonville in 1994, he sponsored a Work-Out session, inviting eighty-five people from around GE to meet with the new director in order to advise him on which courses should be kept and which should not. The main criticism leveled at Crotonville was its country club atmosphere: The Work-Out attendees noted that it had become too ivory-towerish and that its courses were not relevant to GE businesses. To resolve the problem, Steve Kerr created councils, one each for the Americas, Europe, and Asia, made up of the training managers from each GE business. The councils take a hard look at the courseware, coming up with suggestions for new courses, deciding whether a course should be taught at Crotonville or within the businesses. (A sample of Crotonville course material can be found at the end of this chapter.)

The courses at Crotonville

Some businesses run their own mini-Crotonvilles. Kerr and his Crotonville team prefer that the businesses teach technical education. "I don't want to be teaching statistics for Six Sigma," says Kerr, "and I don't want to be teaching how to repair a turbine." Crotonville is responsible for the leadership education. Yet there is some overlap and there are some leadership courses taught in the mini-Crotonvilles. At one time, Crotonville was teaching marketing and the corporate entry course, but Welch decided that both courses should be taught within the businesses. But the businesses offer only so much. They do not teach leadership courses. Those are taught at Crotonville.

Crotonville has also begun courses for non-GE people, including a few thousand customers, suppliers, regulators, and people in joint ventures with GE. They have their own courses and for the most part do not take the regular courses taught for GE personnel. There is concern that the "students" would become less candid if customers were in attendance. Once, however, an exception was made for a high-level general. Most non-GE people take the 2-day course called Partnering with Customers, which is run several times a year; as many as twenty-four customers at once have attended the course.

In that course, customers get a sample of CAP, Work-Out, Six Sigma, and some acquisition-integration material. "We don't whip out our contracts and try to sell them," says Steve Kerr. "It's an honest service." There may be as many as three people representing one customer organization and two or three from their GE business.

Do GE people solicit themselves for the courses?

Sometimes. With respect to the career and leadership courses, employees can ask their bosses for approval to attend a Crotonville course; but usually it is the bosses who propose employees on the basis of merit. For the courses surrounding some corporate initiative, attendance is based purely on what position a person holds.

Crotonville charges tuition and each business is responsible for picking up the tab. There are different kinds of charges. "Full freight" includes all meals, audiovisual equipment and assistance, use of all the facilities, telephone charges, etc. There are also specific tuition charges for courses that vary depending on course length, cost of putting on the course, etc. GE would not disclose the various charges.

Are Crotonville courses needed for promotion?

Not really. The immediate promotion has often just occurred; then the person gets invited to visit Crotonville. Still, some managers might be put off from promoting someone who had not attended the courses. Says Steve Kerr: "We want to know why a good person hasn't been here, because it's a signal and because it's content that we do believe will help him or her be successful."

How have the courses changed over the years?

Past courses were conceived at a time when manufacturing played a big role at GE; today many more courses are devoted to globalization and services. Senior classes tackle projects that are molded on the basis of what's current. So for example the senior officer course—the EDC course—one year benchmarked thirty-four companies around the world on quality practices. The June 1999 global business management course had been dealing with e-commerce.

What about the demands made upon the students?

In some cases students are not required to do anything but listen to the lectures. No exams. No papers. There might be some preparation before the class begins. That's all. Some projects outlive the life of the courses. A few courses have exams. Where there are exams, say, in the finance specialty courses, doing well is vitally important. Not to do well can be a career stumbling block. In finance, those who don't do well keep repeating the course until they pass it.

Not doing well in Green Belt training can be hazardous to one's career. Remember that Jack Welch insisted that all of GE's "professional" employees—some 80,000—had to begin Green Belt or Black Belt training by the start of 1999.

Is Crotonville better than a university?

In some respects, yes. It has the advantage that a university doesn't: it can pick and choose the best faculty people available from anywhere in the country. Traditional universities, in contrast, face strong pressures to use their own faculty for most of their courses. Another advantage of Crotonville: it can switch gears in courseware far more quickly than a university. Some universities require two years before a professor can get a course changed in a catalogue. Steve Kerr says it takes him only a matter of days to change a course at Crotonville. Universities offer a broader spectrum of teaching. Says Steve Kerr: "Universities have a communist, a socialist, radical Marxist thinking. I can't bring such people in here. When the Harvard professor says something stupid, they say that's stupid. When Jack Welch says something stupid, they take notes."

On the following pages is a description of various courses taught at Crotonville. (Parts of the description were deleted at the request of GE.)

Exhibit 16-1 provides details for the global business management course and the executive development course. The BMC course is taught three times a year; the EDC, once a year.

Exhibit 16-2 gives details for the change acceleration process coaches workshops. This is a 2½-day workshop that explains the CAP model in depth.

Exhibit 16-3 describes two courses: the CAP workshop for customers and the CAP tools for Six Sigma. The CAP workshop for customers lasts 3 days and takes places three times a year; the CAP tools for Six Sigma course lasts 2½ days and is offered four to six times a year, depending on demand.

Exhibit 16-4 offers a description of the customer Work-Out/CAP orientation workshop and the customer/partner Work-Out educational programs and visits.

**GLOBAL BUSINESS MANAGE-
MENT COURSE (GLOBAL BMC)**

Overview
Global BMC is held at key business locations throughout the world. During the course, participants meet with prominent business leaders, customers, economists, academics, political leaders, and government officials in the host region. Class members are asked to apply their knowledge to projects sponsored by GE businesses. The results of the projects are presented to GE's senior corporate leadership at the Corporate Executive Council (CEC).

Learning Objectives
- Improve key conceptual business skills, especially in leadership, strategy, human relationships, and working in a global competitive environment
- Participate in building a team capable of successfully conducting a sophisticated project that allows participants to apply their skills to help a GE business with a significant issue and receive feedback on the rigor of their analysis
- Engage in open discussion and visits with key GE business leaders on issues of current strategic importance
- Build their understanding of today's global business environment and the strategic responses of GE's businesses

Who Should Attend
Individuals in the Executive Career Band who have been identified through the Session C process as having strong potential to lead a business or undertake equivalent functional responsibility.

Prerequisites
Must be approved by the leader or Senior HR leader for the business.

Logistics
Global BMC is an action learning course held for three consecutive weeks, three times a year.

 **EXECUTIVE DEVELOPMENT
COURSE (EDC)**

Overview
EDC, the capstone of the Executive Education sequence, is a three-week experiential learning program that has as its focus the creation and leadership of boundaryless, customer-focused, global businesses.

Learning Objectives
EDC is conducted in a global context. In classroom discussions (led by members of the Corporate Executive Council and key business leaders) and in teamwork on a strategic business issue, participants wrestle with:
- Developing customer-focused, global, business strategies
- Leading boundaryless teams and organizations
- Valuing cultural diversity
- Building a personal network of career relationships

Who Should Attend
Individuals in the Executive and Senior Executive Bands who have been identified through the Annual Organization and Staffing Review "Session C" process and have been approved by their Business Leader or equivalent Corporate SVP. Final EDC roster is subject to CEO approval. Please contact your assigned Corporate Human Resources Executive Consulting Manager for more information on this procedure.

Prerequisites
Prior attendance at BMC/MDC is preferred

Logistics
EDC meets for three weeks once a year

Exhibit 16-1. Global Business Management Course and the Executive Development Course

Exhibit 16-5 deals with a pair of courses taught at Crotonville; the facilitation skills workshop, which helps managers and others develop facilitation skills that will allow them to guide staff meetings, and the integration strategy workshop, which helps GE leadership teams develop integration strategies after a business has been acquired.

Exhibit 16-6 focuses on the Master Black Belt training course and a course on partnering with customers: productivity solu-

CHANGE ACCELERATION PROCESS (CAP) COACHES WORKSHOPS

Overview
CAP has proven to be a valuable tool that is helping GE Businesses achieve measurable growth and productivity improvements. The role of the Coach is a key factor in the success of CAP. This 2 1/2 day workshop is designed to provide the participants with an increased understanding of the CAP model, tools, and techniques; develop an understanding of the roles and competencies of a CAP Coach throughout the life-cycle of a change effort; develop proficiency in the use of the CAP tools and develop the ability to conduct CAP briefings within their business.

Learning Objectives
- Setting up CAP Teams for success
- Selecting and defining CAP Projects
- Key principles and tools of CAP
- Instruction and best practices on the use of the CAP tools with groups
- Sharing of best practices about CAP within a GE business and with our customers and partners

Participants learn through interactive presentations, team discussions, exercises, and opportunities to apply, practice leading, coaching the CAP tools with a team.

Who Should Attend
Individuals who are highly skilled at facilitation and group development; are already familiar with, and supportive of, the CAP model and program elements; have a broad view of the business and are willing and effectively able to challenge CAP teams and individuals around the CAP process elements; and are available to serve a GE business and/or a GE/partner team during a CAP program cycle.

Prerequisite
Facilitation skills and knowledge of CAP.

Logistics
The workshop lasts 2 1/2 days. It will be offered 3-6 times in 1998 based on demand.

Exhibit 16-2. CAP Coaches Workshops

CHANGE ACCELERATION PROCESS (CAP) COACHES WORKSHOP FOR CUSTOMERS

Overview
CAP has proven to be a valuable tool that is helping GE's strategic customers drive growth and productivity improvements. The role of the Coach is a key factor in the success of CAP. This 3 day action oriented Workshop provides an opportunity for "change champions" from a GE customer/partner to expand and enhance their facilitation skills, as well as their ability to initiate, lead and manage change using GE's CAP tools and techniques.

Learning Objectives
- Facilitation tools and techniques
- The role of the CAP coach
- Key principles and tools of CAP
- Instruction and best practices on the use of CAP tools with groups
- Practice applying the tools

The faculty is comprised of Crotonville staff and lead Work-Out™ consultants who have experience in coaching CAP teams. Participants learn through interactive presentations/team discussions/exercises, and opportunities to apply/practice leading/coaching teams using the CAP tools.

Who Should Attend
Strategic customers send 4-6 participants, along with a GE sponsor who attend as part of a GE/customer team of change champions.

Prerequisite
Customer coaches must be sponsored by a GE business; a GE business rep attends with them.

Logistics
The workshop lasts 3 days. It will be offered three times in 1998.

 ### CHANGE ACCELERATION PROCESS (CAP) TOOLS FOR SIX SIGMA

Overview
CAP has proven to be a valuable tool that is helping GE Businesses initiate, lead and manage change. CAP, coupled with Six Sigma statistical tools, leads to successful change to support Six Sigma Quality.
This 2 1/2 day workshop is designed to provide participants with an increased understanding of the CAP model, tools, and techniques; to develop an understanding of the roles and competencies of a CAP Quality Project Leader throughout the DMAIC process and to develop proficiency in the use of the CAP tools to support Six Sigma projects.

Learning Objectives
- Using CAP to set up Quality Teams for success
- Selecting and defining Projects
- Key principles and tools of CAP within the context of the DMAIC process
- Instruction and best practices on the use of the CAP tools to support Quality
- Sharing of best practices to drive Quality projects

The faculty is comprised of Crotonville or GE business staff and lead consultants who have experience in coaching CAP teams. Participants learn through interactive presentations, team discussions, exercises, and opportunities to apply, practice leading and coaching with a team.

Who Should Attend
The ideal candidates should have Black Belt/Green Belt level of quality experience and facilitation skills.

Logistics
The workshop lasts 2 1/2 days. It will be offered 4-6 times in 1999 (based on demand).

Exhibit 16-3. CAP Coaches Workshop for Customers and Tools for Six Sigma

CUSTOMER WORK-OUT™/CHANGE ACCELERATION PROCESS (CAP) ORIENTATION WORKSHOP

Overview
This 2 1/2 day workshop provides an opportunity for GE and customer/partner teams to expand and enhance their capability to initiate, lead, and manage change. Participants attend as members of a boundary-less business team working on a strategic change initiative. The workshop covers an overview of the application of tools and techniques of Work-Out™ to culture change. Participants have the opportunity in team break-out sessions to apply this model to their joint change initiative. A critical outcome is an increased capacity to successfully lead change.

Learning Objectives
Examples of typical projects would include:
- Cycle Time Reduction, Establishing Effective Measurements, Organizational Re-structuring, Improved Quality

Expected results would include:
- Increased Productivity, Faster and More Effective Project Delivery, and Heightened Awareness of the Change Process

Who Should Attend
Key customers and partners that have an established relationship with GE and who have a commitment to change.
- Customer teams should include the CEO and/or Executive staff to support and drive cultural change, and the key person(s) of change initiative programs
- GE teams should include high-level functional managers and the Sales Account Management team. In addition, trained CAP coach(es) should attend to help plan and implement the desired results of the GE/customer team

Prerequisite
A change project and a trained CAP coach are required.

Logistics
The Workshop lasts 2-1/2 days. Scheduled to meet demand.

CUSTOMER/PARTNER WORK-OUTS™, EDUCATIONAL PROGRAMS & VISITS

Overview
Crotonville can design and/or customize a wide variety of Work-Outs™, CAP programs, Executive Leadership programs, or visits for customers, JV partners, or suppliers to meet market development and/or business needs.

Learning Objectives
- Depend on the visit or program
- Focused on meeting business objectives, building the customer/partner relationship, and sharing best practices

Who Should Attend
Depends on the visit or program. Typically for visits, individuals from the customer / partner organization plus representatives from the related GE business. Typically for programs, GE / customer or partner participants attend as a member of a business team working on a strategic change project.

Prerequisites
Must have sponsorship of the CEO, GE Business Leaders, Corporate Staff SVPs or Corporate Officers. Representatives from the related GE business must attend with the customer / partner.

Logistics
Half-day or full-day visits are scheduled upon request. Programs vary in length (1 day to 2 weeks) and are scheduled upon request.

Exhibit 16-4. Customer Work-Out/CAP Orientation Workshop and Customer/Partner Work-Outs, Educational Programs and Visits

 ## FACILITATION SKILLS WORKSHOP (FSW)

Overview
FSW helps managers and individual contributors develop the process consultation and facilitation skills necessary to function effectively in the "GE of the '90s." Graduates are better able to guide staff meetings, cross-functional problem-solving teams, task forces, project teams, Six Sigma Teams, and Work-Out meetings.

Learning Objectives
- Facilitation Best Practices
- Group Development and Dynamics
- Peer/Instructor Feedback and Self-Analysis
- Handling Difficult Behavior
- Problem-Solving and Team Building
- Change Acceleration Process
- Teamwork Tool Kit

FSW faculty are external consultants who have been instrumental in supporting Work-Out, Six Sigma and the Change Acceleration Process (CAP). The workshop is an individualized experience with a participant-to-faculty ratio of 8:1. Learning occurs via lectures and group discussions followed by hands-on practice coupled with coaching and video feedback.

Who Should Attend
Team leaders and members who must use a wide range of tools and techniques to influence the performance of groups.

Logistics
FSW is conducted over four days and will be offered five times in 1998 in the Americas.

 ## INTEGRATION STRATEGY WORKSHOP

Overview
This workshop provides the opportunity for the leadership teams of GE and the acquired business(es) or JV partner to develop a strategy for the successful integration of each company's goals, operations, cultures, and strategic focus and/or to enhance their working relationship. Each workshop is customized to meet the business' needs.

Learning Objectives
- Create awareness of each company's strategic focus, operations, and unique strengths
- Assess GE and acquired companies' cultures and identify similarities, differences and future implications
- Develop a successful integration and growth strategy
- Apply Work-Out™ / CAP tools to address key integration issues

Who Should Attend
The leadership teams of GE and the acquired business or JV partner.

Prerequisite
None

Logistics
This 2 - 3 day workshop is scheduled upon request. The ideal timing of this workshop is 4 - 6 weeks after the acquisition / merger occurs.

Exhibit 16-5. Facilitation Skills Workshop and Integration Strategy Workshop

MASTER BLACK BELT TRAINING (MBB)

Overview

This workshop focuses on developing the critical skills needed for success as a Master Black Belt. It addresses Quality from a Strategic Business Perspective and focuses problem solving at Systems level. It will enhance the participants' Consulting skills, Change Management skills, Coaching/Mentoring skills, and Communications/Influence skills.

Learning Objectives

- Apply the key elements of strategic business thinking to link business strategy to strategic objectives, core business processes, identification of potential projects, and determining benefits
- Use systems dynamics and causal loops to enhance problem solving and identify six sigma project translation opportunities
- Practice applying the appropriate influence style and how to tailor their interventions with client groups
- Demonstrate when and how to apply the GE model of change management (CAP)
- Apply the key principles of Coaching and Mentoring to facilitate individual and organizational change
- Develop action plans to address organizational, team, and personal development

Who Should Attend

New Master Black Belts (less than 4 months experience) or Master Black Belt candidates who have completed their DMAIC training. Completion of one or more projects is preferable. *This workshop does not teach any of the advanced statistical tools.*

Prerequisites

DMAIC Training

Logistics

The workshop is one week and will be scheduled to meet the demand of the businesses for MBB training.

 PARTNERING WITH CUSTOMERS: PRODUCTIVITY SOLUTIONS

Overview

This interactive workshop provides an opportunity for the customer to preview GE change management tools and processes. The GE businesses and their partners develop a plan on how to leverage the tools or processes to improve productivity or enhance business relationships. The team will leave with a clear understanding of available tools and a start of a clearly defined action plan for working together.

Learning Objectives

The session is intended to share best practices around the following themes:

- Evolution of Work-Out at GE
- Change Acceleration Process (CAP) Overview
- Building Boundaryless Relationships
- Best Practice Sharing around Strategic Initiatives
- Human Resources Best Practices

Who Should Attend

Strategic customers send one to two participants at the CEO and/or executive staff level in conjunction with the GE Sales Account Manager, Productivity Leader and/or trained CAP Coach.

Prerequisite

None

Logistics

The workshop lasts one evening plus a day. It will be scheduled two times in 1998 (Spring and Fall) with more sessions to be offered as needed.

Exhibit 16-6. Master Black Belt Training and Partnering with Customers

tions. New Master Black Belts and Master Black Belt candidates can attend the former course, which lasts 1 week. As for the partnering-with-customers course, this is an interactive workshop that gives a chance for the customer to learn about GE change management tools and processes.

Exhibit 16-7 describes a course on boundaryless selling. Participants in the course get the chance to develop skills that will assist them with major customer selling situations. The course is 2 to 4 days long.

BOUNDARYLESS SELLING (BS)

Module 1 - Skill Development for Boundaryless Selling
Module 2 - Strategies for Managing Boundaryless Selling
Opportunities
Module 3 - The Drive for Growth in Boundaryless Selling
Through Quality

Overview

Directed at individuals who have prime responsibility
for sales growth through boundaryless selling, this mod-
ularized program offers participants the opportunity to
develop skills, knowledge and techniques to assist them
with major customer selling situations. This program
also provides participants with the opportunity to network across GE businesses and share experiences/best
practices on Boundaryless Selling.

Learning Objectives

Module One (2 days)

- Strengthen knowledge of other GE businesses
  engaged in Boundaryless Selling
- Evaluate the role of the Champion
- Application of SPIN selling approach to
  Boundaryless Selling
- Practice customer presentation skills, selling skills
  and influencing skills, and receive coaching and
  feedback

Module Two (4 days)

- Analyze strengths & weaknesses of your business
  against boundaryless selling opportunities
- Identify GE partnership opportunities
- Create a strategic plan to address a major partnership opportunity
- Test application of boundaryless selling strategies
  using a business simulation
- Develop an influencing strategy to apply back in
  your GE business

Module Three (4 days)

- Positioning skills to drive growth in Boundaryless
  Selling while satisfying GE's quality goals
- Increase your effectiveness in managing change
  through application of the Change Acceleration
  Process (CAP) to Boundaryless Selling

Who Should Attend

- Nominated Cross Selling Champions, Key Account
  Managers and Customer Support

Prerequisites

Participants are obliged to attend all 3 modules before
certification can be awarded.

Logistics

A series of 3 modules offered once a year in Europe.
(Maximum: 30 persons)

Exhibit 16-7. Boundaryless Selling

THE CEO AS COMMUNICATOR

1998 was another terrific year for your company—
another record year.

Opening line of Jack Welch's Letter to Share Owners,
1998 Annual Report

The following chapters are designed to give you a sense of how Jack Welch communicates his message within GE and to the rest of the business community. The opening gives a full-length interview that the author conducted with Welch in April 1999; the next chapter provides two speeches that the GE chairman gave, one in 1998 to GE shareholders, the second a year later, to the same group. We then print in its entirety the document that the business world awaits with great anticipation each year, Welch's letter to share holders, this one taken from the GE 1998 annual report. Finally, we have put together in the last chapter of this section a series of Welch quotes that refer to his business strategies.

In this module, you will learn:

- What Jack Welch is like as he sits through a full-length interview

- What he says to his share owners

- What he writes in his annual letter to share owners, employees, and customers

CHAPTER 17

The Jack Welch Interview

In the course of interviewing Jack Welch over the last 8 years, I have usually found him brimming with energy and enthusiasm, often about his latest corporate initiative. It was no different when we sat down for our interview in late April 1999 over lunch in his private dining room near his office at GE's headquarters in Fairfield, Connecticut. This time he was keen to offer an update on the quality initiative and to talk about the major steps he was taking to give GE a large Internet presence. We have chosen to present the interview in its entirety so that readers can get a better sense of what Welch is like in this setting, how he answers questions, what truly interests him about a certain question: in short, what a complete Jack Welch interview is like.

Q: The last year or two at General Electric have been so excellent. Every year GE gets better and better. How do you account for that?

WELCH: So is this year.

Q: What is it about the last year or two that—?

WELCH: I don't think it's the last two. I think it's been several. I think the best way to describe what's happened here—You have to take the initiatives and you have to understand they've all become broader and deeper. Every one of them. So if you take globalization, we started out doing aftermarkets and expanding

A complete Jack Welch interview. The Chairman addresses a wide range of issues affecting his company.

our horizons. And that was quite successful. International sales have grown two or three times the rate of domestic sales. And that was quite a positive. Then we took globalization to the next step, which was globalizing components, products, sourcing in Mexico, sourcing in eastern Europe, sourcing around the world. That was the next step of globalization. And you take the third step, which we're in now in the last year or so, it's globalizing the intellect. Building research labs in India; dealing with Russian scientists and materials; having medical centers of excellence in China, India, and Korea. Lots of engineers.

Q: Local-hired?

WELCH: Local, local. Building R & D capability at an R & D center in India. GE Plastics is building a new grassroots R & D center in India. Ph.D.s from India. GE Medical is using Israel with Elscint. Getting new product development in nuclear. We kept the engineers there. So that's the globalizing of the intellect. So we've gone from markets, products, and components—we have forty-four plants in Mexico, we have thirteen plants in eastern Europe. We have better metallurgists in Czechoslovakia than we can find in some businesses here. So this intellectual expansion has opened up big new horizons. So that's one thing. If you take services, we started looking originally at OEM, just doing our own services; then we went to third-party, doing other people's services. Now we're migrating from the new platforms like the new CFM56 engine, we're migrating all that technology back down to the old platform. We're changing cores, we're changing blade configurations in engines. We've expanded—instead of leaving the old base, we're upgrading the old base with new platforms back to the old base and the old base is 75 to 80 percent of the product line. We've opened up whole new markets there. Take Six Sigma. We started out with Six Sigma as a quality program, then we turned it into an internal productivity program, saving waste and all that, then we turned it to our customers. What has really happened with Six Sigma? It's the most important management training thing we've ever had. It's better than going to Harvard Business School. It's better than going to Crotonville. It teaches you how to think differently. We had something like 125 managers who had been promoted from quality to Six Sigma. Today we're well over 1,000. Quality leaders have been promoted to management jobs. And I had roundtables with all of them. I go around each place in the session C process and we bring the quality leaders in who used to be quality leaders; they're now running businesses. We had roundtables, and we ask, "What do you do differently now that you wouldn't have done before you had this job?" I talked to a woman down at GE Capital. She came from Citicorp. She was the quality leader. She's gone over to run operations in the vendor business. She said if I went back to Citicorp with what I know, after being a quality leader, I would blow the place apart. So it's become an enormous training ground. It's really gone from a quality program to a productivity program to a customer satisfaction program to changing the fundamental DNA of the company.

Q: At the operating managers meeting in Florida last January you certainly seemed concerned that the quality initiative was missing the boat when it came to customer satisfaction. Why did you feel so strongly?

WELCH: The Six Sigma program clearly got too internal. We had to fix that. The only way I can get attention around here is not to be rational. So if I appear upset, it means nothing. It's just trying to get a fire drill going. If I said (quietly) let's move this to the customer, nothing happens. You know, we have 300,000 and some people. You've got to go to the extremes.

Q: Now that you've got the company up to the 300,000 level, do you have concerns about creating extra bureaucracy?

WELCH: Our mix of employees is totally different. If you look at where they come from today, they're in India, in China, in Hungary. I think you'll hopefully see stories develop about our European and global presence in terms of taking companies and putting GE values in them. GE values work everywhere. It's giving dignity and voice to people; acting faster; and reaching for your dreams. Those aren't some crazy things—they work in any country, so let's face it, I don't see a lot of bureaucracy. I probably create a lot of it. When I'm out going to meetings, people are getting ready for a meeting and all that stuff; that will always happen. But in the end the informality of the company is very real. It's very real.

Q: You don't feel that Six Sigma has created a burden in terms of bureaucracy?

WELCH: Well, let's say that Six Sigma clearly has forced even more chart making into an organization to explain what it's doing. But I find the rigor that it put in may have been healthy because there may have been a little bit of throwing it at the wall and see what sticks; so I'd say it's been helpful. Now in doing this it may get a little too much—but, for example, starting next year Six Sigma success will be measured by monitoring customer satisfaction . . . not just measuring dollars of savings.

Q: And you've started to build Six Sigma into products. How is that working out?

WELCH: We're introducing another one in Medical today. An ultrasound product. Six months ago we introduced the LightSpeed. Unbelievable. Unbelievable. I can show you incredible letters from doctors. By the end of this year Six Sigma will be the way we work. Yesterday I was down at GE Capital doing session C. The quality leaders came in to give a pitch. They were all the best people in the company. No longer do you have to worry about seeing someone come in who isn't a total leader, who isn't going to be a big-deal vice president of the company. You don't see that anymore. It's become a place where diversity's been helped. Because like the financial management program, it's a place for people to get out of the pack. Six Sigma quality is a major program with high visibility and stock options. So the reason why it's all working now is that every one of these initiatives is just so much bigger than when we thought about it, when we started. They just keep growing like a mushroom. I didn't know when I started Six Sigma quality that it would end up being the greatest management training ground that you could possibly have. I had no idea.

Q: You've gone from one initiative to another. And sometimes the initiatives are parallel. I sense that the Internet or e-commerce is becoming another quality-type initiative, isn't it?

WELCH: It's the fourth initiative. It's the newest initiative. We've had three for a long time. We've had globalization. Those initiatives keep expanding. Our view of them gets bigger. Work-Out was really the first kind of corporate initiative. Globalization was not behavioral, but Work-Out was and so is Six Sigma. They define how we work.

Q: Will e-commerce be behavioral?

WELCH: No, it will be enabling—like the service initiative, like globalization. But today Work-Out is still discussed by people at every meeting.

Q: Work-Out has permeated through—

WELCH: It's a way of life. It's a way of life. You get a group of cross-functions. You get seven people across a function. That never would have happened 20 years ago. You stayed in your function.

Q: Are you still doing Work-Out for new employees? How systematic is it today?

WELCH: It's just the way you operate. It's the way you behave.

Q: Are you still doing it?

WELCH: Yes, we'll be initiating Work-Out again in the fall, using the Internet as a resource.

Q: How do you define behaving badly?

WELCH: Selfishly. Self-promoting. Hogging the headlines. Elbowing somebody out of the way.

Q: There is competition, but you're saying it's more gentlemanly?

WELCH: No. People want to excel for the point of excelling and they want to help each other also. You've seen no self-promotion. People want to be the best, but there's no—For example, I'm with guys who say, "I'm copying what Nardelli's [Bob Nardelli, head of GE Power Systems] doing down in Houston. He's doing the greatest boundaryless job in the Houston sales force." They're proud they're copying. Now they say, "I want to do it in Cleveland." Nardelli's the role model. It wouldn't happen.

Q: Since we're talking about succession, are you pretty comfortable with the whole notion that things will go smoothly? I thought I heard you say there won't be any mass defections.

WELCH: No, I didn't say that. There could be all kinds of defections—the world wants our people. What I think I did say had to do with the depth and strength of our team. I hope many will see the opportunity here for this limitless growth that we have—and will stay here and see that being a vice chairman here is a huge job. Some will. Some may not. But that will be determined. What I think I've said is, I have a bench strength that is overwhelming. I brought twelve European business leaders to the analysts. They talked about how they've transformed companies in Europe. Well, the analysts' takeaway was, "My God, I didn't know these twelve guys. And I can't believe how good they are."

Q: Do you have concerns?

WELCH: None. I have concerns about anybody that feels hurt by what the final decision is because I love these guys. And I truly do consider them all my friends. That's the worst part. Three or four people will be selected to run the company in some form or another. So I obviously have feelings about that.

Q: Some are concerned that whoever takes over will be going back to the starting blocks.

WELCH: I won't say it will take the team a week. Probably a month. And they'll wonder who was here before. They'll be walking around saying, "Boy, is this terrific with this new team." And that's the way it will be.

Q: Do you want to do what your predecessor Reg Jones did, which is to choose somebody who's different from him, or do you want to choose someone who has all of your values?

WELCH: Frankly, I think we could pick any combination of six people who have those values. Seven people.

Q: Must it be important that the person have your values?

WELCH: Yeah, but that's—the team that I have today—that's what I was trying to say. I love these people. They're all terrific. They're all a little different here and there, but they're all terrific. Capable. High integrity. Non-ego-crazy.

Q: When you choose the person—

WELCH: The board and I will select the team, the team, the team. [Welch repeated the word team three times to emphasize that the Board would not be selecting simply a new leader, but rather a group of people, most likely a chairman and two vice chairmen) who would constitute the new GE leadership team.]

Q: When you and the board choose your successor, will you use the same criteria as choosing any business leader, or is something different at play here?

WELCH: No, I think the biggest thing is that you have to bet on one thing. And this is the hardest bet in the world. You've got to bet on what's ahead, not what was done. You've got to sort of get a message from what was done. The whole point is, how are they going to see the future—because seeing tomorrow is what it's all about, not writing a history book.

Q: So you want someone who has demonstrated a lot of vision, a lot of foresight?

WELCH: I hope we're able to select a team that has the right combination of foresight and operational skills, because you can't have all foresight and miss out on the numbers. So I hope we can get a team that will have the whole combination. That's what our objective is. But it's very important to think through where it's going. Not where it's been.

Q: The GE of the future is a service company that—

WELCH: Makes products. Very good products. And it's a high-technology service company. Whether it's in financial services, where it's extremely fast-moving, lots of information-based products, whether it's medical systems, where it's software upgrades, whether it's aircraft engines where you're migrating new platforms down.

Q: I know how strongly you feel about the services component, but as I was preparing for this interview, I was wondering, is there any downside to being a service company?

WELCH: Did you find any?

Q: Not so far.

WELCH: What a service company does is, instead of thinking about selling locomotives, you think about selling railroads. Instead of selling equipment to hospitals, you think about serving hospitals. Instead of selling to airlines, you think about servicing airlines.

Q: Someone once said to me that it might be hard to get people excited about services, whereas the engineers always got excited about making a product.

WELCH: I'll show you a chart when you're at Crotonville today, a survey chart that will show the progress we've made. We're not all the way there. This survey we ran is the greatest thing since sliced bread. Because we really get the pulse of the people. It shows that 90+ percent of the company are doing a project or have done a project; 94 percent believe that GE will be a quality leader in the next century. But in service, we're not anywhere near where we are in quality. In globalization they hate every time I talk about the intellectualizing because they think of jobs. Transferring jobs. Why are we taking engineers from India? So you'll see that survey on global sourcing of intellect will be low. Our employees are worried. But the survey helps us so much to manage. We can deal with it. Straight up. But I see an audience, when I talk about sourcing intellect it takes me back to the 1980s when I talked about fix, close, or sell, be number one. You might even be able to watch the body language yourself today. All of a sudden, legs cross. Smiles go to—and there's that bastard doing it again to me. Just when we had it all going well, he's come up with something else to do.

Q: People must be comforted by the fact that GE is growing.

WELCH: We don't have enough people to move fast enough for the opportunities that the whole service horizon opens up. The best summary of all is we entered the 1980s as a $21 billion company serving a $110 billion market, about a 20 percent market share. We enter the year 2000 as a $110 billion company serving a $1 trillion dollar market. So we actually have half the share of the market that we're defining that we had 20 years ago.

Q: And you're comfortable with that?

WELCH: It's grown so big. The growth is limitless.

Q: You've said many times that you felt you didn't move fast enough at GE, and I thought that was quite an admission.

WELCH: It's true.

Q: But I want to ask you specifically, what did you mean by that? Where didn't you move fast enough?

WELCH: If we delayered faster, took out the overhead and the bureaucracy, got leaner, two years faster, started Work-Out two years earlier, we would have had that going. You couldn't have had Six Sigma without Work-Out. You couldn't put Six Sigma on a bureaucratic company doing bureaucratic things. It would have just sunk it. If all those things were moved forward, if we had globalized our intellectual capability in 1994 rather than 1998 and 1999, every one of these things, when you think about it, I mean I've been at this thing for 20 years, just think if I had done it in 10 years, how much better would it have been these last 10 years.

Q: There must be something to be said for going about these things rather deliberately and methodically, rather than—I know you love speed.

WELCH: I'm not going to argue against what's happened. It turned out all right, but I can't help but think how much better it would have been if I had done it faster. You know at the time everything we did was radical. Who knows? I might have gotten fired if I had worked faster.

Q: You also said you couldn't have done a number of these things, say, between 1981 and maybe 1985 or 1986 while you were downsizing. Your starting point for all these things had to be the late 1980s with Work-Out?

WELCH: But it took me 5 years to downsize. Or 4 years. And look, I don't know the answer to this. No one will know the answer.

This is 20-20, but I mean it is clear that all these things that have eventually worked, if we had done them faster, we might be further along.

Q: Let me ask you about stretch. Leaving aside your budget example, what other examples of stretch do you like?

WELCH: I like the BMC class that came in to us one day with a recommendation of their own to the CEC. They said, This number one, number two idea was great for its time; but it's limited our thinking as a company in terms of how big can we be, because everyone is defining their markets smaller so they can be number one and number two. Why don't you have an exercise, just a class, at session 1 that says no one can come to the business with a business that has more than 10 percent market share? That's about as good an exercise as you'll ever get. So everyone tried to go out and find bigger markets. And sure enough, what have they done? They've found products to fill them. It's the ultimate example of stretch, the ultimate. For a class to come in and say everyone's got this one, two, fix, close, or sell memorized. That was good for its time. Let's get off that. It's limiting us.

Q: Other examples?

WELCH: Well, I had no idea that plastics would go to color matching on the Internet. Making chips, putting them away, everytime they make a chip now, they make 500. They put them in a big cold-storage vault. Now they sell chips. Instead of doing the expensive telematching they sell them on the Internet. About three chips around the colors that the guy wants. They put on the Web the different x's and y's of color coordination. Compaq has just made GE colors their true colors for paints or anything else. And they go to our Web site to get their colors, suppliers do. That's not Jack Welch thinking of that; some guy up there came up with this. He's building a $120 million business in a couple of years. That's what stretch is all about. They're thinking beyond the bounds.

Q: When you were asked what you would do after retirement, you said, "Something meaningful." What are your thoughts?

WELCH: I'm not going to tell you. I'm not going to go hit golf balls.

Q: And you still have this 4 or 5 handicap? Scott McNealy is number one, and you're number two?

WELCH: I was lucky enough to beat him twice in a row now. Last year and this year. He just sent me an e-mail. "If I go to one more place and find out that you already told them you beat me this year . . . !!!"

Q: You always disliked Washington.

WELCH: I'll tell you that. I wouldn't go near politics.

Q: It's still, it's still—

WELCH: God almighty.

Q: Or a cabinet post?

WELCH: God almighty. Oh!

Q: But you could tackle one of the world's great bureaucracies. Get rid of all those people.

WELCH: Look, the way you can do it in a company is so much easier—you have a lot of tools at your hands. You can align rewards with desired behavior. Government can't do that. It doesn't have the degrees of freedom that you have. People say to me, "How did you get this company to be so boundaryless? How did that happen?" Very simple. Everyone's got a lot of options. And it's a lot more important what the company does than what their unit does.

Q: There are no similar incentives in government?

WELCH: No, you've got Congress second-guessing you. Someone wants to close a base and he has Congressmen coming around beating him over the head.

Q: So we won't see you in Washington.

WELCH: No way.

Q: We won't see you on the golf course too much?

WELCH: You'll see me plenty. But I'll do something.

Q: Is the idea of people retiring at 65 outmoded now?

WELCH: I think there's another way of looking at it. If I had been in this job 6 years, 7 years, it would be totally outmoded. I feel great. I have more ideas than I ever had. It would be totally outmoded. But I've been here 20 years and an organization needs vitality. And while we've had a lot of vitality below it, this next change will create a lot more vitality because I'll go and some people will leave. We'll get filled in. It will create another fertilization of the company. So 20 years is why I'm leaving, not because I'm 65.

Q: What should be the new age limit, if there were to be one?

WELCH: I have no idea. It's an individual—

Q: Going back to the Internet and e-commerce, I'm struck that you've always described yourself as a Neanderthal when it came to computers, and now you're going to take the company down the Internet and e-commerce road. Are you a big fan of the Internet?

WELCH: This is a crazy thing to say: I've been heavily influenced by my wife, Jane.

Q: She's a big fan?

WELCH: She lives it. And she trades. She shows me her stocks at the end of the day. Her wins and losses. Once she was mad that she hadn't sold something because Internet stocks were down for 2 days. She's almost like a day trader, but she's in there on everything. When we're going to go somewhere, she goes in and shows me pictures of the place. So I've learned how to use it. I almost had to. And I like it a lot.

Q: What do you like about it from a business standpoint?

WELCH: I'll tell you something and it may be a totally age-related and historical thing: I don't feel the same chemistry when I read an e-mail from somebody as I do when they write me a letter.

Q: You handwrite all your notes?

WELCH: Yeah. Now I send e-mails. When I see somebody I like at a meeting, I send him a handwritten note—I don't write him an e-mail—saying I enjoyed meeting him.

Q: You're used to handwritten notes.

WELCH: It makes me feel more comfortable. And it makes me feel closer to someone when I'm getting it that way. Now that's probably age. Last night I was able to communicate with four or five people, you know, in my pecky sort of way [he takes his fingers as he were typing on a keyboard], in a reasonable fashion. My sentences are like baby sentences. They're not very—but I get it done and I enjoy it. I get a kick out of it. It's like a new thing.

Q: Do you agree with those people who say that we're on the verge of a whole new way of doing business because of the Internet?

WELCH: Yeah. I think business will be forever changed. But I don't think every model will work. I think there's a lot of hoopla. What we are in the process of having here is another one of these massive trends. We had one in the industrial revolution when all companies went to crazy price-earning multiples. We had one when they were concepts. We had one in the late twenties in the media thing with RCA, radio, the beginnings of talk, of television. There is a shuffling out as things develop. And now you'll see in these concepts, these are fundamental changes, this is industrial revolution–type stuff. There's no question. Channels will be different. Commerce will be different. People will communicate differently. But I don't want to confuse stock market valuations with the impact.

Q: If it indeed is a revolution, then that means, it seems to me, that it imposes a tremendous challenge to GE and other companies.

WELCH: A tremendous opportunity. A tremendous opportunity.

Q: Do you have any concerns, or do you just think it's a great thing—

WELCH: It's change. And we've got a company that loves change. We never would have had an on-line color-match business that's growing, doubling every 60 days. So we got to find more of those. It will disintermediate lots of channels, no question. It will put pressure on margins. No question.

Q: More competition?

WELCH: More transparency.

Q: You mentioned stock market valuations. You've watched, as we all have, these companies with their market caps going off the charts at the same time that they're losing money. What do you think—?

WELCH: That's what I tried to bring you back to—these concept periods. In concept periods investors bet until the concept is defined, until the earnings profile or the structural profile develops. This is not the first time this has happened. In the old days you did have companies losing money, but doing well in the stock market. I don't know the exact numbers. But in the industrial revolution when you look at the first Dow Jones group, the sugar companies and some of those wild evaluations—genetic engineering stock, biotech stock—that came out in the early rush that roared up in the eighties. And some of them stayed. This has to shuffle out, but some of these are real things and some aren't. Some models won't work, some will. But I don't get upset about valuations.

Q: There isn't a question-and-answer session with you at which a question about NBC doesn't come up. And you're always asked when you are going to sell it. My question is different: What is it that you love about NBC?

WELCH: The media business that we are in has all kinds of opportunities for creativity. Forget just the creativity of a show that enhances the existing channel. But think about MSNBC. Think about cable. Now think about what you can do as you get into the Internet. Think of all the people who have joined up with us. Maybe C-Net or I-Village or a whole series of companies. Because we can drive traffic to sites. We're communicating with millions of people everyday in that business. How many off-shoots can we develop? How many new things? I think CNBC.com will be an incredible property. And we'll have television property. We'll have CNBC.com. We'll be able to send people to both places. It will be remarkable. MSNBC.com is today the largest new site on the Internet, bigger than CNN, bigger than the three networks. Knock on wood, we've been very successful making all these investments in the Internet. A little over a half-billion dollars today, it may be gone tomorrow but gains, gains. So there's all kinds of ways to play this game. It's as big as your appetite again. If you think of it just as an NBC—people still want to tell us that the network audience is shrinking. Next year we'll make $300 million on CNBC. And less than that in the pure network. So CNBC will have gone right by it.

Q: What is it about Crotonville that you like so much?

WELCH: I like it more and more. I think of it as the most important thing in the transformation. We put the money in when we were downsizing the company. We're expanding it.

Q: I was told that you've got about 5,000 to 6,000 people coming through there a year. Do you ever feel that's too few? Or is that the right number? In terms of getting your message across, getting these people educated in GE values. . . .

WELCH: I think it's pretty good. I think it's fine. I wouldn't be smart enough to get the exact right number. But we have a strong educational program there. I don't think I could go there any more. If I went there any more than I do now, that would be my job. For example, I prepared today to go there.

Q: How much preparation do you do?

WELCH: I steal a chart here. I steal a chart there. Make up two or three. To address their questions. They ask the questions. It's a very important part of—For instance, I'll talk today about the vitality chart. And the vitality chart is disturbing. And so it will be a good chance. . . . I had a great discussion with the last class about it. And they felt terrific afterward. They wrote notes about it. They understand it. It's a scary thing.

Q: Some people listen to your thoughts on leadership, the vitality chart, your feeling that people need to be energized; but the ones who are the C's, or the B's dropping to the C's, they say, Well, it's pretty brutal. But this never bothers you, does it?

WELCH: (softly) No.

Q: There's a kind of bluntness to it. You don't want to be soft, do you? You've said that to me earlier.

WELCH: I don't want to be cruel either. I want these people to be treated decently. And one of the great things now is—one of the cruelest things is the company that keeps people around until they're 52 and 53 and 54 and tells them, hey, there's no place for you anymore. Our job is to tell people early and let them go on to great careers in other companies. And not throw them out fast. One of the things I saw was layoffs of people in their fifties, in 1981 and 1982 and 1983. That's cruel. Because they're not as employable. The world doesn't chase them. So from my standpoint, letting everyone know where they are. From now on, every EMS will say, top 10, top 15, middle 50. They'll know. There'll be no more, "Gee, I was always told I was a great employee. And now you're saying, oh ho." My job is to really deal with the extremes of the vitality chart. Principally, the top 10, bottom 10. Kiss them, love them, promote them, reward them, because one great person's worth five mediocre ones. And as for the others on the right side (the bottom 15 percent), get an exit plan for them. I don't think that's cruel.

Q: GE spends so much time hiring the best people, then you have these B's and C's that you don't like and want to get rid of. Is that a contradiction?

WELCH: No. If I could pick the perfect person every time, I'd be better at this job than I am. People change. They don't develop. Some grow. Some swell. All kinds of things happen.

The interview is over. It is vintage Jack Welch. We have talked for 90 minutes about where the company stands in the spring of 1999. It stands in great shape. We have heard him give an honest report on some of the deficiencies that sprang up in the quality initiative. This was Jack Welch following one of his favorite business strategies: face reality. We have listened to him talk about taking GE down a new road. He admits that while he has none of the technological skills of a Bill Gates or a Steve Jobs, he is—as is customary with him—deeply excited about what he thinks of as the next revolution in business: the Internet age. Again, this is Welch at his best, never shrinking from change, but looking at change as a fresh opportunity for GE. So this was, as usual, a Jack Welch starting his day over new, embracing the future and change and the realities that he found. This was as well a different interview from the past I have conducted with him. This one contained a lengthy (lengthy for Welch, that is) discussion on a sensitive topic—his departure from GE at the end of 2000. Welch tries not to show discomfort when addressing the succession issue; but I had the impression that he would prefer staying on as chairman of GE forever. He just loves the job, and he's deeply proud of what he's been able to accomplish. Yet, he faces reality about so many other things. And he faces the reality of December 31, 2000—his last day on the job—realistically as well. He knows he will step down. He even thinks it's the right thing to do. But he's not going to break into a wide smile at the prospect.

CHAPTER 18

The Jack Welch Speeches

Jack Welch gives few speeches. Indeed, for someone for whom communication is a crucial part of his business strategies, Welch seems less a communicator than a man of mystery. That, however, is not the case. He believes in quality over quantity—the old "less is more" approach to business. He also likes to concentrate on GE and the business issues that pertain to the company. In his speeches—as reflected in those that we print here in their entirety—he avoids discussing industrywide issues; he rarely speaks about the American or the international economy. He does talk about leadership and what constitutes ideal business leadership.

We begin with a speech that Welch gave to the business community 6 months after he became GE chairman and CEO. He spoke to a group of financial analysts at the Hotel Pierre on December 8, 1981. In that speech he spent little time on the kind of business strategies and corporate initiatives that he would become famous for, and a good deal of time on GE itself and how it was doing.

We have chosen also to present Welch's talks to share owners in 1998 and 1999; we offer these speeches in large measure because they provide the chance to hear Welch talk about GE, not by simply reciting a bunch of numbers, but by speaking at length about his corporate initiatives—globalization, services, quality. The annual speech to the share owners is one of the highlights of Welch's communications effort over the course of any given year. In these speeches to the share owners he offers his views on business leadership and some of the strategies that he has pursued at GE. So these two speeches help us to get a sense of Jack Welch in action, talking to an audience, delivering his message.

Growing Fast in a Slow-Growth Economy

(Jack Welch speech to the business community, December 8, 1981)

Our purpose today is to give you an update on General Electric, how we are doing—how we've done in 1981—then a sense of our positioning—where we are heading—where we want to go—and last, a feel for how we will get there.

I would like to spend a few minutes covering all this as directly and candidly as I know how, and then turn the meeting over to you for questions. I will be joined for the question and answer period by our two Vice Chairmen, John Burlingame and Ed Hood, and our chief financial officer, Tom Thorsen. We have also invited the Company's Sector Executives and key Corporate Staff officers who will be available during the reception following the formal meeting to elaborate on any issues we may not have covered in sufficient detail.

Let's move first, then, to a look at General Electric in 1981. Most of the estimates we have seen from the people in this room and elsewhere have our earnings per share in the 7.20 to 7.30 range, up 8–10% from 1980. With less than a month to go, we feel very comfortable in saying that our 1981 performance will be within those levels.

One of Jack Welch's first major speeches as Chairman and CEO of General Electric.

In looking behind the total for a perspective on the pieces—each Sector's 1981 performance—I'd like to try to put some balance into that perspective by commenting on the year's low lights as well as the highlights. Of course, I'll be using some natural bias in choosing these "highs" and "lows"!

First, in Consumer the highlights were clearly the strong performances by our Lighting and Audio businesses. Despite general consumer softness, Lighting was able to moderately increase their earnings, while Audio, for the third consecutive year, had major sales and earnings gains.

Our biggest difficulty, our main low in Consumer this year, where overall earnings will be down, was in the Major Appliance business. We were hit harder perhaps than anyone else in the industry as a result of the downturn in housing completions which hurt our contract business. We lost a point or two of share as a result of the relative weakness in the contract versus retail segments.

Looking at the Industrial Sector next, Transportation had strong earnings gains as a result of international strength in locomotives and increased activity in oil and gas drilling. Contractor Equipment had good results principally because of the strength of non-residential construction during most of the year.

The two biggest disappointments in this Sector were the lack of domestic locomotive activity and, in the motor business, the news that Whirlpool is considering phasing us out of some $40 million in annual sales volume over the next 2–3 years.

Power Systems had an excellent 1981. Overall earnings increased and, more importantly, we received several outstanding orders for future delivery. Tokyo Electric Power gave us over $500 million worth of business for the largest gas turbine combined cycle order ever awarded. We also received orders for 125 sets of gas turbine components for the USSR Western Siberian pipeline. Our first order for two 700 megawatt large steam turbine generators for Romania should help us to get orders from this country throughout the decade.

On the disappointing side in 1981, we saw a further decline in domestic utility load growth. This will further postpone the need for domestic utilities to order equipment.

In our Aircraft Engine business, we have had some real breaks in 1981. The military side is very strong. As most of you know, our engines have been selected for both new bomber programs, the B-1 and the advanced technology bomber, with potential sales of billions of dollars during the decade.

Some of this success was offset by the well known weakness in the commercial market, but we still expect that our Aircraft Engine business will be able to record modest earnings increases in both 1981 and 1982.

In natural resources, the major highlight has to be Utah's strong earnings performance, particularly in Australian metallurgical coal, along with the continued exploration successes and earnings growth of Ladd Petroleum.

The biggest disappointment continues to be the Samarco Brazilian iron ore pellet business. We can't operate it profitably as a result of a weak worldwide iron ore demand.

Finally, a look at the two Sectors which came out of our reorganization in September.

Services and Materials had a substantial earnings gain this year. GECC did close to $1.5 billion in tax leases which will provide us with significant cash benefits and net income for a long time. In Materials, sales and earnings were up dramatically as a variety of new applications were found for our products. GEISCO, General Electric Information Services Company, also had very strong 1981 earnings. But, more importantly, this business made four strategic acquisitions to strengthen its ability to provide software solutions rather than raw computing power.

On a less positive note, high interest rates for most of the year kept GECC's earnings growth below the 20+% they had been achieving. Materials, too, is starting to feel in the fourth quarter some of the slowdown that showed up earlier in consumer durables.

Finally, in Technical Systems, earnings overall are down, but for a positive reason—our extensive business development activities: the acquisition of two significant microelectronics companies, Intersil and Calma; the formation of a new joint venture in computer aided engineering with Structural Dynamics; and the development of our automation systems business. These moves, plus the six robots we've announced, were major steps in our drive to become the clear leader in factory automation—one of the mega-markets of the '80s.

Our Aerospace business is doing extremely well, with orders received up 35% over 1980. And, finally, our Medical Systems business continues to grow sales and earnings rapidly on a worldwide basis, principally as a result of our overwhelming success in the CT, computed tomography market. This is, perhaps, the best example of General Electric's ability to couple superior technology with burgeoning new markets. This is the kind of success we are looking forward to in the factory automation market.

I recognize that is a lot to swallow in 5–7 minutes, but I wanted to give you a flavor of the tremendous amount of activity that is going on across this organization. These are businesses and people full of excitement and achievements—clearly recognizing the tough environment that we are in but confident that we have the resources and plans in place to deal with the new realities.

Now, a quick look at 1982.

We have all learned over the last two years that it is impossible to forecast with any precision. But it is clear that most people's crystal balls say that the first half of 1982 will be more difficult than the second half. We feel, nevertheless, that we can more than hold our own in the year ahead.

Perhaps the biggest companywide highlight of 1981 was the organization structure that we put in place September 1. It gave us the opportunity to put together the businesses and people we need to do the job ahead. For example, in our new Technical Systems Sector, we took all our electronics activities from three other organizations and created a critical mass in one entity. The mission of the new organization is to develop leading edge businesses across a myriad of total system fronts, from industrial automation to aerospace to medical systems.

In creating a Services and Materials Sector, we had two objectives. First, an organizational one—to put three very high growth businesses together—each with a unique entrepreneurial cast—each with managements trying to be bigger and better than the best in their industry. Second, we had a strategic objective—to combine the network capability of the General Electric Information Services Company with the financing expertise of the General Electric Credit Corporation and thus secure greater market leverage.

Not only did we form two new Sectors and a new Group aimed more clearly at high growth goals; more importantly, we put new executives in charge who brought track records of high growth and entrepreneurship with them.

So much for what we have done and how we are doing.

Where are we going?—What will General Electric be?—What is the strategy?

If I could, this would be the appropriate moment for me to withdraw from my pocket a sealed envelope containing the grand strategy for the General Electric Company over the next decade. But I can't, and I am not going to attempt, for the sake of intellectual neatness, to tie a bow around the many diverse initiatives of General Electric—initiatives as diverse as the allocation of $1.5 billion for new plastic plants—the acquisition of a CAD/CAM supplier like Calma—the acquisition of four software companies in the last four months—a $300 million commitment for a locomotive plant productivity upgrade and capacity expansion—a new microelectronics laboratory at the Research Center in Schenectady—investments in a microelectronics application center in Raleigh/Durham and a new factory automation laboratory in Charlottesville, Virginia.

It just doesn't make sense for neatness' sake to shoehorn these initiatives and scores of other individual business plans into an all-inclusive, all-GE, central strategy—one grand scheme.

What does relate and will enhance the many decentralized plans and initiatives of this Company isn't a central strategy, but a central idea—a simple core concept that will guide General Electric in the '80s and govern our diverse plans and strategies.

In trying to find a way to express these ideas and to share them with you, we found a powerful letter written by a Bendix planning manager to the editor of *Fortune* magazine. I want to share it with you because it captures, in words I find difficult to improve on, much of my own thinking about strategic planning for a company like General Electric. The letter reads like this:

"Through your excellent series on the current practice of strategic planning runs a common thread: the endless quest for a paint-by-numbers approach, which automatically gives answers. Yet that pursuit continually fails.

"Von Clausewitz summed up what it had all been about in his classic *On War*. Men could not reduce strategy to a formula. Detailed planning necessarily failed, due to the inevitable frictions encountered: chance events, imperfections in execution, and the independent will of the opposition. Instead, the human elements were paramount: leadership, morale, and the almost instinctive savvy of the best generals.

"The Prussian general staff, under the elder Von Moltke, perfected these concepts in practice. They did not expect a plan of operations to survive beyond the first contact with the enemy. They set only the broadest of objectives and emphasized seizing unforeseen opportunities as they arose . . . *Strategy was not a lengthy action plan. It was the evolution of a central idea through continually changing circumstances.*

"Business and war may differ in objectives and codes of conduct. But both involve facing the independent will of other parties. Any cookbook approach is powerless to cope with independent will, or with the unfolding situations of the real world."

Now let me tie this thinking—this notion of "strategy not being a lengthy action plan but the evolution of a central idea through continually changing circumstances"—to the management of the General Electric Company.

The real world, as we see the decade of the '80s, will be a time when inflation is clearly the number one enemy and most countries and most governments will fight that inflation with some form of tight money and fiscal responsibility medicine. The result—slower worldwide growth—slower growth than in any of the past three decades will clearly be the planning base for the 80s.

In this slower growth environment of the '80s, as companies—yes, as companies and countries fight for that reduced volume, fight their own unemployment problems, there will be no room for the mediocre supplier of products and services—the company in the middle of the pack. The winners in this slow-growth environment will be those who search out and participate in the real growth industries and insist upon being number one or number two in every business they are in—the number one or number two leanest, lowest-cost, worldwide producers of quality goods and services or those who have a clear technological edge, a clear advantage in a market niche.

The challenge for General Electric when we participate in these real growth industries, when we are number one or number two, is to ask ourselves—how big, how fast? Yes, how many resources—people and money—can we put behind the opportunity to ensure that we capitalize on this leadership position?

On the other hand, where we are not number one or number two, and don't have or can't see a route to a technological edge, we have got to ask ourselves Peter Drucker's very tough question: "If you weren't already in the business, would you enter it today?" And if the answer is no, face into that second difficult question: "What are you going to do about it?"

The managements and companies in the '80s that don't do this, that hang on to losers for whatever reason—tradition, sentiment, their own management weakness—won't be around in 1990. Think about the fact that in the high growth period between 1945 and 1970, almost one-half of the companies that would have been on a *Fortune* 500 roster disappeared either through acquisition, failure, or slipped quietly off the list due to lack of growth.

We believe this central idea—being number one or number two—more than an objective—a requirement—will give us a set of businesses which will be unique in the world business equation at the end of this decade.

Around this tangible central idea we will wrap these intangible central values—unifying dominant themes that, because of GE's common culture, will become second nature in the organization. One we've termed reality, a second we call quality/excellence, and third, the human element.

Let me try to describe what we mean by reality. It may sound simple, but getting any organization or group of people to see the world the way it is and not the way they wished it were or hoped it will be is not as easy as it sounds. We have to permeate every mind in this Company with an attitude, with an atmosphere that allows people—in fact, encourages people—to see things as they are, to deal with the way it is, not the way they wished it would be. Establishing throughout the organization this concept of reality is a prerequisite to executing the central idea—the necessity of being number one or number two in everything we do—or doing something about it.

When we talk about quality and excellence, we mean creating an atmosphere where every individual across the whole Company is striving to be proud of every product and service we provide. I think it really means all of us stretching beyond our limits, to be, in some cases, better than we ever thought we could be. I see it happening every day in almost every way all over this Company.

This excellence theme leads to our third and final value, what I can only call the human resource element where we have been creating, and will increasingly create, an atmosphere where people dare to try new things—where people feel assured in knowing that only the limits of their creativity and drive, their own standards of personal excellence, will be the ceiling on how far and how fast they move.

The net of these three values—reality, quality, the human element—what could be called soft values—will be a company not simply more high spirited, but more adaptable, more agile than companies that are a twentieth or even a fiftieth of our size. These values will permit us to maintain our common heritage, our common culture, but at the same time, to give ownership to those managers who are leading, operating, and building our stable of number one and number two businesses. We'll give them the resources to take head-on, in skirmish after skirmish, the marketplace competitors they come up against. Yes, give them all the benefits of a company the size of General Electric—financial, technological, and managerial—yet at the same time, provide them the freedom and flexibility that the owners of enterprises their size must have to win in the '80s.

General Electric is a set of diverse enterprises that has to be the envy of every single product line business in America, from oil to high technology. Most of them have been trying to become broader than they are, but most have difficulty finding the route. We are already there—a successful, widely diversified, highly profitable, industrial and financial enterprise. By any measure, we outperformed the GNP and S&P 400 by a good margin in the '70s. We have the commitment and the potential to do better in the '80s. For those of you who like in some way to associate GE and the GNP, if anything, we will be a locomotive pulling the GNP, not a caboose following it.

I predict that you will come to see this Company from the same perspective—and I invite you to measure and judge us by how well we progress along the path I have tried to describe.

Thanks for listening. Now my associates will join me for your questions.

Three Roads to Growth

(Jack Welch speech to GE share owners, April 22, 1998)

Good morning—and welcome once again to our annual meeting. And to those of you who call this lovely city of Cincinnati home, thank you for the welcome and the hospitality you have afforded our Board of Directors in our brief stay here.

Cincinnati is the home of the largest freestanding business in General Electric, GE Aircraft Engines. This is a global business built on a foundation of high technology, manufacturing excellence, and absolute quality of product and services.

Since 1990, over 50% of all jet engine orders placed in the intensely competitive world market have been won by GE; and during the past two years this win rate has grown to over 70%, a trend that is a justified source of pride for our engine people around the globe.

Jim McNerney and his Aircraft Engines team grew both revenues and earnings at a double-digit pace in 1997 and are off to a flying start in '98 with both sales and earnings up over 30%.

Aside from their competitive success, the people of Aircraft Engines have another reason to be proud and another reason why we are proud of them: their involvement in this community. That involvement led to the legendary Aiken High School project that

GE's Chairman and CEO assesses the company in the late 1990s.

began in the mid-1980s when, under the leadership of a real zealot, Principal Jack Shroeder, who is with us today, several hundred GE people—new hires, long-term employees and retirees—decided they were going to make a difference.

GE people like big challenges. They prefer to do things that can be measured. They love keeping score. They had all of these at Aiken High School. The challenge was working with an underprivileged student body that was sending only three seniors a year to college out of a graduating class of 305—just 1%.

The GE volunteers began working alongside Jack and the faculty at Aiken as tutors, advisors, coaches, mentors, and friends, one-on-one with the students. The GE Fund put up a million dollars to support their effort, and in just a few years big changes, great things, began to happen at the school. By 1990 Aiken sent 73 seniors to college. By 1994 a full 60% of Aiken seniors were college bound; and that percentage has remained at that level or higher ever since, as more than 1,000 GE employees have contributed their time and talents to making a bright future possible for the students of Aiken.

And in typical GE fashion, a great idea from one business—in this case, mentoring—spread rapidly across the Company: to Collinwood High School near our Lighting business in Cleveland; to East High in Erie, Pennsylvania, home of our Transportation Systems business; to Parkersburg South High School near one of our Plastics locations in West Virginia; and to the Manhattan Center for Science and Math near NBC in New York.

As of today, 7,500 students who would never have had a prayer of going to college have gone because of our volunteers at 16 high schools—and because of a $20 million commitment from the GE Fund. A few of these students have graduated from college and come back to join GE, and now they themselves are mentoring in the schools.

Our volunteers are active outside the schools as well, building playgrounds, zoo exhibits, environmental projects and, in a unique program here in Cincinnati, 100 volunteers, most of them retired GE engineers, have devoted 80,000 hours of volunteer service focused on repairing and restoring tape recorders for sight-impaired or physically handicapped people. They have repaired 20,000 of these machines to date.

And across our Company, GE volunteers have pledged one million hours a year of service to youth by the year 2000. We're obviously very proud of our volunteers who represent your Company every day in front of the communities our businesses call home. They are, in our view, one of the reasons why GE, in a *Fortune* magazine poll, was named the most admired company in America.

We are quite proud as well of the business achievements of our associates, and I would now like to touch briefly upon just a few of the many numbers that add up to yet another step level of record-breaking, double-digit performance:

- In 1997 revenues rose to $89.3 billion, up 13%.

- Earnings were up 13% to more than $8.2 billion and earnings per share up 14%.

- Operating margins rose to more than 15% for the first time in the history of our Company.

- The Company had operating cash flow of a record $9.3 billion. That cash was used to repurchase $3.5 billion in stock, to increase dividends by 15%, and to finance the more than 100 acquisitions totaling $17 billion that GE made in 1997.

All of this added up to a banner year for GE Share Owners. We received a total return of 51% on our investment, following a 40% return in 1996 and a 45% return in 1995.

1998 has begun auspiciously as well. The first quarter came in two weeks ago with revenues up 12% over last year's first quarter and earnings per share up 14%.

We're headed for yet another record year, a year when we will close in on the $100 billion revenue mark.

The question the sheer size of this enterprise provokes is an important one and one that has been asked us for years: How can GE sustain this type of performance, how can a 120-year-old, $100 billion company have the audacity and the ability to call itself a high-growth company and deliver consistent strong earnings growth as far out into the future as we can see?

Answering that will be the focus of my brief remarks this morning.

Driving the growth of more than two dozen world-class global businesses are three big company-wide initiatives that will accelerate this Company's growth at double-digit velocity. The first initiative is globalization—participating in a big way in the high-growth areas of the world.

Globalization is crucial to our growth, and it is a central focus at each of our businesses. Some of those businesses—among them Plastics, Medical Systems, Power Systems, and Aircraft Engines—already derive a significant share of their revenues from global markets. We've always called ourselves a global company, but even as recently as the 1980s, only 15–20% of our revenues came from outside the U.S. Today, we look at a GE that will do almost half of its business outside the U.S. by the year 2000.

GE Europe is now approaching $23 billion in revenues from a base of less than $10 billion in 1994. With Europe now in the midst of an economic recovery, our strong participation could not have been better timed.

Asia in 1997 produced another $8.3 billion and, while the turbulence and problems in Asia at the present are not to be minimized, we see the changes in that region presenting enormous opportunities as well. We have increased the intensity of our acquisition activity in that great market of the next century.

We are now a truly global company in mind as well as body. The words "foreign," "offshore," and "domestic" have fallen into disuse as antique and meaningless in businesses that operate typically in three poles: Asia, Europe, and the Americas. Our management meetings are conducted in a wide variety of accents, and global experience is now an important qualification for senior leadership.

The reason for the intensity of our globalization effort and the measure of its success are reflected in the fact that GE revenues in the past decade have grown 6% per year in the U.S.— and 17% globally.

Services is the second key growth initiative. Not everyone has noticed it, but the very nature of GE business activity has changed since as recently as 1990. In that year, 55% of our revenues came from sales of products: jet engines, washing machines, CT scanners, locomotives, turbines, and the like; while 45% came from services: GE Capital, NBC, as well as the servicing of our products. We loved to make great things in factories and send them out the door in a box. We still do. But now we have moved, as we like to say, "beyond the box." We have changed the very nature of what we do for a living. Today, services account for two-thirds of our revenues—soon to be 70% or more. We have become a services company that also makes high-quality products.

In this intensely competitive environment there is enormous growth awaiting those companies who can provide true high-technology service solutions to customers, making those customers more productive, lowering their costs, and helping them become more competitive in their marketplaces.

Nowhere has that service transformation been more profound than here at Aircraft Engines. Because when you think of it, in this high-technology culture we live and work in, "real" men and "real" women have always wanted to be at the leading edge of technology; and that edge, in this business, has always centered on pushing into the wild blue yonder with new jet engines, more thrust, more efficiency, and so forth. "Service" seemed to evoke an image of putting on some overalls and going over to the customer's plant to change the oil.

Gene Murphy, and then Jim McNerney and their teams in Cincinnati changed all that. Bill Vareschi, leader of GE Engine Services, led the change. Chuck Chadwell, Corbett Caudill, and Bob Stiber, all traditional "product-side" leaders, changed their headsets when they saw where the growth was and gave Bill the people and the support that allowed him to change the focus of the whole business. Today, the service side of Aircraft Engines is increasingly seen by the best and brightest as the place to be. This transformation from a product to service mindset has been taking place in business after business as these best and brightest, most of them engineers, have come to see that the future of their business lies in finding ways to enhance our customers' productivity, to bring the awesome technical resources of General Electric to bear on the challenge of making our customers win.

This move to high-technology service solutions for customers in increasingly competitive industries such as airlines, railroads, hospitals, and utilities has spread rapidly across GE and focuses on where we can supply high-technology solutions no one else can, while avoiding the low-end, low-value-added "wrench turning" services that anyone can provide.

Our service teams at Aircraft Engines, for instance, can literally sit at computer consoles and monitor the performance of our engines on customer airliners that are flying at 40,000 feet, thousands of miles away. A temperature or some other indicator slightly out of spec prompts a GE repair team to meet the plane when it lands, adjust the engine on the wing, and let it continue on its way, nipping the problem before more serious repairs involving time off the wing become necessary.

Our Medical Systems service people can detect and fix problems with CT scanners and MR machines without even visiting the hospital, and usually before the doctors and technicians even know there's a problem. Thousands of our MR and CT scanners are on line 24 hours a day, allowing a doctor in Tokyo or Bombay to get help in the middle of a procedure from, say, Paris or Milwaukee, anytime, day or night.

The success of the services initiative depends on taking the same creativity, science, and excitement that goes into designing and building the biggest, most powerful, most efficient jet engine and focusing it on improving the thrust, efficiency, and availability of existing engines or, in other businesses, existing CT scanners, locomotives, or turbines. We are doubling our investment in services technology to $200 million in 1998 and will double it again in 1999.

The growth from services has been explosive—from $8.6 billion in revenues in 1996 to $13 billion this year and headed for nearly $18 billion by 2000. Product services growth in 1997 added a full two points of GE top-line growth and delivered operating margins almost twice the Company average.

Our third growth initiative is Six Sigma quality—the transformation of every single product and process that touches our customers into near-flawless quality, in this case defined as less than four defects per million operations. Six Sigma involves massive investment of time, money and leadership talent, very challenging science and statistical analysis, and a whole new facet to our culture.

Six Sigma is now in its third year at GE. Our Company now has begun to converse, globally and effortlessly, in terms that were utterly alien in 1995: "CTQs," for example—which are "Critical To Quality" items important to customers. We speak of DMAIC—Defining, Measuring, Analyzing, Improving, and Controlling processes—from building an engine blade to answering a phone call about a credit card to stocking a customer's shelves with light bulbs. We have thousands of our very best young leaders who are full-time quality leaders, called Master Black Belts and Black Belts.

GE people have again and again answered the call over the past two decades to change the Company, to dismantle the bureaucracy, to globalize, to move into services, to grow a new culture of learning and involvement—challenge after challenge. And they have responded to the great big idea of making GE one of the handful of world-class companies with Six Sigma quality, with an excitement and enthusiasm I have never seen in nearly 40 years with this Company.

By the end of this year, just about every professional in the Company, scores of thousands in number, will be trained—as a minimum—at what we call the Green Belt level. They will have taken two weeks of classes and have completed at least one Six Sigma project. By December, 4,000 full-time Master Black Belts and Black Belts will be in place. Almost all new products will be designed for Six Sigma. Eventually every process of any significance to our customers, scores of thousands of them, will be moved toward Six Sigma levels of highest quality, higher speed, lower cost.

The investment, particularly in training, is huge—$450 million in 1998 alone—but the returns have begun to pour in and they are growing exponentially.

Outside analysts have estimated the return to GE from moving to Six Sigma—in terms of savings, increased margins, and other benefits—to be an $8 to $12 billion bottom-line opportunity. And by the end of this year, just three years from a standing start, we will have captured $2 billion of those benefits. Aircraft Engines captured $70 million in Six Sigma productivity gains in 1997 alone.

Beyond the $12 billion or so of returns from Six Sigma, there lies a virtually endless stream of opportunities for share growth, higher margins, and enhanced product and services reputation.

So, the answers are very clear where the strong growth, the endless summer of growth, will come from as we move into our third century as a company . . . whether it be from globalization, where we have grown revenues nearly five-fold in ten years, or product services, where we are growing at 20% a year, or from the Six Sigma quality initiative, which will return a billion dollars in 1998 and accelerate after that.

Those are the opportunities—but how successfully we capitalize on them will depend on the type of leadership that will take this Company into the era ahead. We use the word "leadership" not as just a fancy euphemism for "management," because it is not. In some ways it's the opposite.

This Company cannot be "managed" to perpetual double-digit growth. Management implies stewardship of an asset, orderly, structured, tightly controlled. With leadership the question at the beginning and at the end of the day is, "How far can we take this . . . how big can we grow it . . . and how fast can we get there?"

A manager controls things, keeps them in channels, builds and respects boundaries between functions and ranks, stays within internal and external Company walls. The leader goes after those boundaries with a hammer, drawing the best ideas from anywhere: the factory floor, other businesses, other companies. The GE leader, in particular, sees this Company for what it truly is: the largest petri dish of business innovation in the world. We have roughly 350 business segments. We see them as 350 laboratories whose ideas are there to be shared, learned, and spread as fast as we can. The leader sees that sharing and spreading near the top of his or her list of responsibilities.

This boundaryless leadership today and in the future can be characterized by what we have come to call the 3 "E's."

The first is Energy. The teams that will lead GE at all levels will be those with very high energy levels, intrigued and excited by ideas, global visions, and reflexively attracted to turbulence because of the opportunity it brings. These are people to whom "business as usual" has no meaning and the words "mature" and "stable" are a great big bore.

These leaders will have the second "E" as well: the ability to energize others, to take their own feverish enthusiasm for an idea, a vision, a goal, and infect everyone—to have everyone dreaming the same big dreams at night and impatient to get to work in the morning to make them come true.

And finally, our leaders will have what we call "Edge": a mental toughness to them, the ability to focus intensely on every issue on the way to every goal, the courage to remove those who don't share our values, and the ability and instinct to excite and encourage those who do, year after year, without ever losing the fire, the intensity, the edge.

I've focused this morning on our clear and simple vision of where your Company is going in the years ahead and the type of leadership that will take us there.

GE today is in terrific shape, roaring with enthusiasm and excitement. We've got big opportunities. We share big dreams.

And we have built across the Company the high-energy leadership that will inspire our quarter of a million people around the globe to take us to what can only be described as a glorious future.

Thanks for being here today and for your continuing support.

A Company to Be Proud Of

(Jack Welch speech to GE share owners, April 21, 1999)

Jack Welch talks to GE's share owners in the spring of 1999.

Good morning—and welcome once again to our annual meeting. Ohio is home to more active GE employees than any state in the Union and is headquarters for two of our world-leading businesses, GE Aircraft Engines in the Cincinnati area and GE Lighting here in Cleveland. Lighting has been here since 1913 at Nela Park, which will soon enter its tenth decade as the world leader in lighting technology, some of which, just a few months from now, will illuminate the first game of what we hope will be a successful season for the Cleveland Browns in their new lakefront stadium.

There are more than 10,000 of our shareowners in the Cleveland area who have cause to be proud of their Company and pleased with its performance in 1998, delivering yet another record year.

For the first time in our history we broke the $100 billion mark in revenues.

We grew earnings 13% to a record $9.3 billion and earnings per share 14%.

We had record operating margins of 16.7%, up from 15.7% in 1997, and a record return on total capital of 23.9%, up about 50% from 16.1% in 1990. This performance generated $10 billion in free cash, cash which allowed us to invest for growth and to increase shareowner value. We invested $21 billion in 108 acquisitions, raised the dividend by 17%, and repurchased an additional $3.6 billion in GE stock.

The bottom line: the total return on a share of GE stock in 1998 was 41%, following a return of 51% in 1997, 40% in 1996, and 45% in 1995.

This strong performance continued into 1999. Two weeks ago we reported first quarter earnings, up 14% to record levels. Operating margins, return on total capital, and cash also achieved new first quarter highs.

Those are great numbers and I'll provide a few more a little later; but, for just a few minutes, I'd like to focus on something a bit softer than business numbers, on subjects that do not get the same level of attention as numbers, from either the business media or the financial analysts that follow GE.

We broke another big round number in 1998 in addition to the $100 billion in revenues. We broke the one million hours per year of GE volunteer service to youth.

At the President's Summit held in Philadelphia in 1997, a very persuasive leader, General Colin Powell, challenged Lloyd Trotter, CEO of our Industrial Systems business and the GE representative to this summit, to raise the bar of GE volunteerism and commit to a pace of one million hours a year of volunteer service to America's youth by April of 2000.

GE people like big round numbers like this and they love to take big swings at what we call "stretch" targets. They knocked this one out of the park. I'm pleased to report today that the GE corporate audit staff finished its review a month ago and certified the numbers. We reached our goal of one million volunteer hours per year, and GE people delivered it a full year ahead of schedule. We're proud enough of this achievement that we've made it part of our corporate advertising, and I've brought the spot along for you to see.

The GE family in Cleveland was particularly active in this campaign, conducting an ongoing and highly successful mentoring and school partnership effort at Collinwood High School.

In 1990, 26% of Collinwood graduates went on to college. GE volunteers set a stretch target of doubling that percentage by 1995. After thousands of hours of working with the terrific Collinwood faculty and students, and a grant of $1 million from the GE Fund, over 67% of Collinwood seniors were college bound by 1995, and that number remains at about that level today.

GE volunteers and donors also participated in several facilities upgrades and construction projects in the schools of this area, including building a playground at the Louis Pasteur Elementary School, which feeds Collinwood, and at the high school itself, including renovating the John D. Opie auditorium, named after our Vice Chairman during his tenure as CEO of GE Lighting.

GE volunteerism on this massive national scale undoubtedly contributed to a great honor given our Company in 1999— our selection for the second consecutive year in a poll by *Fortune* magazine as the Most Admired Company in America, and by the *Financial Times* as the Most Respected Company in the World.

We are very proud of GE people for their efforts in the schools and zoos, museums and playgrounds of the towns we call home—just as proud as we are of them for yet another year of outstanding performance in the laboratories, plants, offices, and global markets where GE does business.

We are equally proud of our Company on another score as well: GE and the environment. This morning I would like to lay out, for those of you who are not familiar with this subject, a few facts and a little history that may serve to frame the discussions that will take place here at our meeting later this morning. The central fact, the most important fact, is that we are a Company of deeply held values and nothing is closer to the heart and core of those values than 100% compliance with the spirit and the letter of the law— with no shortcuts, no winks, just a total commitment to integrity.

Your Company has spent two billion dollars in the past decade, not only on remediating the environment and complying with evolving environmental regulations, but going beyond them voluntarily to improve the air, water, and soil in the communities in which we operate.

What did you get for that two billion?

- In the past ten years GE voluntarily reduced the emission of 600 EPA target chemicals by 64%.

- We achieved a voluntary 83% reduction in a related EPA target list of 17 very widely used chemicals.

- We totally eliminated the use of ozone-depleting CFCs.

- Injury rates in our plants are down by two-thirds.

- And more than 1,000 Six Sigma projects have directly focused on pollution prevention and health and safety compliance.

Now GE globalizes, both to expand markets and to obtain the intellectual capital that exists around the world. Some critics of globalization imply that companies might globalize to avoid strict U.S. environmental regulations. That's not true of your Company. To the contrary, we build any new facility to world-class environmental standards, and when we have taken over existing facilities, GE has received award after award for up-grading their environmental, health, and safety performance, from China to Mexico to Hungary to Ireland. Wherever you go in the world you can be proud of GE's treatment of the environment and of the health and safety record of our employees.

On a more specific issue related to the environment, PCBs (polychlorinated biphenyls), it is important that you understand that your Company has always been a leader in the responsible use, disposal, study, and cleanup of these compounds.

First, we were responsible environmental citizens when we used PCBs in capacitors and transformers. They were specified by many customers and insurance underwriter codes because their flame-retardant characteristics saved lives.

Second, we were responsible citizens in the disposal of PCBs: we had permits whenever permits were required and we discharged or disposed of PCBs in ways considered proper and appropriate at the time.

Third, GE immediately stopped using PCBs in the 1970s when environmental regulations changed, and have worked since then with independent scientists and the government to study the effects, if any, of PCBs on people and the environment.

And finally, we have been and will continue to be a responsible citizen, continuing to develop the appropriate remedies for any PCB contamination resulting from our operations.

Recently, there has been wonderful and encouraging news on the PCB issue, great news for our employees in the plants that used PCBs and for our neighbors in the towns where those plants were located. The largest, most definitive independent study ever done on PCBs and cancer, which tracked over 7,000 GE employees who had been heavily exposed to PCBs over a 30- to 50-year portion of their lives, concluded there was absolutely no increase in deaths from cancer or any other illness, including heart attacks and strokes, among that group.

This study by Dr. Renate Kimbrough, who first raised the issue of possible PCB toxicity 30 years ago, was peer reviewed twice—including by the former head of the National Cancer Institute, Dr. Arthur Upton.

This was the fifth and the largest study of our workers in upstate New York and all have arrived at the same conclusion: that there is no evidence that PCBs cause cancer in people.

This was wonderful news and it was greeted as such by most in the political world and in editorial commentaries. Why would it not be? But, for reasons that puzzle me, it was not good news for some. Those are the people with years invested in one point of view on this subject, and for them "good news is no news." For some, science should never be allowed to get in the way of inflammatory rhetoric.

I take this opportunity, in the middle of what normally would be a routine report on business matters, to address this issue of social responsibility, of GE and the environment, because it's important for you to know that you don't have to make a choice between owning a company that puts up great numbers and a company that is socially responsible. You own both and you have every right to be proud of it on every count.

We passed, as I mentioned, the $100 billion milestone in sales in 1998, an occasion one would expect to be marked by big celebrations or favorable comparisons of our revenues with the Gross Domestic Product of various countries and continents.

There was none of that at GE at the end of '98—none. It was because we instinctively sense that the pomposity and complacency that can result from passing a milestone like this can be the prelude to a stumble or a fall.

And there are some potential disadvantages, as well as advantages, to being as large as we are and as large as we plan to become. Some are obvious: big companies simply cannot communicate as rapidly or clearly as small ones, nor are they generally as quick to act as the smaller ones.

But the biggest potential drawback of size is the temptation it presents to manage it, to consolidate and control it, to try and get bureaucratic arms around it. Managing size in this over-controlled fashion has often spelled decline, or worse, for large companies, and we have no intention of doing it.

But there is one huge advantage in being a big company and that is in using size rather than trying to manage it—taking swings, lots of them, with the confidence that comes from knowing that, unlike many smaller companies, an occasional miss, even a big miss, does not mean the end of the game. We made 108 acquisitions in 1998, for $21 billion, and have averaged over 70 per year for the past five years. The vast majority have been successful, but naturally, a few have not turned out as planned. But it is the pace and intensity of the acquisitions that our size permits, and the knowledge that a "miss" won't be fatal, that keeps GE growing and moving forward.

But a big company must not only be willing to use its size, it must be agile enough to bring that size to bear whenever opportunity presents itself. For us that meant going to Europe in the early 1990s, in the face of a troubled economic situation that was forecast to last indefinitely, a move that took us from under $6 billion in European revenue as we approached the decade to nearly $25 billion as we leave it.

It meant going to Mexico in '95 in the face of economic uncertainty and a collapsed peso, buying 16 companies in six months and participating in the terrific recovery that has followed.

It means seeing the crisis in Asia as a huge opportunity and moving quickly to close $15 billion in Japanese acquisitions in the past six months, and to position ourselves to participate, in a big way, in the $4 trillion Japanese economy and the greatness of that country's future. Japan will assuredly recover in the next few years, the way America's economy rebounded in the 1980s and Europe's and Mexico's did in the 1990s.

Today we have a GE culture that truly understands the benefits of size and the need for agility, and these facets of our culture provide a foundation for our growth.

Positioning ourselves to service the global installed base of high-value products is another path toward sustained high growth for GE. Our service challenge, and the vast opportunity meeting that challenge will create, is to ensure that our customers from utilities to hospitals, from railroads and factories to airlines, win in their markets. We must bring these customers the information-based technology that makes our installed equipment more capable and efficient, making them, in turn, more profitable and competitive.

This is just one element of the total service strategy of your Company. In 1980 GE was 15% services and 85% products. We will leave this decade at 25% products and 75% services. A service focus changes how we go to market and what we do in the market. Today, instead of selling equipment to finite markets, we are selling ideas and solutions to a whole world that hungers for them. This creates a world in which we can envision literally unlimited growth.

Finally, and perhaps most importantly, we have changed how we work. Three and a half years ago we made a decision to immerse this Company in the science and culture of Six Sigma quality, which is a disciplined method of eliminating virtually all defects from every one of the Company's products, processes, and transactions. For those not familiar with Six Sigma, it means, very briefly, going from approximately 35,000 defects or mistakes per million operations—Three Sigma, which is average for most companies—to Six Sigma, fewer than 4 defects per million, in operations that range from manufacturing a locomotive part to servicing a credit card account, to processing a mortgage application, to answering a phone. It means fixing processes so they are nearly perfect and then controlling them so they stay fixed. The common objective in virtually all Six Sigma projects is the elimination of variance.

During the first two years of Six Sigma we invested about half a billion dollars in the training of our entire professional work force. But the commitment, the big bet, was much more than financial. It involved the diversion of the very best talent in the Company—thousands of our best people, high-potential men and women—to multi-year tours of full-time Six Sigma work.

The short version of our progress from a standing start three and a half years ago is this: virtually every professional in the Company is now what we call a "Green Belt," with three full weeks of training and a completed Six Sigma project under his or her belt. Five thousand full-time Black Belts and Master Black Belts are now initiating and coaching projects across the globe. Most importantly, the Master Black Belts and Black Belts are now being promoted to key leadership positions in the Company—big jobs—and they have begun to irrevocably change the DNA of GE to one whose central strand is quality.

The financial returns from Six Sigma have exceeded expectations. In 1998 we achieved three quarters of a billion dollars in Six Sigma-related savings over and above our investment, and this year that number will go to a billion and a half, with billions more to be captured from increased volume and market share as customers increasingly "feel" the benefits of GE Six Sigma in their own businesses.

We are now beginning to see the first major products designed for Six Sigma production, designed in effect by the customer, incorporating every feature he or she considers critical to quality.

The first major Six Sigma-designed product to reach the market—the LightSpeed, a multislice CT scanner—reached our customers in 1998. This lifesaving machine is revolutionizing medical diagnostics. A chest scan that takes a conventional scanner three minutes to perform takes 17 seconds with LightSpeed. A full body scan for a trauma patient, for whom speed can mean life or death, now takes 32 seconds when a conventional scanner could take ten minutes or longer. I brought the tape of the ceremony that marked its introduction.

We've shown that tape to every single senior manager in this Company because it represents the future, when every product in this company will be designed for Six Sigma and every customer will be as delighted as those doctors are.

Six Sigma has forever changed GE. Everyone—from the Six Sigma zealots emerging from their Black Belt tours, to the engineers, the auditors, and the scientists, to the senior leadership team that will take this Company into the new millennium—is a true believer in Six Sigma, the way this Company now works.

In nearly four decades with GE I have never seen a Company initiative move so willingly and so rapidly in pursuit of a big idea.

I've focused this morning on a few characteristics of GE that define the kind of Company you own. I've reported a few of the numbers that describe its impressive financial performance— not just last year—but year after year.

I focused as well on the depth and the seriousness of its social commitments, on both the good its employee volunteers do in their communities and on the Company's adherence to the letter and the spirit of the law. I've described for you, I hope, a Company that does most things right and always tries to do the right thing.

I've outlined our view of the one decisive advantage a big global Company has: the ability to take big swings in the pursuit of growth.

But are there limits to that growth? GE in 1999 will be well over $100 billion in revenues, over $10 billion in net income, and people will ask, as they have asked for a decade or more, what are the limits to this growth? There might have been an answer to that question two decades ago when our served markets were a fraction of what they are today. We were then a $25 billion Company serving about a third of our available market. As we enter the millennium we'll be a well over $100 billion Company serving a small fraction of our newly defined market opportunities. The size of our potential market is growing even faster than we are because our definition of the market we serve becomes bigger and broader every day.

Our global reach has expanded enormously. We are positioned at the center of every high-growth region on the globe.

Our services initiative has immensely expanded the market to be served. We service airlines rather than just engines, railroads rather than locomotives, hospitals rather than CT scanners. We sell solutions and answers rather than just products.

Our Six Sigma initiative is growing share and opening markets, even in its relative infancy, as customers see the solutions it brings to their lives and are drawn to a Company that knows how to help them win in their markets.

The next time we gather again, on this occasion in April of 2000, as GE begins operations in its third century, you can be certain that your Company will never have been newer, fresher, or more energized.

And you can be equally certain that this new GE will be looking forward with excitement to limitless opportunities of a number and size that would have been the stuff of dreams just a few years ago.

Thanks for your support—and for being with us today.

CHAPTER 19

The Jack Welch Letter to Share Owners, Employees, and Customers

The letter that Jack Welch wrote to share owners, employees, and customers on February 12, 1999 (Exhibit 19-1, printed here in its entirety) ranks as one of the most important documents of American business in this era. Awaited each year with great anticipation by financial analysts, the media, and hundreds of thousands of business people around the United States, and indeed the world, the letter constitutes Jack Welch's once-a-year effort to describe how he has been carrying General Electric forward. In his earlier letters, Welch devoted much space to the company's financial results over the previous year. But over the years, he began to focus more and more on the various business strategies he has employed, and dealt only fleetingly with the "numbers." This letter is an excellent example of Welch discussing strategy, and downplaying the financials.

One of the most anticipated business communiques of the year—the Jack Welch letter.

To Our Share Owners, Employees and Customers

1998 was another terrific year for your Company — another record year.

- Revenues rose to $100.5 billion, up 11%.

- Earnings increased 13% to $9.3 billion.

- Earnings per share grew 14% to $2.80.

- Operating margin rose to a record 16.7%, up a full point from the record 15.7% of 1997. Working capital turns rose sharply to 9.2, up from 1997's record of 7.4.

- This performance generated $10 billion in free cash flow, which, in combination with a "AAA" debt rating, allowed us to invest $21 billion for 108 acquisitions in support of two of our three Company-wide initiatives: Globalization and Services.

- Record cash flow allowed us to raise dividends by 17% and to further increase share owner value by repurchasing an additional $3.6 billion in GE stock.

- In 1998, GE was named *Fortune* magazine's "Most Admired Company in America" and "The World's Most Respected Company" by a worldwide business audience in the *Financial Times*.

Our share owners — including our active and retired employees, who now own more than $17 billion in GE stock in their savings plans — were rewarded for these actions and this performance — the total return on a share of GE stock was 41% in 1998. GE has averaged a 24% per-year total return to share owners for the past 18 years.

Exhibit 19-1. Letter to Our Share Owners, Employees, and Customers, February 12, 1999

This performance, year after year, is the product of a diverse and powerful portfolio of leading global businesses. This performance has been driven this decade by three big Company-wide growth initiatives: Globalization, Services and Six Sigma quality.

These initiatives, in turn, have been rapidly advanced by a General Electric culture that values the contributions of every individual, thrives on learning, thirsts for the better idea, and has the flexibility and speed to put the better idea into action every day.

We are a learning company, a company that studies its own successes and failures and those of others — a company that has the self-confidence and the resources to take big swings and pursue numerous opportunities based on winning ideas and insights, regardless of their source.

That appetite for learning, and the ability to act quickly on that learning, will provide GE with what we believe is an insurmountable and sustainable competitive advantage as we pursue our three big growth initiatives.

Globalization is the first of those initiatives.

Last year we wrote to you as the difficulties in Asia were causing global uncertainty and unease.

We, like everyone else, had not foreseen these difficulties, but we quickly viewed Asia as similar in many respects to the Europe of the early 1990s — in need of various structural remedies but rich in opportunity. In the case of Europe — and in the case of Mexico in the mid- 90s — we moved decisively and were rewarded with significant and rapid growth. We have grown fourfold in Europe, from a relatively small GE presence in 1990 to $24 billion in revenues in 1998.

The GE of the next century must provide high-value global products and services, designed by global talent, for global markets.

We learned from our European successes and saw in Japan the opportunity to do it again — only faster.

We acquired the business infrastructure and sales force of Toho Mutual Life, and — because of the high respect the Japanese have for Thomas Edison — we renamed it GE Edison Life and quickly became a force in the Japanese insurance industry. We also acquired the consumer loan business of Japan's Lake Corporation, with $6.2 billion in assets, and added it to our already rapidly growing consumer finance business there. These acquisitions, along with several other ventures, partnerships and buyouts by our industrial businesses, together with the growth of our ongoing existing businesses in Japan, should allow us to more than double our over $300 million in 1998 Japanese earnings within three years.

Our Japanese initiatives are part of an intense multiyear focus on globalization that produced $43 billion in revenues in 1998 and a growth rate for GE outside the United States that has been double our U.S. growth rate for 10 years.

Growth Through Globalization

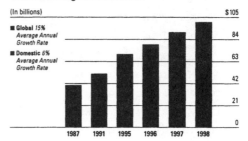

But market success is only part of globalization. We must globalize every activity in the Company. We've made some progress in sourcing products and components so critical to survive and win in a price-competitive deflationary world, but our challenge is to go beyond that — to capitalize on the vast intellectual capital available around the globe. In 1999, we will move aggressively to broaden our definition of globalization by increasing the intensity of our effort to search out and attract the unlimited pool of talent that is available in the countries in which we do business — from software designers in India to product engineers in Mexico, Eastern Europe and China.

The GE of the next century must provide high-value global products and services, designed by global talent, for global markets.

Product services is a second continuing growth initiative. This initiative has already changed the headset of the Company from that of a provider of products augmented

Exhibit 19-1. *(Continued)*

by ancillary services to a Company that is overwhelmingly a source of customer-focused, high-value, information technology-based productivity solutions — as well as a provider of high-quality products.

With this initiative, as with globalization, we are broadening our definition of services — from the traditional activities of parts replacement, overhauling and reconditioning high-value machines like jet engines, turbines, medical equipment and locomotives, to a larger and bolder vision. We have the engineering, the R&D, the product knowledge, the resources and the management commitment to make the series of hundred-million-dollar investments that will allow us to truly change the performance of our installed base, and by doing so upgrade the competitiveness and profitability of our customers: utilities, hospitals, railroads, factories and airlines.

By adding higher and higher technology to the customers' installed base of machines, we will have the capability of returning them to operation not just "overhauled" but with better fuel burn rates in engines, higher efficiency in turbines, better resolutions in CT scanners, and the like.

The ability to go beyond "servicing" to, in essence, "reengineering the installed base" will dramatically improve our customers' competitive positions.

Growth Through Product Services

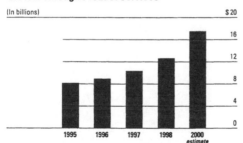

In product services, as with globalization, the new expanding view of both initiatives is driven by the insatiable learning culture inherent in the Company today, learning from each other, across businesses, across cultures, and from other companies.

Six Sigma quality, our third growth initiative, is, in itself, a product of learning. After observing the transforma-

tional effects this science, this way of life and work, had on the few companies that pursued it, we plunged into Six Sigma with a Company-consuming vengeance just over three years ago. We have invested more than a billion dollars in the effort, and the financial returns have now entered the exponential phase — more than three quarters of a billion dollars in savings beyond our investment in 1998, with a billion and a half in sight for 1999.

The Six Sigma-driven savings are impressive, but it is the radical change in the overall measures of operating efficiency that excite us most. For years — decades — we have been straining to improve operating margin and working capital turns. Our progress was typically measured in basis points for margins and decimal points in working capital turns. Six Sigma came along in 1995 when our margins were in the 13.6% range and turns at 5.8. At the end of 1998, margins hit 16.7% and turns hit 9.2. These numbers are an indicator of the progress and momentum in our Six Sigma journey.

The ratio of plant and equipment expenditures to depreciation is another measure of asset efficiency. This number in 1998 dropped to 1.2 and will be in the .7–.8 range in the future, as "hidden factory" after "hidden factory"— literally "free capacity" — is uncovered by Six Sigma process improvements.

All this has taken place in just over three years, after the quarter million of us hurled ourselves into this unknown way of life and work.

Six Sigma Progress

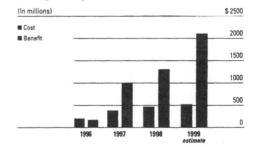

Year three of Six Sigma shows how far we have come in training ourselves — with 5,000 full-time "Master Black Belts" and "Black Belts" driving scores of thousands of quality

Exhibit 19-1.

projects around the globe, and with virtually every single professional in the Company a Green Belt," extensively trained and with a project completed.

As measured by internal performance improvements, and the enhancement of share owner value, Six Sigma has been an unqualified success.

The first major products designed for Six Sigma are just now coming into the marketplace and beginning to touch some of our customers. The new LightSpeed™ CT scanner and the new TrueTemp™ electric range, to name two, are drawing unprecedented customer accolades because they were, in essence, designed by the customer, using all of the critical-to-quality performance features (CTQs) the customer wanted in the product and then subjecting these CTQs to the rigorous statistical Design For Six Sigma process.

The LightSpeed scanner, the first multislice CT to reach the market, is a godsend to patients who, for example, now have to endure a chest scan for only 17 seconds compared with the 3 minutes it takes with a conventional CT. A patient with a pulmonary embolism, usually in breathing distress, must lie in a conventional scanner for nearly half a minute compared with 6 seconds for the LightSpeed. A trauma patient, for whom time-to-diagnosis is a literal life-or-death matter, can have a full-body scan in 26 seconds instead of the 3 minutes a single-slice CT scanner requires. Hospitals, for their part, now get a much higher utilization rate and hence lower per-scan costs. The reception of this product has been remarkable, with $60 million in orders in the first 90 days and with customer acceptance levels and endorsements never before seen.

Every new GE product and service in the future will be "DFSS" — Designed For Six Sigma. These new offerings will truly take us to a new definition of "World Class."

Yes, we've had some early product successes, and those customers who have been touched by them understand what this Six Sigma they've heard so much about really means. But, as we celebrate our progress and count our financial gain, we need to focus on the most powerful piece of learning we have been given in 1998, summarized perfectly in the form of what most of our customers must be thinking, which is: "When do I get the benefits of Six Sigma?" "When does my company get to experience the GE I read about in the GE Annual Report?"

Questions like these are being asked because, up to now, our Six Sigma process improvements have concentrated primarily on our own internal processes and on internal measurements such as "order-to-delivery" or "shop turnaround time."

And in focusing that way — inwardly on our processes — we have tended to use all our energy and Six Sigma science to "move the mean" to, for example, reduce order-to-delivery times from an average of, say, 17 days to 12 days, as reflected in the example below. We've repeated this type of improvement over and over again in thousands of GE processes and have been rewarded for it with less "rework" and greater cash flow. The problem is, as has been said, "the mean never happens," and the customer who looks at this chart, or charts like it, is still seeing variances in when the deliveries actually occur — a heroic 4-day delivery time on one order, with an awful 20-day delay on another, and no real consistency. The customers in this chart feel nothing. Their life hasn't changed; their profitability hasn't increased one bit. These customers hear the sounds of celebration coming from within GE walls and ask, "What's the big event; what did we miss?" The customer only feels the variance that we have not yet removed.

Example

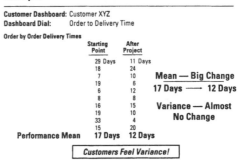

Customer Dashboard: Customer XYZ
Dashboard Dial: Order to Delivery Time

Order by Order Delivery Times

	Starting Point	After Project	
	29 Days	11 Days	
	18	24	
	7	10	**Mean — Big Change**
	19	6	**17 Days ⟶ 12 Days**
	6	12	
	8	8	**Variance — Almost**
	16	15	**No Change**
	19	10	
	33	4	
	15	20	
Performance Mean	**17 Days**	**12 Days**	

> **Customers Feel Variance!**

Our challenge, as we move toward 2000, is to turn our Company vision "outside in," to measure the parameters of the customers' needs and processes and work toward zero variability in serving them. ***Variation is evil in any customer-touching process.*** Improvement to our internal processes is of no interest to the customer.

Exhibit 19-1. *(Continued)*

In 1999, our customers will feel and enjoy the same benefits of Six Sigma that we have been experiencing internally. We will improve variability. We will make this happen. The impetus for this change will come not only from the business leaders but also from the first of the pioneering Six Sigma GE leaders who have now completed their "tours" and have been promoted into leadership positions in the businesses. They are now General Managers, Directors of Finance, Vice Presidents of Sales, Vice President of the Audit Staff, President of GE Mexico, and the like — big jobs.

This next generation of senior GE leadership, and the succeeding waves of Black Belts, share a camaraderie and an esprit forged by their Six Sigma training and the experiences of their tours. They are already predisposed toward hiring only those fluent in Six Sigma language and adept at its methodology. Within a few years, the work culture and the management style of General Electric will be indelibly, irreversibly, Six Sigma — and it will be focused on the customer's success.

These new leaders are changing the very DNA of GE culture. Work-Out, in the 80s, opened our culture up to ideas from everyone, everywhere, killed NIH (Not Invented Here) thinking, decimated the bureaucracy, and made boundaryless behavior a reflexive and natural part of our culture, thereby creating the learning culture that led to Six Sigma. Now, Six Sigma, in turn, is embedding quality thinking — process thinking — across every level and in every operation in our Company around the globe.

Work-Out in the 1980s defined how we behave. Today, Six Sigma is defining how we work.

The two initiatives — Services and Six Sigma — have one common theme: Only when tomorrow's product and service offerings from GE significantly reduce the plant and equipment expenditures of our customers and increase their productivity will we have fulfilled the GE Services and Six Sigma vision.

These, then, are the three initiatives — Globalization, Services and Six Sigma — fueling powerful growth in your Company and transforming its culture and its soul.

These initiatives are being driven across the businesses and across the globe by a unique brand of 21st century business leader — the GE "A" player, the leader who embodies what we call the four "E's": high *E*nergy; the ability to *E*nergize others; "*E*dge," the ability to make the tough calls; and finally *E*xecute, the consistent ability to turn vision into results.

These "A" players, driving these initiatives, have transformed the very nature of GE — what it does and how well and how quickly it does it.

With our three initiatives, these "A" players will broaden our globalization vision beyond markets and products to the pursuit of the best intellectual capital in the world.

"A" players will see the mission of product services as investing in technology to change our customers' productivity equation and enhance their competitiveness.

And finally, they will turn the face of Six Sigma outward toward the customer and make that customer's profitability the number one priority in any process improvement.

What does a Company with an incredible array of leading global businesses, a learning culture and a depth of "A" player leadership talent have to worry about as we approach the next century? What should keep it awake at night?

Not much, but history points a warning finger toward the arrogance and complacency that have caused others to stumble. It points to the sheer size that has slowed them and limited their agility to change quickly in this era of rapid change.

Already, as we approach the millennium, the pundits are hard at work. Predictions of trends and megatrends are in full production. Their record for accuracy has been spotty, at best. Most recently, less than two years ago, the conventional view of Asia was still one of "onward and upward" without interruption.

Exhibit 19-1. *(Continued)*

Looking back much further, to 20 years ago, when a new GE team moved into leadership, the prognostications were, in many cases, spectacularly inaccurate.

- In 1980, with oil at $35 a barrel, the big questions were when would it hit $100 or if it would be available at all.
- Japan in 1980 seemed to be in inexorable ascendancy, invading and dominating complacent industry after industry. Future American generations were doomed to menial work. The U.S. was losing confidence, experiencing "malaise."
- Twenty years ago, everything was predicated on the expectation of a never-ending double-digit inflationary environment.

Obviously, these trends did not play out — quite the reverse. Oil is at record lows, Japan is struggling, and the U.S. has moved from "malaise" to exuberance — irrational or not. Inflation has yielded to deflation as the shaping economic force.

So what does this tell us about the future? It tells us that what's as important as predicting trends is a company's ability to cope with any trend.

Sure, early in the next century, Japan will rebound. Oil prices are bound to rise again. Inflation is probably not dead. But spending a lot of time putting too fine a point on the "how" and "when" any of these might happen is less important than growing a culture that is both challenged by the unexpected and confident in, as well as capable of, dealing with whatever comes along.

That's why so much about leading a big company is about assuring that it stays agile, unencumbered by bureaucracy or lulled by complacency — keeping it a company that breathes information, loves change and is excited by the opportunity change presents. It means never allowing a company to take itself too seriously, and reminding it constantly, in the face of any praise or good press, that yesterday's press clippings often wrap today's fish.

Crossing the $100 billion mark in revenue, as we did in 1998, was a milestone, just as the $10 billion mark in earnings will be, but that's all they are — good for a quick pat on the back.

Yes, GE has become a very big company, and with the growth initiatives we have under way, we have every intention of becoming a lot bigger.

But bigger is only better if a company understands and is committed to using the unique advantages of size.

As a big, global, multibusiness company, we have access to an enormous amount of information — and with our learning culture, we have the ability to acquire, share and act rapidly on that information to turn it into marketplace advantage.

Size gives us another big advantage: our reach and resources enable us to go to bat more frequently, to take more swings, to experiment more, and, unlike a small company, we can miss on occasion and get to swing again.

What size cannot be allowed to do to a big company is to let it fall to the temptation of "managing" its size rather than "using" it. We can never stop swinging! At the same time, we must always be striving to capture the best of a small company — its energy, excitement and speed.

We move into 1999 filled with high expectations and with the confidence that we have the right initiatives, the right culture and the right leadership teams — teams with the agility and speed to seize the big opportunities we know this changing world will present us.

Thanks for your continuing support.

John F. Welch, Jr.
Chairman of the Board and
Chief Executive Officer

Eugene F. Murphy
Vice Chairman of the Board
and Executive Officer

February 12, 1999

Dennis D. Dammerman
Vice Chairman of the Board
and Executive Officer

John D. Opie
Vice Chairman of the Board
and Executive Officer

Exhibit 19-1. *(Continued)*

CHAPTER 20

From the Files of Jack Welch

This section features the thoughts and insights of Jack Welch on everything from leadership to quality to the impact of the Internet on business. His words are taken from a large variety of sources, many of which have never been published. For a complete listing of sources, see the notes at the end of the book.

Jack Welch took a bold step in the late 1980s when he began the process of empowering his employees. Here he talks about the need to involve employees in company decision making:

Involving everyone [has been a key Welch strategy]. I went back and looked at the annual reports that I've written over the last 18 years. I talked about individual ownership in the first, in 1981, that we had to give people the feeling that they could make decisions, that they were controlling their own destiny, that they were the people who had to be involved. You can't wait for instructions. The command-and-control structures that were built after the war that practically sunk American business in the 1970s and 1980s had to be decimated. We had enormous layers. We had bureaucrats checking on bureaucrats, people evaluating reports by the cover—literally, you'd get grades for the cover. We had fifty-five planners sitting there planning. . . . all that stuff was part of a shedding that had to be shed because the world was getting closer, information was more available, foreign competition was everywhere and you don't have time for that stuff.

Jack Welch had been no big fan of quality programs. He thought they accomplished little. Here he talks about the old quality programs he dismissed as useless, and the new one, Six Sigma, which he came to love:

I thought they were a bunch of slogans, a bunch of nonsense, a bunch of consultants running around trying to sell hats to one another on quality. . . . Now only one person hated quality programs more than I did and that was Larry [Bossidy]. And he called me one day and he said, "Jack, I've got to eat crow." He said, "I've been to Motorola. It's fabulous what this quality program is." He said, "You've got to look at it." . . . Larry was the biggest skeptic in the world, so for him to say, "I apologize, it works," made it very easy. And we bought into the program. . . . Quality is like every other initiative in GE. You've got to go after it like a lunatic. You can't say, "Look, let's get everybody together here. We have them here tonight. Quality's a very good thing. I think it's good for your families. I think it'd be good for our company. And let's drive it." You have to say only the A players are the quality leaders. The best, the very best that you've got in the company. Only the quality leaders get options this year. Everyone in the company must be Green Belt–trained, including myself, within two years. And we put an auditor on every program so that every quality program isn't quality for quality's sake; it's quality for net income sake and quality's sake. So all these things have to be done with a crazed passion.

Welch became a champion of the Six Sigma quality program. He insisted that it become GE's number one priority in the mid- and late 1990s:

Simply put, quality must be the central activity of every person in this room. You can't be balanced about this subject. You've got to be lunatics about this subject. You've got to be passionate lunatics about the quality issue. You've got to be out on the fringe of demand and pressure and push to make this happen. This has to be central to everything you do every day. Your meetings. Your speeches. Your reviews. Your promotions. Your hiring. Every one of you here is a quality champion or you shouldn't be here. It's no different than boundaryless behavior. People who weren't boundaryless shouldn't have been here in the 1980s. Shouldn't be here in the 1990s. If you're not driving quality you should take your skills elsewhere. Because quality is what this company is all about. Six Sigma must become the common language of this company. Only your best can be Black Belts. Black Belts must be in the middle of things. They can't be an upgraded quality organization. They've got to be central to the heart of the business. Measure the hell out of it. . . . This is all about better business and better operating results. In 1997, I want you to promote your best people. Show the world that people that make the big quality leadership contribution are the leaders we want across the business. In the next century we expect the leadership of this company to have been Black Belt–trained people. They will just naturally only hire Black Belt–trained people. They will be the leaders who will insist only on seeing people like that in the company. . . . So in quality the warm-up is over. The intensity level has to come up tenfold from where it is today. It's your central activity. It's the company's future. So 2000 will be tough as hell. But we're all going at it with an intensity never seen in business history.

It was only when he paid a visit to a GE business in England in late spring of 1997 that Jack Welch truly understood the power of his own quality initiative. It took a man named David Curren, then the European director of GE Capital's mortgage business, to make Welch sit up and take notice of just how ingrained the quality effort was becoming at GE. Welch was highly impressed, first of all, that Curren had made the effort to become a trained Black Belt in quality. This appeared to be solid evidence that upper management was heeding Welch's insistent call to take the Six Sigma program seriously. Second, Curren had actually invited some customers to participate in the meeting with the GE chairman, a strong indication that GE managers had grasped a key point about the quality initiative—that it was aimed at customers primarily. This, thought Jack Welch, is truly the wave of GE's future:

> Everything's got to be lined up to go consistent with what you believe. And for us, quality meant everything. So if you're going to pick any initiative, all your compensation plans have to be aligned with it, all of your promotional opportunities—you have to promote people out of quality to show that's the place to be. Because you're breaking years of tradition where people put somebody

that couldn't do any work, put him over there looking at quality. So now you've got to break all those paradigms that are out there. So you've got to change the game so that the highest-potential young vice president becomes the quality leader. Then they will say, "Jesus, they really mean it. They're serious about it." So every one of these initiatives takes enormous overreaction. If you're going to move the needle from here to here, you've got to be over here or the needle's just not going to go. The needle doesn't go with a nice, moderate presentation in large organizations. . . . You know, "quality's good" isn't going to make it.

The learning organization that Welch pursued at GE was based on the notion that it was legitimate to hunt down good ideas inside or outside the company, and then implement those ideas as fast as possible. Here are two citations from Welch extolling the learning culture:

When you sit here, and look at how we've got 150 laboratories of business in this company, and people are going from place to place to place as natural acts to grab ideas and move them, we really have found a better way to behave. We're not the chimney-oriented place we used to be. From Capital, to Appliances, to business after business, we move around and get these things done. It is a remarkable, remarkable collection of people who have the self-confidence truly to go across businesses to pick up better ideas, and you ought to feel very, very good about yourselves.

The Badge of Courage

People today look for an idea anywhere. It is a badge of courage if I learn from Larry Bossidy, the CEO at Allied Signal, or Motorola, or somewhere else. It used to be a badge of weakness. Rank isn't important. Title isn't important. It's the idea that wins. And that's a big deal. Everything we've done is leading up to a learning organization. The fact that we are a learning organization, that we accept it as our value. What's the value of having all these businesses? We're a library of ideas. And I'm the facilitator. It's a whole different way of thinking. Let me learn. I don't use the word synergy because it's a trite little word. If everybody in our place gets up every day trying to find a better way, it'll all take care of itself.

In March 1999, he talked fervently about what it was like to work in a learning culture. He enjoyed the fact that he was challenging the old ways, that he was deflating the not-invented-here attitude that had prevailed at GE and other American firms:

> I know if I pan this room tonight and talk to everyone here, I'd learn a zillion things about how to do my job better. And I come to work every day knowing that Hewlett-Packard's doing something smarter than I'm doing, that Sam Walton was doing something smarter and I'd go down and spend days with Sam Walton to understand what he was doing. Mano Kapurason, American Standard over here, is an LBO—he knows how to generate cash better than anybody alive because he can't survive without it, so we send teams down there to learn about inventory turns and other things. So finding a better way every day is in the culture. It's a badge of honor to say you found something from somebody and then spread it. Motorola taught us Six Sigma. We're proud of that. We made it better we think but we learned from them.

The kind of leaders found at GE was of primary importance to Welch. At the January 1997 operating managers meeting, attended by the company's 500 top managers, he offered a heartfelt plea, urging the executives to keep the A's, those who are team players, who subscribe to the company's values. He made an equally compelling plea to get rid of the C's, those managers who have no business hanging around GE because they don't buy into the company's value system. As for the B's, he wanted to make sure they remained productive and continued to grow:

> Too many of you work too hard to make C's into B's. It is a wheel-spinning exercise. Push C's on to B companies or C companies and they will do just fine. At session C this year we're going to be reviewing not only the A's, but the out-placement activity on the C players. We're an A-plus company. We want only A players. We can get anyone we want. Shame on any of you who aren't facing into your less-than-the-best. Take care of your best. Reward them, promote them, pay them well, give them a lot of options. And don't spend all of that time trying to do work plans to get C's to be B's. Move them out early, it's a contribution.

Later that year—in September 1997—during his appearance at Crotonville, Welch talked lengthily about what kinds of features A, B, and C managers should have. He asked junior executives from GE, seated in the audience, to suggest what defines an A. The answers came one by one.

Trust.

Impact on decisions.

Leaders who seek to develop high value in other leaders below them.

Welch wrote each feature on a white board, a sign that he agreed with the suggestions.

What defined C's? More suggestions from the audience.

They don't know they are C's.

They're afraid of A's.

They're blah. Neutral.

What counsel does Welch give to junior executives to help them become future great leaders?

> The biggest advice I give people is you cannot do these jobs alone. You've got to be very comfortable with the brightest human beings alive on your team. And if you do that, you get the world by the tail. . . .
>
> It's too bad that we can't define people in business as easily as you can on a basketball court or a hockey rink. If the guy couldn't skate, you wouldn't have him at left wing. If the guy couldn't shoot, he wouldn't be the forward. Or he wouldn't be on the team. And it's no different in the business team you have to build. . . . Always get the best people. If you haven't got one who's good, you're short-changing yourself.

But isn't it hard to tell a young person who wants to make a name for him or herself that the main thing is to become a team player?

Very hard, Welch acknowledges:

> A lot of them don't get it. That's why I always talk self-confidence because you've got to have the self-confidence to hire brilliant people, many times smarter than you are sometimes. You've got to feel very comfortable with that situation.

In the spring of 1999, Welch modified the way he talked about the kind of managers he wanted at GE. The message remained the same. He wanted only the best people to remain; the rest he wanted to let go. Now, Welch relied on an organization vitality chart, a tool used to rank executive-level employees by differentiating their abilities and potential into five categories: top 10 percent, next 15, middle 50, caution 15, and bottom 10, least effective. A normally distributed population would chart a traditional bell-shaped curve. One purpose of the organization vitality chart during 1999 was to make sure that the best GE executives were being rewarded properly; and to make sure as well that rewards were not being handed out to the weaker players:

The organization vitality chart. It is used to make sure that GE is nurturing the right people in its organization.

> Last year we started out with 25 percent top, 50 middle, 15 percent in the caution, 10 percent lower. We did quite well, but didn't do quite as well as we'd like. Eight percent of our people in the bottom 10 got options [which we saw] when we went back and looked at the grids afterward. Twenty-three percent of the people in the caution area got options. No more, no more. You will live by 10, 15, 50, 15, 10—and that bottom 25 ain't getting an option. It ain't going to happen in GE anymore. Your job is going to be, and I'll pound this over your head, take care of those A's until you can't stand it. Those A's have got to be kissed, hugged, loved. It's going to be an absolute sin to lose one, none of you can do that; and you are going to stop drizzling little bits out to C's.
>
> In 1998, we made real progress on our top 25, our mid 50, our caution 15, and our bottom 10 people identification. In 1999, we are cutting it finer: top 10, next 15, mid 50, caution 15, and the bottom 10. Be sure that top 10 percent in every business is being rewarded, nurtured. Make it a real sin to lose any one in this category. There is no excuse. We are growing, our compensation plans are flexible. You must not lose an A player. The game is all about A players. Make every encounter you have, every meeting you have here and everywhere else, a session C. Talk about your best every time, stretch them, excite them, reward them. They are your future and they are the key to our employees' well-being.
>
> On the other side, C players on any team, at any level, should be an embarrassment. No one in this room can be an A if you are carrying a C. And as you move the obvious C's and the bar for a 38 P/E company is raised, some of your B's will become your new C's. You must relentlessly repeat the process. A 38 P/E company can only afford world-class athletes. As I said before, this is not about Wall Street. It's about GE people, their families, their

dreams—and they are counting on you. So, let's commit ourselves again to avoid these two things that can worry us. Complacency—recognize that yesterday's press clippings wrap today's fish. Tomorrow is all that counts. It's all that counts. And to provide our employee owners with the assurance they expect and deserve we must execute, and execute better than ever before. And to do that you must have the guts, the guts to remove those who are not the very best, and have the courage to hire the best—better than you—and to take big risks on high-potential people all around the globe. We have more career growth and more opportunity in more places in the world than anyone else. Take advantage of it. Treasure those A's.

The kind of manager Jack Welch admires bears little resemblance to the type found so frequently in American business. The kind who feel they've been rewarded with the title of manager in order to do just that—manage. The kind who feel they've got to stick out in the crowd—and not merge their identity in "the team." Welch is indeed a revolutionary in defining a new type of manager for the twenty-first century. He wants managers who can swallow their egos, blur their identities, and work for the good of the company. He wants managers who can energize others, and allow them to be free to think and work creatively. Above all else, he wants managers who are going to manage less and who are going to wake up every morning looking at their work with a fresh eye.

When a *Fortune* magazine interviewer asked how it was that he was still bursting with energy even after being General Electric's boss for 17 years, he replied:

> There are a thousand things, I think. I have the greatest job in the world. We go from broadcasting, engines, plastics, the power system—anything you want, we've got a game going. So from an intellectual standpoint, you're learning every day.
>
> We get a great kick out of the fact that we have made this company think outside itself. We want people who get up every morning with a passion about finding a better way: finding from their associate in the office, finding from another company. We're constantly on the search. We brag about learning from Motorola, HP, Allied. Wal-Mart—we learned quick market intelligence from them. Toyota—asset management.

> So we've designed a culture that gets people to look outside the company, and we've designed a reward system that's aligned with that.

Jack Welch speaks frequently about the need to create a boundaryless organization, an enterprise that has no impediments, that allows each and every employee to do his or her job without interference, without obstacles. Sometimes, the GE chairman practices a little boundaryless behavior himself.

He was determined to make his meetings boundaryless. But what could he do about those people who, upon hearing that they were scheduled to make a presentation before the new GE chairman, would prepare page after page of possible answers that Welch might put to them? He knew what he could do. He ordered a stop to the practice. Executives would no longer prepare long answers for potential questions. Grudgingly accepting the decree of the chairman, the executives were still too nervous to comply fully. So they kept a person in reserve outside the meeting site, someone who would be able to get an answer speedily. Welch found out about the person waiting outside the meeting. He put a halt to that practice as well. The chairman was pleased. He had erased a few boundaries, and he was sure it was for the better. Soon after all the boundaries were removed, Welch was at a meeting when one of his executives simply could not answer a question the chairman had thrown at him. That's OK, said Welch, just make sure you find out the answer and let me know what it is.

All through the 1990s Jack Welch has strengthened the service side of the GE business. In an interview with the author, Welch was asked if he was prepared to abandon certain product lines. No, he replied emphatically because that would cause his service business to wither:

> We offer them complete solutions, not so much in order to increase our equipment sales but because they have a need for them. That said, we will always be a company that sells high-tech products. Without products, you're dead. You go out of business and become obsolete. If I fail to introduce a new medical scanner, how many hospitals are likely to come and see me for new services? Take aeronautics. I don't know how far my

guys would go, but one day they could end up maintaining a whole plane. But if that's what the customer wants, they'll find a way to do it. The market is bigger than we ever dreamt. However, one thing remains absolutely certain: we will continue to expand and to manufacture aircraft engines.

The importance of globalization to GE.

During the late 1980s and 1990s GE has increased its global position enormously. Globalization has been one of Jack Welch's major strategic initiatives. Here he talks about the payoff to GE:

Globalization has been a common theme here for more that a decade and the payoff has been clear: a growth rate three times the U.S. rate. I have two points to make on this subject: First, doing business in developing Asia is somewhere between 100 and 1,000 times harder than it is doing business in the United States for this company. Yes, you're putting more and better people into the game. But it's a fraction of what you need. We had a presentation by the BMC class at Crotonville and Jim Smith, who's a region manager for Lighting, had been out in the Los Angeles region and he went on a sales call in the BMC class somewhere in Thailand or Indonesia with a salesperson. He couldn't believe the tools they had. Jim's whole experience had been in the United States—going with planagrams, monthly programs, weekly . . . all laid out and planned centrally. He walked in with a briefcase empty to a call in Indonesia or Thailand. No tools. No kit. No backup. No plan. He couldn't believe after his many years in Lighting, watching it done right, compared to the limited tools those poor souls have out there. So everything you have done, you're not even close to the training and staffing that has to go on. Go back and look again because we're going to be looking at just exactly what that is. We're going to be looking at the staffing outside the United States versus the United States, and the historic growth rates between the regions. Think of the details. Jim Smith's point comes to life better than anything: A regional manager in Lighting, calling on Lighting customers in the United States for 20 years, with all of the backup and the plans and the detailing, to deal with the customer. And going in and making a call and knocking on the door with *nothing* in Asia. If we could bring *half* of the planning and the infrastructure that we have here, we could change the ball game.

The next challenge in globalization, Jack Welch suggested in January 1999, was getting more and more local nationals in place in GE's overseas businesses:

> This next phase of globalization. Getting markets was easy. Sourcing intellectual capital. Doing more products outside the United States. More R&D outside the United States and then personnel. Reducing FSE [foreign service employees] . . .
>
> We want more local national promotions. If we're going to be a global company we don't want to just send your next-door neighbor and the person down the hall. We want local nationals who can do the job. We've been out there for years. Now we've got talent. Let's give them a chance. Let's give them the same chance we give people here.
>
> We'll get a two-pronged hit. We'll get a global face on the company. We'll get global culture and we'll also get enormous cost saving.

In this passage Welch talks about the frustration of mounting a globalization drive in a deflationary period. Welch is determined to conquer the ill effects of deflation, and he sees globalization as part of the cure:

> On globalization, we've had six [GE] CEOs make the case as to how they are going to deal with this deflationary world by using low-cost global reach for direct and indirect buys; plus, as Jeff [Immelt, president and CEO of Medical Systems] and Lloyd [Trotter, president and CEO of Industrial Systems] described, low-cost intellectual capital to drive new products. Why have CEOs get up and talk about this? Because it's obviously the toughest thing I've ever seen us try to tackle in the 18 years I've been on this job. I've never seen us put so much energy into something and get as little yield out of it as we have on this. It's the toughest one we've ever had. I've never seen people fight any harder than they did this year to make it happen, but it's the only survival that we can possibly have in a deflationary world. There is no other way to fight deflation than this way. Global brains in the past have referred primarily to markets and marketing. In GE in the next century it will mean global products designed by global engineers serving a global world. We have to think globally in every aspect of the business, not in just markets, and not in just products, but in the entire thing.

Finally, Jack Welch looked at GE and the world in a question-and-answer session at the 92nd Street Y in March 1999.

In the 1990s everyone said Europe was dead, so we went and spent $25 billion buying companies when Europe was dead and now Europe's fine. When the peso devalued in the mid-1990s, we went down and bought 18 companies in four months. Mexico's doing just fine because the United States can't let Mexico go down the drain. In the last six months we've spent $16 billion in Japan. Why did we go to Japan? People said, "Why are you going to Japan?" Japan has a highly educated workforce, like Europe did. It has a smart crowd. It has money. And it has regulation. Let me tell you, the only time you like regulation is when you go to a country that doesn't have it. And try China and Russia—there's two. That's when you love regulation and laws. . . ."

The Japanese Will Do Better

I can't predict Japan in three years. I'll tell you this though—over the next five to seven years and probably sooner, you will see a robust, strong Japanese economy. I would guarantee you that. . . . The Japanese have too much resilience, too much capital, too much brain power, too much capability, too much of a society working together to ever think they're down for the count so that will be back. . . . In Europe in the 1990s, Jurgen Shremp and others began to change Daimler Chrysler—Daimler at that time, now Daimler Chrysler—Europe has changed dramatically. Japan this week, just yesterday, Sony announced 10 percent layoffs, closing forty-four factories. Toshiba did it three months ago without much notoriety . . . you'll see Japan changing the exact same way. They will restructure. Their white-collar productivity is terrible. That'll all change. The facts are in a global world, smart countries see what the answer is. It's a more productive, open society that generates jobs and volume and other things for success and Japan is starting to see that. . . . The only thing I like about Russia is the intellect. I don't find the society to be one where you'd want to put capital in. . . . Maybe my successor will think Russia's a hot spot. But I go back to the rules of the game. If there are no rules, stay out of the place. I really think it's that simple.

Jack Welch accepted the point that a new push had to be given in January 1999 in the quality initiative—a push that aimed at making sure customers felt satisfied as a result of all the quality improvements being worked out in the Six Sigma program.

Changing the Game

The focus on the customer that we are launching today, which we launched in October really, will change General Electric forever. It will absolutely make this company totally different. "Outside in" is an enormous thought. "Outside in" is a big, big idea. We've been "inside out" for over a hundred years. Forcing everything around the "outside in" view will change the game . . . with the company focused on the customer, no one in this company can ever again at the end of a month, at the end of a quarter, at the end of a year do anything—whether it be with inventories or whatever—to make a financial number at the expense of customer satisfaction. That is something we cannot do. You want to put that down as a commandment. You talk about sins—that's the ultimate sin. . . .

Every business I've been associated with has generally operated on a "promises kept" basis. What is "promises kept"? It's the most massive internal negotiation between eleven GE people, all trying to make their own operating plans and budgets, getting together to agree upon something that they will finally commit to, that will safely save their butt, and eventually the product gets to the customer. We must drive that out. . . . All of us have got to look within our businesses to see whether or not the measurements we are using are, in fact, coming from the "outside in" or inside.

Denis Nayden made a huge point on Six Sigma. And we all laughed when he gave the quote from a customer who said, "I want to deal with the company I read about." And we all had a chuckle. I'm going to talk about this in the annual report because I am embarrassed by it. Because I've been blowing in the annual report about our Six Sigma progress. And as I said in the beginning, if you are a share owner, you'll love it. If you are a share owner/customer you'll like it, but not as much. If you are a customer and not a share owner, you say, "I want to deal with the company I read about." So, I want every one of you in this room to be committed to changing this, to be humiliated if that's the comment that is being made about your business. Or at least be irritated as hell by anybody who says, "I want to deal with the company I read about." That isn't funny. That is big-league stuff you want to be ashamed about. I am ashamed about it. I am ashamed that I write annual reports and talk about Six Sigma and customers aren't feeling it. That's why this whole day is all about getting people to feel it. You have got to want every customer you have to feel Six Sigma and want it and get it and understand it. And you've got to have every one of your employees caring about those customers; 1999 is the beginning of the journey to make that statement never ever true again in this company.

THE CEO AS STRATEGIST

What size cannot be allowed to do to a big company is to let it fall to the temptation of "managing" its size rather than "using" it.

In these chapters we examine a series of Jack Welch's strategic initiatives, covering the early ones in the 1980s in Chapter 21 among which are downsizing, delayering, and the number one, number two approach; and then we move on in Chapter 22 to the later ones, such as services, globalization, and the Internet.

In this module, you will learn:

- What Jack Welch meant by "number one, number two"

- Why the GE chairman felt so strongly about "getting rid of the layers"

- How globalization and services have become two crucial strategies at GE for the 1990s

CHAPTER 21

Early Strategic Initiatives at GE: The 1980s

We found in the 1980s that becoming faster is tied to becoming simpler.

No other American CEO has launched as many strategic initiatives as Jack Welch. From the early days of his tenure as chairman and CEO of General Electric, Welch was bent on propelling the company through massive strategic change. Though GE appeared to be doing well in Welch's first year at the helm, 1981, he was immediately concerned that, without significant change, GE would falter.

The very fact that Welch was prepared to undertake *change* in the company had strategic implications. Change, in fact, became Welch's first strategic initiative. Ever a realist, Welch sensed that change was a critical ingredient of the business environment. He knew that undertaking change would not be easy. Change, he liked to say, has no constituency—no fans to root for it. Change was uncomfortable to most people. They were used to the status quo.

GE had to transform itself, Welch believed, because major changes had been occurring in the business environment during the 1970s and early 1980s. These changes—specifically the rise of high-tech industries and global competitors—could have caused big trouble for GE. Products enjoyed higher quality; workers were becoming more productive. To cope, Welch felt that the change he envisioned for GE would have to be revolutionary. In pursuit of his goal of making GE more competitive, Welch sensed that he would have to launch strategic initiatives on a scale never undertaken in an American corporation before. The very changes that he envisioned for GE had no name back then, but in time Welch's strategic initiatives would be called *restructuring*.

He first took on GE's vaunted electrical and electronic manufacturing businesses, which as late as 1970 still represented as much as 80 percent of GE's earnings. Though a major component of GE's businesses, these manufacturing enterprises contributed only one-third of GE's total 1981 earnings.

To make sure that GE had the right businesses, Welch launched a path-breaking strategy—from now on, GE businesses would have to be first or second in their market—and, if the company could not rehabilitate weakened businesses quickly, it would close or sell them. The strategy was aimed at delivering growth, and deliver growth it did.

Welch believed there was a definite competitive advantage to being the best—or the second best—in a market. More to the point, Welch wanted to establish the highest-possible standards in order to assure that mediocre players within GE would fall by the wayside.

Number One, Number Two

One of Jack Welch's earliest and most important business strategies—being number one or number two in the market.

The "number one, number two" strategy was meant to defeat the great enemy of the early 1980s, inflation, which was crippling American business growth. Inflation made it impossible, in Welch's view, for the mediocre supplier of products and services—the company that found itself in the middle of the pack—to survive.

Business leaders at GE were supposed to ask what they could do to make their business dominant in its market. Then they had to make tough decisions: Which businesses were worth nurturing, which were not? Welch's strategy did not sit well with GE's executives, who felt that there was no reason to discard a business simply because it was *only* number three or four in its market. But none of their complaints budged Jack Welch.

A Leaner GE

Along with the "one-two" strategy, Welch undertook a second bold strategic initiative as part of the reshaping of GE. He decided to reduce its size dramatically. Keeping so many GE employees—the number had mushroomed to 404,000 when he took over—was a flawed strategy and had cost the company huge amounts of money. GE's main competition was now coming from foreign enterprises whose employees had become efficient and productive. Only by rationalizing its businesses, and paring its payrolls—a two-pronged strategic initiative that was called *downsizing*—did GE have a chance of remaining a superior company.

The downsizing initiative was unique. No other American business leader thought it important to reduce the payroll of a company that was not confronting a crisis. In the past, downsizing had been the last resort of a firm that was on the verge of failure; getting rid of employees carried the shameful stigma of defeat. People had been hired for life, and the popular American ethic had been to treat the worker as sacred. But Welch was not moved by such arguments.

The effect of his downsizing initiative was to put thousands of GE workers out of work; by 1988, seven years after Welch took over, the company had reduced its workforce by 100,000 employees. Conscious of the pain he was causing people, Welch argued that not to downsize would have brought far more suffering to all of GE's employees. He felt he simply had no choice.

Welch was forced to take a good deal of grief from critics who labeled him Neutron Jack after the deadly weapon that destroyed people, while leaving buildings intact. But the criticism had no impact on Welch. It amuses him that today people get praised for laying off 10,000 employees. But just the thought of what he had to put the company through gives him little joy. Firing people, he acknowledges, was the worst part of the job for him.

The Layers Must Go

It was not good enough to invoke change, pare the payrolls, and strip away all but the top businesses. Jack Welch wanted to get rid of the management layers that he felt were keeping senior managers from functioning at their best. This strategic initiative that he called *delayering* was aimed at creating an informal, open organization. The excessive management layers at GE created unnecessary barriers to that informality and openness.

It was all too easy in an overly bureaucratic atmosphere to lose sight of what the company's fundamental purpose should be—to get lean and agile so that it could become competitive again. Too many controls limited managers, slowed down their decision making, and prevented them from keeping pace with the fast-changing business environment.

GE's managerial structure had grown so diffuse that one had the impression that almost everyone in the company had some kind of title. Some 25,000 people bore the title of manager; another 500 were senior managers; and another 130 were vice presidents or higher. The main job of these managers was to check up on their subordinate managers. Memos went back and forth which, to Welch, seemed only to slow down the decision-making process. Managers were too busy reading those memos to spot trouble when it first occurred. For all the strategic planning and control that went on, the fundamental effect was to rob GE of the entrepreneurial spirit that Welch wanted to foster. During the 1980s GE's business leaders were forced to report to senior vice presidents; those senior vice presidents in turn reported to executive vice presidents; all of these vice presidents, senior and executive alike, had their own staffs. Welch decreed that the business leaders would report directly to the CEO's office—Welch and his two vice chairmen.

By abolishing many of the managerial layers that existed between his business leaders and himself, the corporate CEO, Welch could talk directly to his business leaders without management layers getting in the way. The number of management levels dropped from nine to eleven to between four and six.

Once those managerial layers were considered valuable. Having a management layer supervise the one just below it was considered the right way to run a business. No wonder, then, that critics assailed delayering for reducing GE's needed command-and-control system, but Welch countered that all he was doing was getting rid of the control portion of the system; he wanted to retain the command portion.

In delayering GE's management, Welch decided to transfer the strategic planning function away from senior managers and give it over to his business leaders; the whole idea was to become lean and agile.

Going for the Quantum Leap

Welch's other major strategic initiative in his early years was the concept known as the *quantum leap*. Essentially, what he meant was a swift, surprising business decision that improved the company's financials dramatically and in one single bound. The classic example of a "quantum leap" at GE was the purchase of NBC.

Going for the quantum leap.

Back in the early 1980s, Welch was not averse to buying a large company if the fit and price were right—to making a quantum leap, in his own phrase. He liked RCA, the Radio Corporation of America, one of America's most famous corporate names.

But up to that time, the idea that a General Electric would even think of buying an NBC, or one of the two other major television networks, was ridiculous. These television monoliths had owners who could not fathom parting with these highly profitable, very visible properties.

But Welch was not overwhelmed by such thinking and in December 1985 he went ahead and purchased RCA. The purchase was the largest countercultural step Welch's GE had ever taken. Yet he felt that buying the communications giant made great sense. GE paid $6.28 billion (or $66.50 a share) for RCA. Together, GE and RCA formed a new corporate entity that by the very act of merging had collective sales of $40 billion, putting it in seventh place on the *Fortune* 500. The merger enhanced GE's drive into the service and technology fields, and at the same time lessened its dependence on manufacturing businesses.

That purchase had seemed strange to many. But it was not strange to Jack Welch. His conquest of RCA, and with it the purchase of the NBC television network, was for him a bold ploy, a surprise move, an adventurous move that he liked to call a "quantum leap."

To Welch the RCA purchase had great logic. After all, he was searching for new cash flow to overcome his faltering manufacturing businesses. Many were surprised by the GE purchase, recalling that General Electric, throughout most of its history, had grown from within. GE policy had been against growing by acquisition. Yet Welch felt no obligation to cling to old ways; he cared largely about earnings, so he had no trouble taking on all those sacred traditions.

CHAPTER 22

Late Strategic Initiatives: The 1990s

Services . . . fueling powerful growth in your company and transforming its culture and its soul.

Turning to Service

In the last decades of the twentieth century the manufacturing economy has been transformed into a service-oriented economy. In 1980, the year before Jack Welch took over as chairman and CEO of GE, the company was almost entirely a manufacturing enterprise: 85 percent of its revenues came from manufacturing, and only 15 percent from services. GE had always been involved in some service work, but it was little more of an afterthought. Indeed it was known as an "aftermarket." For decades GE's growth was linked inextricably to the company's manufacturing side. The shift away from manufacturing and toward services began in the 1980s and gained huge momentum in the 1990s. At first it was seen as a way of giving GE some extra business. But in time GE executives understood that the focus on services had the effect of enlarging the potential markets of GE businesses by many times.

The GE Refresher Course

To Jack Welch and other GE executives, it was not so much that the company was doing less manufacturing; it was rather that the service sector potentially had a far higher rate of growth. One reason for this: There were just so many steam turbines and aircraft engines that could be sold in the world. Moreover, GE gets a great dividend from the service initiative since margins are typically 50 percent higher on services compared with the sale of its manufactured products.

Service has become a new GE growth engine.

Exhibit 22-1 demonstrates GE's remarkable shift from a manufacturing company to a service company. In 1980, only 15 percent of the company's revenues came from services; but in the year 2000 it is projected that 75 percent of GE's expected $120 to $125 billion revenues will derive from services.

GE in 1990 derived only 45 percent of its revenues from its service businesses. We used the word "only" though this 45 percent figure constituted a 300 percent increase as a percentage of its total business over the previous decade.

Five years later, in 1995, GE's manufacturing business had gone from 55 percent to 45 percent and financial services had

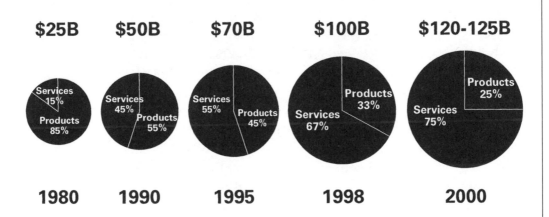

Transformation to a Service Company

$25B — 1980: Services 15%, Products 85%

$50B — 1990: Services 45%, Products 55%

$70B — 1995: Services 55%, Products 45%

$100B — 1998: Services 67%, Products 33%

$120-125B — 2000: Services 75%, Products 25%

Dramatic Transformation from Product Oriented Company to Higher Margin, Higher Growth, Services Oriented Company

Exhibit 22-1.

streaked from 25 to 38 percent. The aftermarket service aspect held steady at 12.3 percent, as did broadcasting at 6 percent.

In 1998, GE continued to expand its service component:

1. Aircraft Engines created joint ventures with Eva Airways in Taiwan, Varig Airlines, and AAR Corporation and won a total of $2.4 billion in multiyear service contracts.

2. Power Systems completed the acquisition of Stewart & Stevenson's turbine packaging business and won $2.4 billion in multiyear service contracts.

3. Medical Systems completed sixteen global acquisitions and alliances, which further expanded the size of its services business.

4. Transportation Systems was awarded multiyear railroad service contracts totaling $1 billion.

By the year 2000 manufacturing is expected to make up a smaller part of the GE business mix—the guess is only 33.2 percent of the entire GE mix—while financial services could rise as high as 45.8 percent, with aftermarket service as high as 16 percent; broadcasting is likely to hover around 5 percent.

Jack Welch pushed a business strategy to turn GE into a service-oriented company, knowing that GE's manufacturing businesses were experiencing slow rates of growth. As manufacturing did less and less well, GE's revenues grew on average only 5.4 percent a year from 1990 to 1995. By that latter year, when the service initiative was gaining fresh impetus, revenues increased a highly respectable 11 percent; earnings rose 11 percent to $6.6 billion. The following year was equally impressive: In 1996, revenues grew 13 percent to a record $79.2 billion and earnings were up 11 percent to a record $7.28 billion. The most important engine of service growth—indeed the key engine of growth for all of GE—has been GE Capital Services.

Helping GE enormously in the service field was the fact that it had what might be deemed a hidden asset: its installed base of equipment, which included 9,000 GE commercial jet engines, 10,000 turbines, 13,000 locomotives, and 84,000 major pieces of medical diagnostic equipment. By October 1996 GE was bringing in $7.8 billion—fully 11 percent of its total revenues—from servicing that installed base of industrial equipment. At the end of 1998, its product service revenue exceeded $12 billion a year.

No GE business better illustrates the shift to services than does Aircraft Engines. GEAE decided to enter the service business in the early 1990s on the heels of large government cutbacks in defense spending as well as a recession. Pressure built on GEAE as some commercial airlines filed for bankruptcy. Those airlines that survived wanted more value from their already-purchased engines.

So, Aircraft Engines went into the service business, and that side of the aircraft engine business produced double-digit growth in 1996, with annual revenues above $2 billion.

GEAE concluded deals that included ten-year maintenance and overhaul awards from British Airways, US Air, and Atlas Air. The business also bought a major interest in Celma, a rapidly growing overhaul operation in Brazil and set up joint-venture accords with airlines and other leading engine maintenance providers.

In 1995, Aircraft Engines integrated the overhaul and component repair services and spare-parts businesses into GE Engine Services; this was part of Jack Welch's plan to give the service effort independent status within General Electric.

And, in a ten-year, $2.3 billion deal between GE and British Airways PLC in March 1996, GE agreed to perform 85 percent of the engine maintenance work on BA's fleet, which included engines made by rivals Rolls-Royce PLC and Pratt & Whitney.

By entering into these acquisitions and joint ventures, Bill Vareschi, president and CEO of GE Engine Services, has, since 1996, created a nearly $5 billion parts and service business with 14,000 employees, leveraging GEAE's installed fleet of 9,000 commercial engines.

The business got off the ground in 1995 when Welch urged senior executives to optimize their service potential. GE Engine Services was established in mid-1995 with 4,300 employees. Since then GE Aircraft Engines has become largely a service business, with 55 percent of its business in 1998 coming from the service sector.

In 1998, GEAE invested more than $43 million just in R&D for repair technology—a 360 percent increase from 1996. Traditionally, the engine development side got all the company R&D money. But in order to create a differential with its competitors, GEAE is pouring money into advanced repair technology. In addition, because it has this huge installed base of GE and CFM engines, it is also investing in upgrade kits to make its veteran engines far more cost-effective by keeping them in service longer.

General Electric's fresh emphasis on services is not entirely consistent with one of Welch's earlier business strategies—that all GE businesses must be either number one or number two in their markets. As GE executives explain, once a GE business leader tries to be number one or number two, the leader is likely to make a point of defining the market quite narrowly. But when the business provides services as well, its market can grow ten times as large—and market share will drop to one-tenth the previous size—because now GE is competing with other service-oriented firms.

How Globalized Is Your Business?

Exhibit 22-2 is a questionnaire designed to find out just how globalized your business is. You are asked to assess, among other things, to what extent your managers have a global outlook; whether you communicate well across borders; and whether you accept international assignments as promotions.

If you scored 4 or 5 in most categories, you can feel good about your globalization efforts. You are clearly moving in the right direction. But if you came up with scores of 1, 2, and 3 in a majority of cases, you have a lot more work to do in the globalization field.

Self-Assessment Exercise

Taking a Global View

In addition to services and Six Sigma quality, the other major initiative Welch has been promoting during the 1990s revolves around globalization.

In the early 1980s globalizing a business was largely an unknown concept to many American businesses. Most of those

Questionnaire #5

Stepping Up to the Line: How Far Along the Path to Globalization Is Your Organization?

Instructions: Assess your organization's efforts to remove global boundaries and operate across space, time, and nationality. Use the scale to indicate the extent to which each of the following statements characterizes your organization, circling a number from 1 (not true at all) to 5 (very true).

	Not true at all				Very true
1. Managers in our company have a global outlook.	1	2	3	4	5
2. Managers in our company speak more than one language.	1	2	3	4	5
3. We have managers responsible for global products, services, or customers.	1	2	3	4	5
4. We communicate well across borders.	1	2	3	4	5
5. We respect cultural differences in management styles.	1	2	3	4	5
6. Top management constantly stresses its desire to become a global competitor.	1	2	3	4	5
7. We routinely engage in cross-border task forces on projects.	1	2	3	4	5
8. Top management's calendars (daily schedules) reflect their commitment to globalization.	1	2	3	4	5
9. Training programs include significant exposure to global issues.	1	2	3	4	5
10. Leadership positions in our company include people from culturally diverse backgrounds.	1	2	3	4	5
11. Accepting international assignments is a stepping stone to future success.	1	2	3	4	5
12. Information about global competitors and customers is well known throughout the company.	1	2	3	4	5
13. Travel budgets enable us to take necessary international trips.	1	2	3	4	5
14. Our structure allows us to operate seamlessly across borders.	1	2	3	4	5
15. Our customers recognize our ability to operate across borders.	1	2	3	4	5
16. We operate across borders significantly better than our competitors.	1	2	3	4	5
17. We recruit in places where "globally minded" candidates can be easily found.	1	2	3	4	5
18. We have many examples of culturally diverse teams.	1	2	3	4	5
19. Our culturally diverse teams generally work together in a way that the whole is greater than the sum of the parts.	1	2	3	4	5
20. Other companies have, or could, benchmark our efforts to remove geographic boundaries.	1	2	3	4	5

Exhibit 22-2.

businesses had done well enough focusing on the American market; there seemed little reason to change. Operating on a global basis seemed difficult, complex, perplexing.

Not, however, to Jack Welch. He watched with growing concern as GE's most important competitors were not American. He understood that his company's only sensible response was to attempt to penetrate non-American markets as fast and as aggressively as possible.

As was the case with some of his other business strategies, Welch knew that it would have been unthinkable for GE to globalize in the early 1980s when it was going through its fix, close, or sell phase, when the entire company was going through a revolutionary restructuring. Before he could take General Electric overseas, Welch had to build and solidify a strong base at home. He was all too aware of that.

The big breakthrough occurred in the summer of 1987. It was then that Jack Welch's globalization revolution got started. It took the GE chairman only a half an hour to nail an agreement with Alain Gomez, chairman of Thomson S.A., the largest French electronics company.

The deal went like this:

GE turned over its television set business to Thomson S.A.

In turn, GE acquired a Thomson company called CGR, which specialized in medical imaging, pretty much dominating the French market.

When he took GE overseas, starting in the late 1980s, the face of the company began to change. Its global revenues grew from 20 percent of GE's total in 1985 to 38 percent just a decade later. In 1996, General Electric's globalization effort came to $33.3 billion, an 18 percent hike over the previous year. In 1997, the effort rose to $38.5 billion.

Despite the serious economic turmoil in Asia, General Electric's globalization effort in 1998 grew 10 percent over the year before, reaching $42.8 billion in revenues—representing 43 percent of total GE revenues. GE businesses increased their global reach that year by acquiring seventy businesses abroad.

The 1998 overseas revenues broke down by region this way:

1. Europe—$21.6 billion

2. Pacific Basin—$5.1 billion ($1.2 billion of that came from China; $4 billion from Japan)

3. Americas—$5 billion

4. Other—$1 billion

5. Exports from the United States to external customers—$8.7 billion

6. RCA residual licensing income—$250 million

In 1998, GE Capital Services announced an agreement to acquire Eagle Star Reinsurance Company Ltd. of the United Kingdom; the aim was to strengthen its Employers Reinsurance broker business. GE also completed the acquisition of the $4.4 billion consumer loan business of Lake Corporation in Japan. And the company agreed to acquire WTB Westdeutsche Kreditbank GmbH, an important German provider of equipment leasing products and services with some $670 million in financing assets.

Exhibit 22-3 indicates how GE's globalization program has gone from strength to strength. It was only $8.7 billion in 1987; but just 11 years later, in 1998, the global side of GE had grown to $42.8 billion. As the exhibit shows, GE's globalization drive has certainly been paying dividends.

With the lifting of the Iron Curtain in 1989, GE was in a position to improve its position in Europe, so in 1990, it acquired a majority interest in the Hungarian lighting company called Tungsram. Until 1990, GE's lighting business was almost completely American—it had only a 2 percent market share in Europe. Early in 1991, GE gained a majority of the THORN Light Source business in the United Kingdom as well. Thanks to those additions, GE owned the top lamp business in the world—its market share in western Europe now reached nearly 20 percent.

By the early 1990s, GE's global presence grew even larger as its operating profits abroad had been increasing 30 percent a year since 1987.

Europe was always a prime focus for GE's globalization initiative. Starting in the late 1980s, the company invested nearly

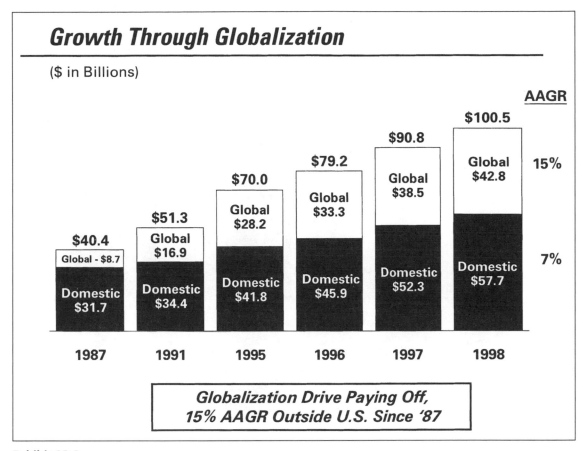

Growth Through Globalization

($ in Billions)

Exhibit 22-3.

$10 billion in Europe, half of which went into the financing of fifty or so acquisitions. Revenues in Europe had grown from $9.9 billion in 1994 to $21.6 billion in 1998 (nearly 25 percent of the total GE revenues for that year). Net income had risen during that same period from $500 million in 1994 to $1.8 billion in 1998. By the year 2000 Welch was hoping that GE would reap $30 billion a year in revenues and $2 to $2.5 billion in profits from Europe.

Exhibit 22-4 provides a graphical illustration of how GE turned poor-performing, fragmented assets (the ten businesses mentioned in the exhibit) into major players. Revenues in those ten European businesses rose from $6.4 billion in the first year

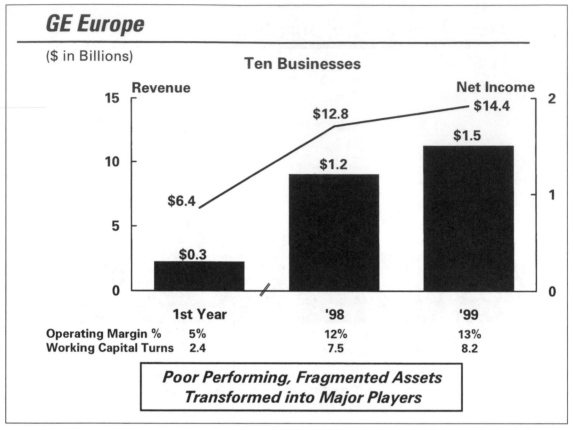

GE Europe

($ in Billions)

Ten Businesses

Revenue — $6.4 → $12.8 → $14.4 — Net Income

$0.3 ($0.3) | $1.2 | $1.5

	1st Year	'98	'99
Operating Margin %	5%	12%	13%
Working Capital Turns	2.4	7.5	8.2

**Poor Performing, Fragmented Assets
Transformed into Major Players**

Exhibit 22-4.

to $12.8 billion in 1998. Operating margins during that same time frame rose from 5 percent to 12 percent.

As the exhibit clearly suggests, GE has achieved a good deal in Europe, after much effort. Europe has been a key to the company's globalization objectives. As Exhibit 22-5 demonstrates, fully $24.3 billion of GE's total globalization revenues of $42.8 billion in 1998 came from Europe.

GE and Welch are proud of these achievements. It is quite an accomplishment, in GE's view, that European revenues have reached just under 25 percent of the company's total revenues.

In pursuit of GE's global strategy, Welch has made sure to promote a number of non-U.S. nationals to senior management

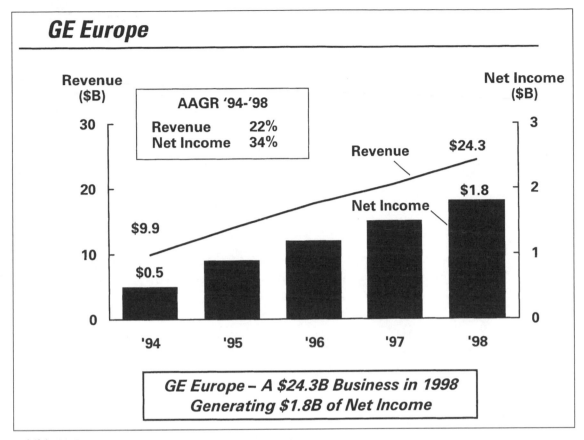

GE Europe

AAGR '94-'98

Revenue	22%
Net Income	34%

Revenue ($B)

Net Income ($B)

Revenue $24.3

$9.9

Net Income $1.8

$0.5

'94   '95   '96   '97   '98

**GE Europe – A $24.3B Business in 1998
Generating $1.8B of Net Income**

Exhibit 22-5.

positions. Today, half of GE's dozen divisions in Europe are held by locals.

In September 1997, Welch appointed Swedish-born Goran S. Malm as president of GE Asia Pacific and senior vice president of GE. He also appointed Japanese-born Yoshiaki Fujimori as president and CEO of GE Medical Systems Asia and vice president of GE Asia Pacific, succeeding Malm. That same week Welch selected Cuban-born Ricardo Artigas to be vice president of Global Parts and Services for GE Power Systems; and Spanish-born Joaquim Agut president and CEO of GE Power Controls, succeeding Artigas. In December 1998, he appointed Patrick Dupuis as CFO of GE Medical Systems; and in May 1999, Claudio

Santiago was made president of GE's Nuovo Pignone, the Italian electrical equipment (turbine and compressor) manufacturer.

In June 1999, Welch declared that the best way to globalize the company was to bring as many of its American expatriate employees home and give local nationals the chance to assume key leadership roles. He planned to expand that part of the globalization program over the next year.

Welch had been watching the global marketplace grow and grow during the 1990s. Back in 1992, he observed that the reality of the global marketplace as GE's true arena was underscored by a major shift of senior management and resources toward India, Southeast Asia, China, and Mexico. A year later he commented that GE's business strategy of emphasizing speed in all of its operations had allowed GE to shift the center of gravity of the company quickly toward the high-growth areas of the world, especially in Asia.

In 1994, Welch noted that GE's "globalization" revenues continued to outpace its domestic growth, totaling in Europe alone over $9 billion that year. Double-digit top-line growth was occurring for GE in the important emerging markets of Mexico, India, China, and Southeast Asia. GE was competing in many major world markets:

1. *Aircraft engines* GE is the world's largest producer of large and small jet engines for commercial and military aircraft, including the GE 90, the largest jet engine ever built, which powers the new Boeing 777 twin jet. In 1995, more than half the world's large commercial jet engine orders were awarded to GE and its joint venture, CFM International.

2. *Appliances* GE serves some of the world's fastest-growing markets, including India, China, Asia, Mexico, and South America.

3. *Capital services* Financial Services is expanding its operations globally, with special emphasis on Asia and Europe.

4. *Lighting* GE is a world leader in lighting products for consumer, commercial, and industrial markets, with a

complete line of incandescent, fluorescent, quartz, high-intensity, tungsten-halogen, and holiday lighting. Its global operations include joint ventures in China, Indonesia, India, and Japan and acquisitions in the UK, Germany, Italy, and Hungary.

5. *Medical systems*   Its global operations include sales, service, engineering, and manufacturing organizations in the Americas, Europe, and Asia.

6. *Media*   NBC International ventures include entertainment and news channels in Europe and Asia. It also includes NBC's highly rated coverage of the Atlanta Olympics.

7. *Power systems*   GE Power Systems serves customers in 119 countries.

GE Online

Finally, in the spring of 1999, GE was gearing itself for another corporatewide initiative, this one dealing with the Internet. When the new phenomenon of e-commerce gained widespread attention in the winter of 1998, GE, along with a host of other American companies, realized that it was time to figure out how to use the Internet—and fast. "If you're not ahead," says Gary Reiner, senior vice president and chief information officer, "you could get killed. You see somebody come ahead of you and before you realize it, they took away your game. It's a matter of controlling your destiny." Getting GE involved in the business side of the Internet became a major concern for Jack Welch in the first half of 1999. He genuinely believed that GE was in the midst of one more business revolution—this one brought about by the Internet. He predicted that the years ahead, as GE moved into Internet business activity, would be the most exciting in the company's history. The Internet, in short, provided one more chance to implement one of Welch's key business strategies: take advantage of change, or to put it a different way, see change as opportunity.

He instructed each of GE's ten businesses to select an e-commerce leader. The topic of e-commerce dominated the con-

GE and the Internet. Jack Welch hopes the Internet will be the next big business tool to drive the company's growth.

versation at the Corporate Executive Council meeting in June; the Internet came up frequently in Welch's conversations both inside and outside GE. Welch instructed Crotonville's staff to make sure that every class coming to the leadership institute in the next year focused intensively on some aspect of e-business.

One quick decision emerging from the June CEC meeting was for Welch to issue via the Internet an update each quarter on the CEC meeting since it was now possible—through the Internet— to spread the word about the company instantaneously. In that first "e-brief" issued on June 7, 1999, Welch noted: "We must have a 'break-the-glass' mentality to get on top of this fast-moving subject. You will see fanatical commitment from the business CEOs and from me on this subject."

CHAPTER 23

The Grand GE Tool Kit

What is it that makes GE work?

**What makes
GE work?**

There seem to be many reasons, not the least of which is the leadership of Jack Welch.

But what does Welch himself think are the reasons for GE's success? Interestingly, we have a quick and easy way to find out in a chart that summarizes his best thinking on the subject. In Exhibit 23-1 Welch offers in thumbnail form the various reasons why GE works as successfully as it does. Interestingly, he puts the Work-Out program first on the list.

GE also works, as this exhibit notes, because of its quest to become a true learning organization, because of its agility, and because of its size. Finally, there is leadership. Putting this last may be pure modesty on Jack Welch's part. Some might put it first on the list.

Exhibit 23-2 gives the content of GE's values. These are the values that have sustained GE during the late 1980s and throughout the 1990s and they represent the major business strategies and thinking of Jack Welch. The values set forth here appear on a laminated business card that GE employees are encouraged to carry in their wallets. Not everyone does of course. But even those who don't have a pretty good idea of what GE's values are.

To understand Jack Welch, one must take into account the importance that he attaches to company values and the right kind

What Makes GE Work

Everyone Counts

- Workout

Learning Organization

- Values
  - Boundaryless, Speed, Stretch
  - Four Types of Managers

- Initiatives
  - Globalization, Services, Six Sigma

Agility

Size

- "Use It" – Don't "Manage It"

Leadership

- 4 E's

Exhibit 23-1.

of corporate culture. He dwells on these things, and leaves the numbers to take care of themselves. If he can instill the right values in individuals, the company will prosper. That is his belief, and the Jack Welch era has proven him right. The numbers have indeed been spectacular. Exhibit 23-3 indicates just how spectacular.

Exhibit 23-3 charts the financial performance of the company from 1993 to 1998 and from 1980 to 1998. The charts appear in the 1999 GE proxy statement. The chart on the left compares the 5-year cumulative total return of GE, S&P 500, and the Dow Jones Industrial Average. The graph on the right compares the 18-year cumulative total return of GE, S&P 500, and the Dow Jones Industrial Average. Both charts show that GE got far better results than either the S&P 500 or the Dow Jones Industrial Average.

GE Values

GE Leaders ... Always with Unyielding Integrity:
- Have a Passion for Excellence and Hate Bureaucracy
- Are Open to Ideas from Anywhere ... and Committed to Work-Out
- Live Quality ... and Drive Cost and Speed for Competitive Advantage
- Have the Self-Confidence to Involve Everyone and Behave in a Boundaryless Fashion

- Create a Clear, Simple, Reality-Based Vision ... and Communicate It to All Constituencies
- Have Enormous Energy and the Ability to Energize Others
- Stretch ... Set Aggressive Goals ... Reward Progress ... Yet Understand Accountability and Commitment
- See Change as Opportunity ... Not Threat
- Have Global Brains ... and Build Diverse and Global Teams

Exhibit 23-2.

Jack Welch is most pleased about having created an organization that is lean and agile, one that can spring into action quickly despite its size. GE's functional simplicity and straightforwardness are immediately apparent in Exhibit 23-4, a one-page chart that gives an overview of GE's corporate and business structure. (Note that Information Services is shown as a separate business here, while in the 1998 annual report, it is not.)

The chart reflects how easy it is for GE to explain its corporate and business structure to the outside world today. It was not always so—not when it had 350 different business units. Welch is extremely proud of the user-friendly look of the GE Company, as reflected neatly in this chart.

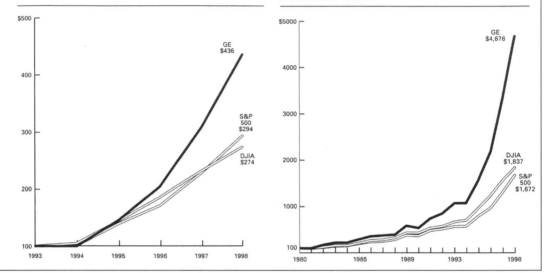

FIVE-YEAR PERFORMANCE GRAPH: 1993 – 1998

Comparison of Five-Year Cumulative Total Return Among
GE, S&P 500 and Dow Jones Industrial Average (DJIA)

The annual changes for the five- and eighteen-year periods shown in the
graphs on this and the opposite page are based on the assumption that $100
had been invested in GE stock and each index on December 31, 1993 (as
required by SEC rules) and 1980, respectively, and that all quarterly dividends
were reinvested at the average of the closing stock prices at the beginning and
end of the quarter. The total cumulative dollar returns shown on the graphs
represent the value that such investments would have had on December 31,
1998.

EIGHTEEN-YEAR PERFORMANCE GRAPH: 1980 – 1998

Comparison of Eighteen-Year Cumulative Total Return Among
GE, S&P 500 and Dow Jones Industrial Average (DJIA)

The graph below shows the cumulative total return to GE share owners since
December 31, 1980, shortly before Mr. Welch became Chairman and Chief
Executive Officer in April 1981, compared with the same indices shown
on the five-year graph, thus illustrating the relative performance of the
Company during his tenure in that position. As with the five-year graph, this
comparison assumes that $100 was invested in GE and each index at the start
of the period and that all dividends were reinvested. The total cumulative
dollar returns shown represent the value that such investments would have
had on December 31, 1998.

Exhibit 23-3. GE's Financial Performance, 1993–1998 and 1980–1998

Creating a lean and agile organization did not solve every one of GE's problems. The company could look uncomplicated, but Wall Street wasn't going to hand out credit to a CEO just for establishing an uncomplicated enterprise. Wall Street wanted to know that an organization, especially a large organization, was not overly dependent on any one of its component parts. If it were, the enterprise could be resting on shaky foundations. It appeared to Welch during the first half of 1999 that Wall Street was developing such an impression of GE, an incorrect one in his view. Wall Street seemed to think that one GE company—GE Capital—was carrying the other nine GE companies, both in terms of revenues and earnings. Of GE's $9.2 billion in earnings, fully 40 percent came from GE Capital. Some questioned whether GE could continue to

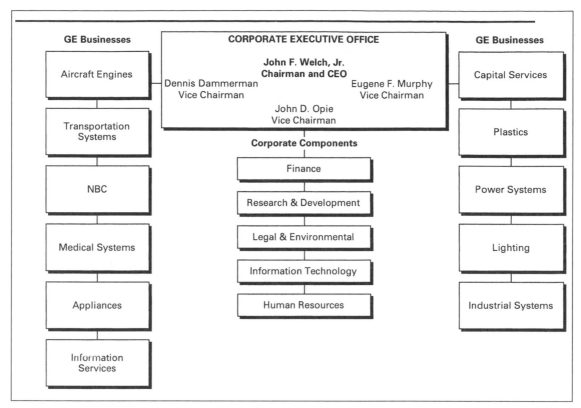

Exhibit 23-4. GE Corporate and Business Structure

grow under these circumstances, when financial markets and other less diversified financial firms (bank and insurance companies, among others) face economic challenges.

Welch argued that there are two ways to look at GE. One is the annual report view, which shows that GE has ten major businesses. The other, more accurate view is the portfolio view, which includes GE's top twenty businesses—which together contribute 90 percent of earnings (see Exhibit 23-5). Of the top twenty businesses, ten are within GE Capital. It would appear that Wall Street accepted Welch's argument. GE stock's continued to rise through the first half of 1999 and hit a new high in late 1999.

It is the fall of 1999. Jack Welch is readying his company for action once again. He's very pleased with the progress made thus far in the corporate quality initiative that he launched a few years earlier. Now he's planning to take the company down the

GE Earnings Power and Diversity

Annual Report View

1. GE Capital
2. Aircraft Engines
3. Plastics
4. Power Systems
5. NBC
6. Medical Systems
7. Lighting
8. Industrial Systems
9. Appliances
10. Transportation

GE Portfolio View

Business

1. Aircraft Engines
2. Plastics
3. Power Systems
4. Employers Reinsurance
5. NBC
6. Medical Systems
7. Commercial Equipment Finance
8. Lighting
9. Industrial Systems
10. Global Consumer Finance
11. GE Financial Assurance
12. Appliances
13. Commercial Real Estate
14. Aviation Services
15. Structured Finance Group
16. Mortgage Services
17. Transportation
18. Vendor Financial Services
19. Retailer Financial Services
20. Railcar

90% of Earnings from Top 20

Exhibit 23-5.

Internet path. Though not an early convert to the Internet, Welch has observed the amazing growth of the Internet in 1999 and wants to get on board. He is gearing up his businesses, urging them to act quickly to take advantage of this remarkable business tool. There is nothing unusual in Welch acting aggressively on a new front. What is unusual—and even Welch senses this—is the realization that in a year he will have to give all of this up. He will retire, as is customary for GE CEOs to do, at age 65 at the end of 2000. He's not letting up. He seems to be saying, "I still have a lot of initiatives left in me. I still have a lot of energy. Don't write about me in the past tense quite yet."

October 15, 1878 Thomas A. Edison establishes the Edison Electric Light Company and effectively founds General Electric.

April 15, 1892 The Edison General Electric Company and Thomson-Houston Electric merge and create the General Electric Company. Edison envisioned a company that would produce the components of electrical power stations and electric lamps in quest of his goal to light up the entire country. In its first 7 months, ending on December 31, GE earns nearly $3 million.

1894 GE produces a fan.

1895 GE builds the largest electric locomotive in the world (90 tons).

1896 General Electric is included in the first index of the Dow Jones Industrial Index; in March 1999 it remains the only company still on that index.

December 1900 Charles Steinmetz opens the GE Research Laboratory; it is the first industrial research laboratory in the United States.

1905 GE produces an iron. The company controls 97 percent of the U.S. lamp business.

1908 GE produces a toaster.

Summer 1909   Irving Langmuir, a Brooklyn-born chemist, joins the GE laboratory and, 3 years later, produces a major advance in lighting: a lightbulb filled with inert gas, tripling the hours of light and reducing the problem of bulb blackening.

1917   GE produces the first household refrigerator.

1922   GE's annual sales, $12 million in 1892, grow to $243 million.

Late 1920s   GE broadens its consumer product line to include an electric mixer and a vacuum cleaner.

1930   The GE laboratory produces the first American photoflash lamp. Four years later comes the high-pressure gaseous-discharge lamp line; 8 years later, the fluorescent lamp.

1930s   GE adds clocks, clothes washers, dishwashers, air conditioners, radios, and food waste disposals.

November 19, 1935   John F. Welch, Jr., is born in Peabody, Massachusetts, across the city line from Salem, where he grows up.

1942   GE builds and tests the first jet engine.

1950   GE has 183,000 employees, 117 plants, and sales of $1.96 billion.

April 1953   An actor named Ronald Reagan, a newly appointed spokesman for GE, hosts *GE Theater*, which debuts over 120 CBS-affiliated stations. The future president appears six times each year in the program's dramas.

1950s   GE is producing toaster ovens, portable hair dryers, table-top broilers, and pocket radios. "Progress Is Our Most Important Product," becomes its advertising slogan.

Early 1956   Crotonville, GE's leadership institute on the Hudson River, is founded. It becomes an indoctrination center that is used to disseminate GE's views on strategic planning.

1956   GE introduces the microwave oven.

1960   Welch is hired by GE to develop new businesses in GE's Chemical Development Operation.

December 1963   Fred Borch takes over as CEO. To accommodate the boom of the 1960s, he increases GE's bureaucracy.

1963   Revenues stagnate and reach only $4.9 billion, a mere $200 million increase from 1962 and a $500 million increase from 1961.

1968 Welch is named the general manager of GE's plastics department; in the past 8 years, he is promoted through four management layers. He is only 33 years old.

1970 As much as 80 percent of GE's earnings still come from its traditional electrical and electronic manufacturing businesses. And manufacturing is on the slide.

Late 1971 Welch becomes general manager of the GE Chemical and Metallurgical Division.

1971 Thanks to the economic boom of the late 1960s, GE nets $471.8 million in profits and sales of $9.4 billion.

December 15, 1972 Reg Jones becomes CEO of GE.

1974 GE moves its corporate headquarters from New York City to Fairfield, Connecticut.

December 1977 Welch is promoted to senior vice president and sector executive of the Consumer Products and Services Sector and vice chairman of the GE Credit Corporation.

August 1979 Welch is named one of three GE vice chairmen.

September 1979 GE is the world's largest manufacturer of electrical equipment and among the world's leaders in electronics, nuclear power, consumer goods, and aerospace.

1979 Between 1968 and now, GE sales double to $19.6 billion and its net income triples to $1.23 billion. It has 401,000 employees and 562 stockholders.

1980 The year before Jack Welch takes over, GE has sales of $25 billion and profits of $1.5 billion.

April 1981 Welch becomes chairman and CEO of GE at the age of 45.

1981 GE is only tenth in market value among U.S. public companies.

Early 1980s Only three GE businesses—Lighting, Motors, and Power Systems—lead their markets. Only Aircraft Engines and Plastics are global.

1983 Welch scraps GE's housewares business: an unpopular move, but one that the CEO felt was essential.

December 12, 1985 GE purchases RCA, the communications giant, which includes the NBC television network, its jewel in the crown, for $6.28 billion. At the time GE is the ninth largest

U.S. industrial firm; RCA is second among the country's service firms.

1985 Annual sales at GE increase from $27.24 billion in 1981 to $28.29 billion and GE is the tenth largest of the *Fortune* 500 companies, up a notch from the year before. Earnings rise 2 percent to $2.33 billion, making GE the fifth most profitable U.S. company.

The 1980s Welch sells $10 billion and purchases $19 billion worth of businesses. And he pares the 1981 workforce from 404,000 to 229,000.

1987 Welch takes a major countercultural step: he discards one of GE's most cherished businesses, the $3 billion-a-year Consumer Electronics division, the leading maker of television sets and video recording equipment in the United States, and acquires a company in the medical diagnostics field, Thomson-CGR medical imaging.

1988 100,000 positions are eliminated at GE from 1981 to 1988.

1989 Welch begins corporatewide initiative called Work-Out, a program designed to give everyone at GE a chance to propose ways of improving the company's day-to-day operations.

1993 GE, with roughly $80 billion in market value, shares the lead with Exxon and AT&T. Twelve of the 13 GE businesses are number one or number two in their markets (NBC is the lone exception). Annual corporate productivity rises from 2 percent in 1981 to 4.5 percent. It has revenues of $60.6 billion and net earnings of $5.2 billion.

August 1995 NBC works out a billion-dollar package that gives it the rights to cover all Olympics through 2008 except for the 1998 winter games at a cost of $3.55 billion.

January 1996 Welch announces a new initiative to improve quality based on the Six Sigma statistical system of measurement.

July 1996 The debut of MSNBC Cable, a 24-hour news-and-information channel, and MSNBC, a comprehensive, interactive, on-line news service.

1996 GE has its best year ever: revenues rise to a record $79.2 billion, a 13 percent increase over the previous year's revenues; profits increase 11 percent to a record $7.28 billion.

1996 GE Capital Services earns $4 billion and NBC earns $953 million; together, they account for almost half of GE's $10.8 billion in operating profits, as the GE service initiative picks up steam.

Spring 1997 More than 40 percent of GE's revenues are derived from non-U.S. markets.

December 31, 1997 GE's market value reaches $240 billion, $50 billion more than the next highest in the world, Royal Dutch/Shell. Revenues reach a record $90.84 billion, making GE the fifth-largest American company in revenues (after General Motors, Ford Motor, Exxon, and Wal-Mart Stores); its net earnings increase to more than $8.2 billion, another record figure, making GE the second most profitable U.S. company (after Exxon).

December 1997 NBC's Jerry Seinfeld lets it be known that he wants to discontinue his show at the end of the 1997–1998 season. It had been one of the most successful shows of all time. Even Jack Welch's personal intervention with Seinfeld doesn't convince the sit-com star to change his mind.

March 1998 GE's market value rises to $250 billion.

First quarter, 1998 GE profits reach $1.67 billion, more than the company earned ($1.65 billion) during all of 1981, the year Jack Welch took over as chairman and CEO of GE.

Third quarter, 1998 GE's profits of $2.01 billion lead all American companies, ahead of Exxon ($1.82 billion) and Intel ($1.574 billion).

December 31, 1998 GE has annual revenues of $100.5 billion and net earnings of $9.3 billion; its market value stands at $327 billion, second-highest in the world. Its international revenues have grown to $42.8 billion, 43 percent of total revenues.

November 19, 1998 Jack Welch turns 63 years old. He plans to step down as chairman and CEO of GE at the end of the year 2000. (GE CEOs have customarily retired at the age of 65.)

January 1999 Welch sets in motion a new companywide initiative involving e-commerce and the Internet. Welch orders each business to select an e-business leader.

March 1999 GE employee rolls grow to 293,000, including 163,000 in the United States.

1999 General Electric ranks as the world's most admired company (*Fortune* magazine); the world's most respected company (*Financial Times*); American's greatest wealth creator (*Fortune*); it is first in the *Business Week* 1000 and the *Financial Times* FT500. Jack Welch is called the most respected CEO by *Industry Week*. The company ranks fifth on the *Fortune* 500. If ranked independently, nine of GE's businesses would be on the *Fortune* 500.

June 1999 Jack Welch launches e-briefs over GE's Intranet as he prepares the company for the new Internet-based initiative. E-commerce is discussed intensively at this month's Corporate Executive Council.

July 1999 GE's stock hits a record-high 118 early this month. Predictions are that revenues will reach $110 billion for the year and profits will approach the $10 billion figure.

Fall 2000 GE will announce Jack Welch's successor. In all likelihood, the new chairman and CEO will be one of the GE's business leaders. A majority of those leaders appear to be in contention.

December 31, 2000 Jack Welch, having turned 65 a month earlier, will retire as chairman and CEO of General Electric. As for what he will do in retirement, all he will say is "something meaningful."

Acknowledgments

It is always good to give credit where credit is due—especially when it is to one's editor. When my long-time editor Jeffrey Krames proposed that I write *The GE Way Fieldbook,* I quickly agreed. After all, he and I had worked closely and productively on ten previous books, spanning 15 fruitful years. Routinely, it is the author to whom attention is naturally drawn when a book is written—and when it enjoys a measure of success. Yet, it is the editor who takes a good idea and turns it into a great one. It is the editor—and here I am speaking specifically of Jeff—who, like a talented sculptor, molds the author's best effort into a final product that is vastly greater than the simple sum of its parts.

The editor who accomplishes such feats can rightly take pride in being an editor, the noblest and most unsung part of our profession. The editor—and again I refer especially to Jeff—who helps produce a book of substances deserves far more recognition than we authors tend to give. It is sometimes asserted that a truly good author does not need an editor at all. The truth is that a truly good author understands just how much a highly skilled editor can do toward improving a book. My thanks to my editor

Jeffrey Krames both for his unwavering sense of what makes a good book and for investing so much time and effort in all of the books we have done together, including this one.

I also wish to think some other members of the McGraw-Hill team: Philip Ruppel, vice president and group publisher, Business and General Reference, who has been as much a friend and adviser as publisher; John Morriss, who as editing manager has played a large share in assuring that my McGraw-Hill books look as good as they do; Laura Libretti, a special thanks for her tireless efforts in helping to assemble and coordinate the final manuscript; and Lydia Rinaldi, who has been both enthusiastic and efficient in past promotion efforts of my McGraw-Hill books. I also wish to thank my agent, Chris Calhoun at Sterling Lord Literistic, who has provided me with his keen judgment and warm support over the past three years.

Now a word of acknowledgment to the other factor without whom I could not have written this book—Jack Welch and General Electric. I group the man and the enterprise together because for the past 8 years of my writing about the two, they seem inseparable. Authors always hope to get close to the people about whom they write. That is, after all, how we acquire the best information and how we gain the most important insights. I am grateful for having had so much access to Jack Welch and his senior colleagues over the years, and specifically in the case of this book. With regard to *The GE Way Fieldbook,* I asked Jack Welch to grant a request that was at the core of this book: to make available a number of hitherto-unpublished internal charts and documents. I wanted to use those charts and documents to give "flesh and bones" to the organizing idea of this book—helping readers to judge how far along they were in implementing Welch's business strategies and how they might make even more progress toward implementing those strategies.

Both Jeffrey Krames and I believed that a fieldbook ought to rely as much on visual material as on text. Hence, the need for those charts and documents. GE agreed to provide me with a large selection of charts and documents. I then selected those I wished to use and submitted the smaller list to Jack Welch for approval. He personally decided on those I could use, and the GE-approved ones appear in this book.

I also want to express thanks to Beth Comstock, GE's vice president for public relations. She, along with her staff (especially Bruce Bunch, Beth Coley, and Jay Pomeroy, were always so helpful, efficient, and cheerful, responding to my many phone calls and e-mails.

Others who played a significant role at GE in helping me to shape this book were William Conaty, Steve Kerr, Lloyd Trotter, Piet van Abeelen, and Gary Reiner.

I also want to thank the Jossey-Bass Publishers for permitting me to reprint a number of questionnaires that appeared originally in the book *The Boundaryless Organization: Breaking the Chains of Organizational Structure*, by Ron Ashkenas, Dave Ulrich, Todd Jick, and Steve Kerr (Jossey-Bass Publishers, San Francisco, 1995).

Finally, a word about my family. By now they know how grateful I am to them for being of such good cheer and understanding as I make my trips for interviews and as I barricade myself in my study to do the writing. Yet, I want to say it once more. Thank you. To my wife, Elinor, who shows such good judgment and deep understanding of the writing process (she has been my co-author for three other books), making my work easier and more pleasurable.

To my children, Miriam, Shimi, Adam, and Rachel, a very warm, appreciative thank-you. Also to my grandchildren, Edo and Mayo, who are still too young to read, my thank-you to them. When they get older, they will read this—I will make sure of that—and then they will know how glad I was that they were around while I moved through this book.

Endnotes

Leadership Module Opener

13 "All of management . . . ," Jack Welch, question-and-answer session, 92nd Street Y, New York City, New York, March 8, 1999.

Chapter 1

15 "The command-and-control structures . . . ," Jack Welch, question-and-answer session, 92nd Street Y, New York City, New York, March 8, 1999.

21 "This is real common . . . ," William Conaty, interview with author, March 11, 1999.

21 "When I went around to . . . ," Ibid.

Chapter 2

24 "An A leader has enormous . . . ," Jack Welch, Letter to Share Owners, General Electric Annual Report, 1997.

26 "We said we want . . . ," William Conaty, interview with author, March 11, 1999.

26 "It's great to think about . . . ," Ibid.

Chapter 4

39 "Rewarding your employees . . . ," Jack Welch, speaking to a class at the GE Leadership Institute, Crotonville, April 29, 1999.

42 "Doesn't want to micromanage . . . ," William Conaty, interview, March 11, 1999.

43 "When you look . . . ," Ibid.

Chapter 5

49 "After a decade . . . ," Jack Welch, Letter to Share Owners, General Electric Annual Report, 1997.

Chapter 6

55 "People closest to the work . . . ," Letter to Share Owners, General Electric Annual Report, 1995.

65 "Our organizational 'attics,' " Jack Welch e-briefs, GE Intranet, June 7, 1999.

66 "You walk before you run . . . ," Steve Kerr, interview, April 27, 1999.

The Organization Module

71 "We want people who get up . . . ," Jack Welch quoted in Fortune *Jack and Herb Show,* January 1, 1999.

Chapter 7

73 "We described our emerging . . . ," Jack Welch, Letter to Share Owners, General Electric Annual Report, 1995.

Chapter 8

87 "It's a badge of honor . . . ," Jack Welch, question-and-answer session, 92nd Street Y, New York City, New York, March 8, 1999.

Chapter 9

93 "The ultimate competitive advantage . . . ," "Face to Face: Jack Welch," *FOCUIS, the Journal of Egon Zehnder International,* January 1997, pp. 3–12.

94 "We had to take . . . ," Lloyd Trotter, interview, April 30, 1999.

97 "If you are a . . . ," Ibid.

98 "Shamelessly stealing . . . ," Ibid.

98 "Now it's used . . . ," Ibid.

Chapter 10

101 "We poll 10,000 . . ." *Jack and Herb Show,* op. cit.

104 "We continue to win . . . ," Bill Conaty, interview, March 11, 1999.

104 "We know we're going . . . ," Ibid.

105 "We don't want the survey . . . ," Ibid.

The Customer Module

109 "Six Sigma . . . is the most important . . . ," Jack Welch, interview with author, April 29, 1999.

Chapter 11

111 "Six Sigma training . . . ," Jack Welch e-briefs, GE Intranet, June 7, 1999.

117 "Jack, this ain't . . . ," *Jack and Herb Show*, op. cit.

Chapter 12

119 "We're basically changing . . . ," Jack Welch, question-and-answer session, 92nd Street Y, New York City, New York, March 8, 1999.

Chapter 13

124 "Six Sigma has spread . . . ," Jack Welch, Letter to Share Owners, General Electric Annual Report, 1997.

Chapter 14

130 "So it's become . . . ," Jack Welch, interview, April 29, 1999.

134 "Our customers' own voices . . . ," Denis J. Nayden, speech, General Electric Operating Managers Meeting, Boca Raton, Florida, January 4–5, 1999.

134 "Hear the sounds . . . ," Jack Welch, Letter to Share Owners, General Electric Annual Report, 1998.

135 "The lesson learned . . . ," Piet van Abeelen, interview, April 29, 1999.

138 "Now we have come . . . ," Ibid.

The CEO as Strategist

158 "I don't want . . . ," Steve Kerr, interview, April 27, 1999.

158 "We don't whip out . . . ," Ibid.

159 "We want to know why . . . ," Ibid.

160 "Universities have a communist . . . ," Ibid.

Chapter 20

221 "Involving everyone . . . ," Jack Welch, question-and-answer session, 92nd Street Y, New York City, New York, March 8, 1999.

222 "I thought they were a bunch . . . ," Ibid.

222 "Simply put, quality must be . . . ," Jack Welch, speech, General Electric Operating Managers Meeting, Boca Raton, Florida, January 6–7, 1997.

223 "Everything's got to be . . . ," Jack Welch, question-and-answer session, 92nd Street Y, New York City, New York, March 8, 1999.

224 When you sit here . . ." Jack Welch, speech, General Electric Operating Managers Meeting, Boca Raton, Florida, January 6–7, 1997.

224 People today look for . . . ," Jack Welch, interview, July 22, 1997.

225 "I know if I plan . . . ," Jack Welch, question-and-answer session, 92nd Street Y, New York City, New York, March 8, 1999.

225 "Too many of you . . . ," Jack Welch, speech, General Electric Operating Managers Meeting, Boca Raton, Florida, January 6–7, 1997.

226 "The biggest advice I give . . . ," Jack Welch, interview, December 12, 1997.

226 "A lot of them . . . ," Ibid.

227 "Last year we started . . . ," Jack Welch, speech, General Electric Operating Managers Meeting, Boca Raton, Florida, January 4–5, 1999.

228 "There are a thousand things . . . ," *Jack and Herb Show*, op. cit.

229 "We offer them complete . . . ," Jack Welch, interview, "The Secrets of the Finest Company in the World," *L'Expansion*, July 10–24, 1997, pp. 26–39.

230 "Globalization has been a common . . . ," Jack Welch, speech, General Electric Operating Managers Meeting, Boca Raton, Florida, January 6–7, 1997.

231 "This next phase of . . . ," Jack Welch, speech, General Electric Operating Managers Meeting, Boca Raton, Florida, January 4–5, 1999.

231 "On globalization, we've had . . . ," Ibid.

232 "In the 1990s everyone . . . ," Jack Welch, question-and-answer session, 92nd Street Y, New York City, New York, March 8, 1999.

232 "I can't predict . . . ," Ibid.

233 "The focus on the customer . . . ," Jack Welch, speech, General Electric Operating Managers Meeting, Boca Raton, Florida, January 4–5, 1999.

The CEO as Strategist

235 "What size cannot be allowed . . . ," Jack Welch, Letter to Share Owners, General Electric Annual Report, 1997.

Chapter 21

237 "We found in the 1980s . . . ," Jack Welch, speech, General Electric Annual Meeting of Share Owners, Greenville, South Carolina, April 26, 1989.

Chapter 22

243 "Services . . . fueling powerful growth . . . ," Jack Welch, Letter to Share Owners, General Electric Annual Report, 1998.

255 "If you're not ahead . . . ," Gary Reiner, interview, April 29, 1999.

256 "We must have a . . . ," Jack Welch, e-briefs, GE Intranet, June 7, 1999.

Index

Index